T0305080

Growth and Cohesion in the European Union

Growth and Cohesion in the European Union

The Impact of Macroeconomic Policy

Edited by

William Mitchell

University of Newcastle, Australia

Joan Muysken

Maastricht University, The Netherlands

Tom van Veen

Maastricht University, The Netherlands

Centre of Full Employment and Equity

Edward Elgar

Cheltenham, UK • Northampton, MA, USA

Published by
Edward Elgar Publishing Limited
Glensanda House
Montpellier Parade
Cheltenham
Glos GL50 1UA
UK

Edward Elgar Publishing, Inc.
136 West Street
Suite 202
Northampton
Massachusetts 01060
USA

A catalogue record for this book
is available from the British Library

ISBN-13: 978 1 84542 611 8
ISBN-10: 1 84542 611 8

Printed and bound in Great Britain by MPG Books Ltd, Bodmin, Cornwall

Contents

Contributors

Philip Arestis
Director of Research at Cambridge Centre for Economic and Public Policy, United Kingdom.

Lucio Baccaro
Researcher, International Labour Organization, International Institute for Labor Studies, Geneva.

Anna Batyra
Researcher, Institut de Recherches Economiques et Sociales (IRES), Catholic University of Louvain, Louvain-la-Neuve, Belgium.

Julie Castonguay
Researcher, Maastricht School of Governance, The Netherlands.

Henri de Groot
Associate Professor of Economics, Faculty of Economics and Business Administration, Free University, Amsterdam, The Netherlands.

Clemens J.M Kool
Professor of Financial Markets, Utrecht School of Economics, Utrecht University, The Netherlands.

Jan Kregel
Distinguished Research Professor of Economics, Department of Economics, Universitý degli Studi di Bologna, Italy; Adjunct Professor of International Economics, Johns Hopkins University Paul Nitze School of Advanced International Studies and Distinguished Research Professor, Center for Full Employment and Price Stability, University of Missouri – Kansas City, USA. He is currently serving as Chief of Policy Analysis and Development at the Financing for Development Office in the United Nations Department of Economic and Social Affairs.

William Mitchell
Professor of Economics, University of Newcastle and Inaugural Director of CofFEE, Australia.

Paola Monperrus-Veroni
Researcher, French Observatory of Economic Conditions (OFCE) and National Political Science Foundation, Paris, France.

Joan Muysken
Professor of Economics, Faculty of Economics and Business Administration, Maastricht University and Director of CofFEE-Europe, The Netherlands.

Richard Nahuis
Program Leader, Public Organizations, CPB Netherlands Bureau for Economic Policy Analysis, The Hague and Post-doc, Utrecht School of Economics, Utrecht University, The Netherlands.

Chris de Neubourg
Professor in Economics, Faculty of Economics and Business Administration, Maastricht University and Director of Maastricht School of Governance, The Netherlands .

Diego Rei
Junior Researcher, International Labour Organization, International Institute for Labor Studies, Geneva.

Francesco Saraceno
Researcher, French Observatory of Economic Conditions (OFCE) and National Political Science Foundation, Paris, France and Dipartimento di Scienze Economiche (Department of Economics) Facoltà di Economia (Faculty of Economics), Università degli Studi di Roma La Sapienza, Roma, Italy

Malcolm Sawyer
Pro-Dean for Learning and Teaching and Professor of Economics, Leeds University Business School, United Kingdom.

Henri Sneessens
Professor of Economics, Department of Economics, Catholic University of Louvain, Louvain-la-Neuve, Belgium.

Paul Tang
Program Manager European Analysis. CPB Netherlands Bureau for Economic Policy Analysis, The Hague, The Netherlands.

Tom van Veen
Associate Professor of Economics, Faculty of Economics and Business Administration, Maastricht University and Deputy Director of CofFEE – Europe, The Netherlands.

Acknowledgements

In the preparation of this volume we had great help from a number of institutions and individuals whom we would like to thank.

First, we would like to thank the participants to the CofFEE-Europe workshop for their contributions to the various discussions. We deeply regret that one of the authors, Richard Nahuis, passed away soon after the workshop. Second, both the Research Institute METEOR of the Faculty of Economics and Business Administration in Maastricht and the Netherlands Organisation for Scientific Research (NWO) have provided a grant for the CofFEE-Europe workshop in which the first drafts of the papers which have been included in this volume have been presented. Moreover, NWO has contributed to finance the preparation of the current volume.

The final manuscript for this volume has been produced by Jaakko Kooroshy and Akshay Regmi, who also helped with the editing. Also enormous assistance in editing the manuscript has been provided by Ellen Carlson from the Center of Full Employment and Equity at the University of Newcastle in Australia. All three have pointed out numerous inconsistencies in the text and unclear passages. Moreover, Ellen Carlson made many useful suggestions to improve the use of English. We thank them for their continuous efforts, patience, expedience and efficiency.

Introduction

William Mitchell, Joan Muysken and Tom van Veen

Macroeconomic policy is often hotly debated within the European Union (EU). On the monetary policy side, the actions (or lack of actions) of the European Central Bank (ECB) are frequently commented upon by political leaders. Moreover, the ECB activities are monitored by various political (for example, the European Parliament) and academic (for example, the European Shadow Financial Regulatory Committee) bodies. Overlaying this scrutiny is that fact that some European countries have shown a reluctance to surrender their monetary independence to the ECB. On the fiscal policy side, the failure of France and Germany to abide by the constraints imposed by the Stability and Growth Pact (SGP) has been controversial. In fact, the SGP has been plagued by controversy from its inception, especially after EU president Prodi dubbed it as being 'stupid'. However, the major policy discussions have started from a shared view of how the economy works and then argued about the implementation of the policy. The Sapir report refers to this shared view as the 'Brussels–Frankfurt Consensus' in macroeconomics (Sapir et al., 2004, p. 41). There are several important components of this view. First, the economy tends to fluctuate around the NAIRU such that when unemployment lies below the NAIRU inflation occurs. Second, economic growth and the level of economic activity are determined by supply factors. As a consequence, fiscal policy should be as neutral and supportive of monetary policy as possible, which should manipulate the interest rate to neutralize demand shocks.

Consistent with this macroeconomic consensus is the notion that fiscal and monetary policy should be detached from the political process. This underlies the idea of an independent ECB and the SGP that restricts the room for fiscal policy discretion. Macroeconomic policy should only have an accommodating role in economic growth. As the Sapir report puts it: 'To expand economic growth potential requires first and foremost reforms of microeconomic policies' (p. 4). This emphasis on microeconomic policies is also found in the Lisbon Strategy 2000 and in the recommendations by the European Employment Taskforce 2003, which evaluated Europe's recent disappointing performance in light of the targets of sustainable growth and more and better jobs.[1] The Consensus considered that the changes to monetary policy conduct together with adherence to the SGP would solve the macroeconomic problems. However, it also required the European Monetary Union (EMU) countries to reform their labour market institutions to make the labour markets more flexible and more competitive. In addition, microeconomic reforms aimed at increasing competition in the goods market would put downward pressure on mark-ups.

The implementation of the Lisbon Strategy is challenged by the need to balance the tension between efficiency and equity, which are represented by its central goals of sustainable growth and cohesion, respectively. The latter goal aims in part to abolish social exclusion, eradicate poverty and enhance gender equality. The Sapir report recognizes this tension and criticizes the tendency of EU policy-makers to try to 'kill two birds with one stone'. 'Policy instruments are assigned two objectives at the same time: for example, fostering growth and improving cohesion. It would be better to assign one objective to each policy instrument' (p. 4). In that context macroeconomic policy can play a somewhat larger role than is currently envisaged, but the report is not very clear about how this might be achieved and remains close to the Brussels–Frankfurt Consensus.[2]

The Centre of Full Employment and Equity – Europe (CofFEE-Europe) is by its very nature concerned with the twin goals of achieving full employment and equity across European society. We also think that macroeconomic policy should have a larger role in achieving these aims because aggregate demand has a large and lasting impact on the macroeconomic performance of a country (Modigliani, 2000; Mitchell and Muysken, 2002). For all of these reasons, it is essential to scrutinize the Brussels–Frankfurt Consensus from various angles and to discuss the implications of it for macroeconomic prospects.

A main concern in the context of the current European situation is the persistently high unemployment. Over the last decade (1990–2002) unemployment averaged 9.3 per cent, while the OECD average was 7.1 per cent. Given the current economic slowdown, EU unemployment is on the rise again. In addition, the level of European unemployment has persisted at this unacceptably high level since the 1980s while unemployment in the US has decreased from an average of 7.2 per cent in the 1980s to an average 5.5 per cent over the period 1990 to 2002.

According to the Brussels–Frankfurt Consensus, European labour markets are too rigid by comparison to the US labour market. Hence, the unemployment problem can be solved by increasing incentives, improving the returns on schooling, and redefining the role and the necessity of labour market institutions. However, in this volume we make a case that it is not at all clear which institutions cause labour market rigidities and to what extent. While the Consensus considers these institutions to be transitory market imperfections, the reality is that most of them have evolved over a long period where cultural values (for example, about pay equity) have played as important a role as economic values in determining social and economic outcomes. As a consequence, any processes designed to change the labour market institutions require complicated and slowly evolving dialogues and are unlikely to be a short-term remedy for significantly reducing unemployment. We therefore argue that the problem of unemployment requires a much broader set of microeconomic solutions, including active labour market policies, policies concerning schooling and the development of skills (see Agell, 2003; Baker et al., 2002). But microeconomic policies will not in themselves provide the solution to what is essentially a macroeconomic problem. First and foremost the role of aggregate demand in the determination of unemployment has to be placed at the forefront of the debate. The achievement and maintenance of full employment requires macroeconomic policy action which may be supported by active labour market policies and income policies to assist in smooth transitions.

Within this context, CofFEE-Europe dedicated its October 2004 workshop in Maastricht to the role of macroeconomic policy in the European Union. The aim of the workshop was twofold. First, we aimed to promote an in-depth discussion on the Brussels–Frankfurt Consensus and the impact of macroeconomic policy, in particular for full employment. Second, we aimed to present a comprehensive analysis of the interaction of macroeconomic policy with the welfare state, with a focus on the implications for cohesion. We invited papers from reputable researchers on these subjects, which have been rewritten on the basis of discussions in the workshop. The present volume presents the results of these efforts and provides a coherent basis for further debate and policy development.

In the opening chapter, 'The Brussels–Frankfurt Consensus: An Answer to the Wrong Question', Bill Mitchell and Joan Muysken criticize the Brussels–Frankfurt Consensus for its overriding priority on the maintenance of price stability – reflected in low rates of inflation – and the implied constraints on the fiscal options of sovereign states – reflected in the SGP. They argue that the Consensus provides an 'answer to the wrong question' because the major economic problem facing most economies is persistently high unemployment and the accompanying income and social losses. Unfortunately, EU politicians do not consider this malaise to be a major issue that needs to be given the highest priority. They show that, in fact, the current policy emphasis is opposite to this: unemployment, at best, is seen as an unfortunate consequence of the need to maintain a low-inflation environment and is a symptom of rigidities which hamper a proper functioning of the economy. At worst, it is seen as a voluntary state where individuals choose life paths emphasizing leisure. Never is it constructed as the systematic macroeconomic failure of governments to ensure there are enough jobs created in their economies.

Against this background Mitchell and Muysken show how the NAIRU - approach and the Brussels–Frankfurt Consensus gained its influence on European policy through the OECD Jobs Study, the European Employment Study, the Maastricht criteria and the Stability and Growth Pact. They challenge the basis of this dominant paradigm in conceptual terms, emphasizing that European governments have abandoned full employment in favour of the diminished goal of full employability. In addition, they argue that key components of the Consensus are not in accord with the data.

The latter point is elaborated with respect to the SGP in the chapter 'Whither Stability Pact? An Assessment of Reform Proposals' by Paola Monperrus-Veroni and Francesco Saraceno. These authors examine different proposals for reforming the SGP by extending a counterfactual experiment performed in Eichengreen and Wyplosz (1998). Using estimated coefficients from a reduced-form model, they simulate the path of the output gap for the largest Euro Zone countries (France, Germany, Italy) after imposing limits to structural deficits according to different fiscal rules (structural deficit rules, golden rules and rules that incorporate the stock of debt). For each of these countries they rank the different reform proposals in terms of output loss over the period considered. The main result of the seemingly robust analysis is that the structural golden rule would be the most beneficial in terms of both an individual country's criteria and global criteria. The nominal golden rule is a close second. The *status quo*, the Maastricht rule, does not perform very well and is seen as a second-best alternative.

In the chapter 'Alternatives for the Policy Framework of the Euro' Philip Arestis and Malcolm Sawyer juxtapose the role of monetary policy with the role of fiscal policy. They emphasize that the achievement of full employment and sustainable and equitable growth should be the major objectives for economic policy in the European Union. The achievement of these objectives requires, amongst other things, the use of macroeconomic (monetary and fiscal) policy to secure high levels of aggregate demand and the building of adequate productive capacity. Moreover, the aims of the ECB should better reflect these concerns and the bank should be more accountable for its actions. They conclude that the ECB needs a reformulation of its objectives to include high and sustainable levels of employment and economic growth. The bank should also broaden the set of instruments with which it aims to achieve these objectives, beyond interest management.

Clemens Kool does not agree with the conclusions in Arestis and Sawyer's chapter. In the chapter 'What Drives ECB Monetary Policy?' Kool claims that contrary to popular belief and continuous ECB statements, the ECB has not acted as an obsessive inflation-fighter. His claim is based on simulations with different Taylor rules, and Kool shows that output considerations do play a significant role in the ECB's policy rule. In terms of actual policy, Kool claims the ECB has erred on the 'loose' side, especially since 2001. According to conventional wisdom, the Euro Area as a whole needed a higher interest rate than was provided by the ECB. Kool argues that actual interest rates have been consistent with German preferences, which suggests that the ECB has put a dominant weight on German economic developments. The claims that small peripheral countries get their way within EMU are clearly rejected by the data. If anything, their interests are given a lower weight. Finally, the Fed and the ECB appear to behave in very similar ways in terms of actual operations, even though the Fed in the end may be a little more aggressive than the ECB. Kool concludes that there is little reason to criticize the ECB for not following the Fed's example.

A totally different perspective on the role of monetary policy is provided by Jan Kregel in the chapter 'Interest Rates, Debt, Counter-Cyclical Policy and Monetary Sovereignty'. Kregel criticizes the policy of interest management, usually with an explicit or implicit inflation target pursued via some sort of Taylor rule. This policy takes a very limited view on the impact of interest rates on the economy, focusing on the link between the rate of change in goods prices and interest rates. However, there is a long tradition of analysis that focuses on the impact of interest rates on other aspects of the economy such as income, the value of assets, debt burdens and international stability. In particular Kregel considers the relation between interest rates and growth rates and conditions for sustainability of debts and transfers of resources. The relevance is that, according to Kregel, the EU-15 looks very much like the US in the 1950s in its attempt to replace government expenditure-led growth with export-led growth. However, this policy is only sustainable if this does not cause any exchange rate pressures between the euro and the dollar. Kregel argues that only if the rate of capital outflow from Europe exceeds the rate that is being earned by Europeans on their investments in the US, is an export-led growth policy sustainable. Kregel doubts that this stability condition is fulfilled and therefore concludes that a pure export-led growth, although not impossible, is probably unsustainable. Hence, the government needs to consider alternative policies like monetary and fiscal policies, to foster economic growth and development in the Euro Area.

In the second part of the book, the focus shifts from the direct role of macroeconomic policy to the interaction of macroeconomic policy with labour market institutions. In the chapter 'Institutions and the Labour Market: Examining the Benefits', Tom van Veen discusses the costs and the benefits of labour market institutions. Van Veen argues that in the discussions about the appropriate labour market institutions, the debate tends to focus on the costs rather than the benefits of these institutions. However, most institutions are the result of long struggles between the government, employers' organizations and employees' organizations, and reflect values like consensus building and decent treatment of employees. These values constitute the benefits of institutions.

Van Veen concludes that different types of labour market institutions exist depending on whether societies are more collectivist or individually oriented, and therefore differences in labour market institutions may be related to differences in societal preferences. For that reason, it is not sensible to impose a 'one-size-fits-all' approach to reforming labour market institutions. The upshot is likely to be significant resistance because labour market institutions are part of a broader social and cultural setting and the concept of the 'welfare state' has differing connotations among societies. Thus in a broader context, according to van Veen, the discussion about the role of labour market institutions links up with the equity-efficiency debate.

A complementary view to van Veen is provided by Lucio Baccaro and Diego Rei in the chapter 'Institutions and Unemployment in OECD Countries: A Panel Data Analysis'. In this chapter, the empirical plausibility of the popular view that unemployment is caused by labour market institutions and should be addressed through systematic institutional deregulation is assessed. Baccaro and Rei argue that such strong policy conclusions are not supported by the empirical evidence. They find that increasing interest rates raises unemployment and is higher where the level of independence of the central bank is higher. Changes in employment protection, benefit replacement rates and the tax wedge appear to be negatively associated with changes in unemployment, even though the coefficients are (mostly but not always) insignificant. Although the union density change variable is positively associated with changes in unemployment, the bargaining coordination variable turns out to be mostly insignificant. As a consequence, the claim that systematic deregulation of labour markets would solve the unemployment problem faced by several advanced countries is not supported by their results.

Henri de Groot, Richard Nahuis and Paul Tang also argue in the chapter 'The Institutional Determinants of Labour Market Performance: Comparing the Anglo-Saxon Model and a European-Style Alternative' that the European social models can be considered both interesting and successful in comparison to the US model, which is typically offered as the role model for countries to aspire to. They argue that the substantially higher GDP per capita of US citizens compared to those of Europe follows mainly from a difference in the number of hours worked per employee. In terms of productivity per hour and employment per inhabitant, several European countries score equally well or even better than the US, while at the same time they outperform the US with a more equal distribution of income. Based on an empirical analysis for OECD countries the authors show that income redistribution (through a social security system) does not necessarily lead to lower participation and higher unemployment, provided that countries supplement it with active labour market policies. Furthermore, the results suggest that generous unemployment benefits of short duration contribute to employment without widening the income distribution.

Van Veen, Baccaro and Rei, and de Groot et al. all implicitly or explicitly discuss the efficiency and equity considerations relating to labour market institutions. The mainstream view considers there to be a trade-off between equity and efficiency in the design of labour market institutions: more income redistribution is achieved at the cost of a less efficient economy. The existence of such a trade-off between equity and efficiency in the design of social policy is discussed by Chris de Neubourg and Julie Castonguay in the chapter 'Enhancing Productivity: Social Protection as Investment Policy'. De Neubourg and Castonguay argue that under certain conditions, social protection enhances competitiveness through productivity increases. One important argument is that social protection reduces poverty and consequently increases the willingness of people to invest in skills, which, in turn, results in productivity increases. As de Neubourg and Castonguay show, the levels and developments of poverty rates differ remarkably between continental Europe and the Anglo-Saxon countries. In addition they discuss the idea that the risks that are covered by social insurances have to be covered anyway, and public provision of insurance is neither necessarily less effective nor less efficient than private provision. Therefore social protection expenditures must be viewed as investments in society whose returns are not necessarily negative. However, this being said, the labour force participation rate and the employment–population rate are major concerns within the EU member states. For that reason de Neubourg and Castonguay propose a revision of the benefit systems, which they term the Generalised Income Loss Insurance system. The aim of this system is to stimulate increases in participation rates.

In the final chapter, 'Labour Market Adjustments and Macroeconomic Performance', Anna Batyra and Henri Sneessens analyse the impact of differences in labour market institutions on low-skilled unemployment. Although they focus on results for the Belgian economy, their analysis could be extended to other countries that are characterized by similar problems. Batyra and Sneessens argue that biased technological change in conjunction with relative wage rigidities has increased low-skilled unemployment. As a consequence, they propose decreases in labour taxes for low-skilled workers.

Their theoretical model is based on a labour market flow model where labour flows are separated into job creation and job destruction flows. The model calibration is based on quarterly data for the Belgian economy, and the results show that it is important to take into account the effect of cuts in employers' taxes on both job creation and job destruction rates. They argue that the failure to do so in many models may explain the gap between macro- and microeconometric evaluations of such policies. In addition, their results suggest that cutting taxes for a specific group of workers (low skilled in their case) is superior to a general tax cut (on all workers notwithstanding their skills level) in terms of increasing employment and welfare. This chapter links up with the equity–efficiency debate as well and shows how both equity and efficiency can be improved with a relatively small change in tax policies.

Several important conclusions can be drawn from the book, although not all authors would fully agree with each of them. First, the 'Brussels–Frankfurt Consensus' of macroeconomics, based on the view that the economy tends to fluctuate around the NAIRU and economic growth and the level of economic activity are determined by supply factors, is not supported by robust empirical evidence. This failure is highlighted in the chapters by Baccaro and Rei, de Groot et al., and Mitchell and Muysken. This view is primarily based on ideological preferences. The same holds for the implied notion that fiscal and monetary policy should be detached from the political process, which underlies the idea of an independent ECB and the SGP. Both restrict the room for fiscal policy which is essential for the achievement of full employment.

Following the arguments put forward by Arestis and Sawyer, Kregel, and Mitchell and Muysken we support the notion that both fiscal and monetary policy should play a more active role. Both policies should be coordinated to ensure full employment and sustainable growth. In line with the view of functional finance, government spending should compensate for aggregate demand levels below full employment. With respect to monetary policy the ECB should be less focused on inflation. Although Kool suggests that this is already the case, recent comments by the OECD on the rigid interest rate policy do not support his view. The aims of the ECB should be reformulated to include full employment as a goal and the ECB should also be publicly held accountable for its actions. Monetary policy should be coordinated with fiscal policy and use a wider range of instruments, including direct intervention.

While macroeconomic policy plays a crucial role in the achievement and maintenance of full employment, this policy should be supported by active labour market policies and income policies to smooth transitions. As the second part of this volume shows, labour market institutions play an important role in this respect. The chapters by van Veen, Baccaro and Rei, de

Groot et al., and de Neubourg and Castonguay show, first, that labour market institutions do not necessarily hamper economic growth, and second, that some institutions related to income policies can even foster economic growth. The results also suggest that the 'one-size-fits-all' approach is not the most appropriate way to reshape the European welfare states. In addition, Batyra and Sneessens show that the actual design of the policy matters as well. In their study, for example, different methods of policy financing clearly generate different results.

NOTES

1. See the report of the Spring European Council 2004 and the report of the European Employment Taskforce, 'Jobs, Jobs, Jobs', November 2003.
2. Sapir et al. (2004) recommend 'increasing the role for fiscal policies in bad times ... and more effective and flexible implementation of the Stability and Growth Pact, while sticking to the 3% ceiling ... the conditions under which the 3% deficit threshold can be breached should be modified' (p. 5). See also the recommendations on pp. 144–5 in the Sapir report and the discussion preceding these recommendations.

REFERENCES

Agell, J. (2003), 'Efficiency and equality in the labour market', *CESifo Forum*, No. 2/2003, pp. 33–42.

Arestis, P. and M. Sawyer (2003), 'Macroeconomic policies of the Economic and Monetary Union: theoretical underpinnings and challenges', *Levy Economics Institute Working Chapter*, No. 385.

Baker, D., A. Glyn, D. Howell and J. Schmitt (2002), 'Labor market institutions and unemployment: a critical assessment of the cross-country evidence', *Center for Economic Policy Analysis Working Chapter*, No. 2002–17, New School University, New York.

Blanchard, O. and J. Wolfers (1999), 'The role of shocks and institutions in the rise of European unemployment: the aggregate evidence', *NBER Working Chapter*, No. 7282.

Eichengreen, B. and C. Wyplosz (1998), 'The Stability Pact: more than a minor nuisance?' *Economic Policy: A European Forum*, **26**, 65–104.

Kok, W. (2003), 'Jobs, jobs, jobs: creating more employment in Europe', Report of the Employment Taskforce chaired by Wim Kok, November.

Mitchell, W.F. and J. Muysken (2002), 'Aggregate demand should do the job', in E. Carlson and W.F. Mitchell (eds), *The urgency of full employment*, The Center for Applied Economic Research, UNSW Press, pp. 133–157.

Modigliani, F. (2000) 'Europe's economic problems', *Carpe Oeconomiam Chapters in Economics*, 3rd Monetary and Finance Lecture, Freiburg, 6 April.

Nickell, S. (1997), 'Unemployment and Labor Market Rigidities', *Journal of Economic Perspectives*, **11** (3), pp. 55–74.

Sapir, A., P. Aghion, G. Bertola, M. Hellwig, J. Pisani-Ferry, D. Rosati, J. Vinals and H. Wallace (2004), *An Agenda for a Growing Europe: The Sapir Report*, Oxford: Oxford University Press.

PART ONE

Monetary Policy, Fiscal Policy and the Stability and Growth Pact

1. The Brussels–Frankfurt Consensus: An Answer to the Wrong Question

William Mitchell and Joan Muysken

1.1 INTRODUCTION

Figure 1.1 depicts Okun Misery Indexes (the sum of the inflation rate and unemployment rate) for the periods 1980–89, 1990–99 and 2000–2003 for several countries. The average misery index has fallen from 14.7 per cent in the 1980s to its recent value of 8.6 per cent. The average unemployment rate corresponding to these misery indexes increased from 7.3 to 8.3 per cent, and subsequently declined to 6.4 per cent in 2000–2003.[1] By implication, the weight of inflation in the index decreased from 50 per cent in the 1980s to about 25 per cent in recent times. Unemployment now constitutes by far the largest part of misery in the portrayed OECD countries.

Many countries (particularly in Europe) still experience near to double-digit unemployment rates. This is illustrated in Figure 1.2 which shows the post-WWII unemployment experience in the US and in Europe, the latter represented here by France and Germany.

Against this background it is rather surprising that the ongoing macroeconomic losses that arise from the persistent unemployment, not to mention the massive social and personal costs, are not considered by EU politicians to be the most compelling policy problem that needs their highest priority. Sadly, it appears that the politicians and policy-makers have the totally opposite construction of events. Unemployment is seen, at best, as an unfortunate and ephemeral consequence of policies that are required to maintain low-inflation economies and is largely attributed to either rigidities (overly generous welfare and other regulations and out-of-touch unions) or to individual choice. This construction has allowed governments in Europe (and elsewhere throughout the OECD bloc) to abandon the goal of full employment and replace it with the diminished goal of full employability, which then generates a bevy of wasteful training programmes that relentlessly churn the unemployed without enhancing their participation

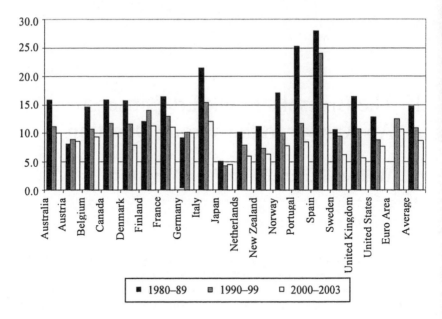

Source: OECD Main Economic Indicators.

Figure 1.1   Misery indexes (%) for selected countries, 1980–89, 1990–99, and 2000–2003.

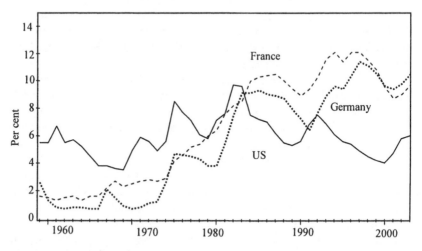

Source: OECD Economic Outlook.

Figure 1.2 Unemployment rates in 'Europe' and the US, 1959–2003

in paid employment. It is a policy agenda bereft of hope and its clear failure stands as an indictment of the governments that introduce it.

The underpinning of the bankrupt policy framework is dubbed in the influential Sapir et al. (2004, p. 41) report as the 'Brussels–Frankfurt Consensus' and represented as follows:

> The maintenance of price stability – reflected in low rates of inflation – facilitates achieving higher rates of economic growth over the medium term and helps to reduce cyclical fluctuations. This shows up in a lower variability of output and inflation. In turn, sound public finances are necessary both to prevent imbalances in the policy mix, which negatively affect the variability of output and inflation, and also to contribute to national savings, thus helping to foster private investment and ultimately growth. The latter beneficial effect is magnified as low deficits and debt, by entailing a low interest burden, create the room for higher public investment, 'productive' public spending and a low tax burden. Finally, the beneficial effects of price stability and fiscal discipline on economic performance reinforce each other in various ways. On the one hand, fiscal discipline supports the central bank in its task to maintain price stability. On the other hand, prudent monetary and fiscal policies avoid policy-induced shocks and their unfavourable impact on economic fluctuations while ensuring a higher room for manoeuvre to address other disturbances that increase cyclical instability.

The Sapir report is broadly sympathetic of the view underlying this Consensus, although it stresses that some of the recommendations following from it should consider the possibility that shocks may be asymmetric, which implies that the policy 'rules' it espouses might be applied differently across countries to consider 'specific' circumstances.

The overwhelming priority of price stability has enormous implications for unemployment in that the latter has become an instrument of policy rather than a policy target. The use of a 'buffer stock' of unemployment to control inflation reflects the dominant 'faith' in the NAIRU (Non-Accelerating Inflation Rate of Unemployment) construct. The adherents of this 'faith' have largely dismissed these 'costs' as adjustments towards equilibrium and therefore a transitory phenomenon without long-term relevance. Implicit in the Brussels–Frankfurt Consensus is the view that there is no relevant sustainable trade-off between inflation and unemployment (Sapir et al. 2004, pp. 44–5). In other words, unemployment will converge to the NAIRU and needs little separate policy action. This view also underlies the highly influential OECD Jobs Study (OECD, 1994) which has shaped labour market policies in many OECD countries. For the EU countries, the Jobs Study and its underlying 'faith' became especially important after the Luxembourg Summit of 1997. The European Employment Strategy which was implemented at the Summit is largely modelled along the lines set out by the OECD Jobs Study (Dostal, 2004).

Our view is quite different and much more in line with that of Modigliani, who introduced the term 'NAIRU' to the economics profession (Modigliani and Papademos, 1975). Modigliani recently argued that:

> Unemployment is primarily due to *lack of aggregate demand*. This is mainly the outcome of erroneous macroeconomic policies ... [the decisions of central banks] ... inspired by an obsessive fear of inflation ... coupled with a benign neglect for unemployment ... have resulted in systematically over tight monetary policy decisions, apparently based on an objectionable use of the so-called NAIRU approach. The contractive effects of these policies have been reinforced by common, very tight fiscal policies. (Modigliani, 2000, p. 3)

We would emphasize that one of the outcomes of governments adopting the 'ideology' of inflation control via interest rate policy has been their failure to use fiscal policy in appropriate ways to ensure there are enough jobs created in their economies. We will further argue that the Brussels–Frankfurt Consensus has also led to a narrowing of 'acceptable' monetary policy activity, such that foreign exchange operations which may have been previously necessary to maintain competitive currency values have been abandoned.

In the light of these policy deficiencies, we identify two major policy challenges that make the Brussels–Frankfurt Consensus unsustainable. First, by 'artificially constraining' European governments to eschew public deficits, policy-makers have created a situation where desired net savings in euro-denominated financial assets by the private non-government sector is unable to be achieved and the result is lack of spending, sluggish production and entrenched unemployment. Second, the European Central Bank (ECB) is reluctant to provide the appropriate underpinning to European exporters through direct foreign currency market intervention because it has an ideological objection to building stores of US dollars. The result is that the euro is overvalued and exporters cannot achieve the necessary growth that is required to boost the domestic economies.

From our perspective it is obvious that the Brussels–Frankfurt Consensus is an answer to the wrong question. The focus should not be on inflation, but on unemployment. Moreover, it should be recognized that contractionary policies with the aim of containing inflation can have very harmful effects on both unemployment and economic growth. We do not support the use of a 'buffer stock' of unemployment to maintain inflation targets as being an acceptable policy in modern democracies. It violates the human rights of those who are the victims of this policy.

The aim of this chapter is threefold. First, we will analyse the background to the NAIRU approach and the Brussels–Frankfurt Consensus and trace its rise to the dominant position in European policy through the OECD Jobs

Study, the European Employment Study, the Maastricht Criteria and the Stability and Growth Pact (SGP). Second, we challenge the basis of this dominant paradigm in conceptual terms emphasizing that European governments have abandoned full employment in favour of the diminished goal of full employability. Third, we will argue that key components of the Consensus are not in accord with the data. Our argument is organized as follows. Section 1.2 outlines the background to the macroeconomic policy debate and the attitudes towards unemployment against which the Jobs Study was developed in the early 1990s. We present in section 1.3 some evidence, partly referring to our earlier work, to demonstrate the deficiencies that we see in the NAIRU approach that has the European policy framework in its vice-like grip. In section 1.4, we argue that the ideology underpinning the OECD Jobs Study has dominated the way policy-makers have constructed the problem of unemployment and led to the implementation of active labour market policies which emphasize supply-side factors but fail to enhance paid employment opportunities. We show how these views have shaped and driven the European Employment Strategy. In section 1.5, we review the various arguments which have been presented in the literature against the Stability and Growth Pact. Section 1.6 presents a more fundamental critique of the various claims that are implied by the Brussels–Frankfurt Consensus. Concluding remarks follow.

1.2 THE EUROPEAN DEBATE ON MACROECONOMIC POLICY AND INFLATION

The oil crises in the early and late 1970s had a very different impact on the economies of either side of the Atlantic, as can be seen from Figure 1.2. It seems plausible to us that these divergent economic developments were instrumental in shaping the debates about unemployment that took a rather different direction in Europe relative to the way the debate unfolded in the US. In the US, the rational expectations revolution dominated the economic debate with New Classical economics emerging out of it as a popular framework. Accordingly, unemployment was analysed from the perspective of inter-temporal substitution and real business cycle theory, all of which contributed to a denial of the concept of involuntary unemployment. This view was challenged by New Keynesians who sought to found the existence of involuntary unemployment in an explanation of wage rigidities and coordination failures. Whatever, by the 1990s, the focus of the US macroeconomic policy debate was on inflation rather than unemployment (Chang, 1997).

In Europe, New Classical economics never really played a serious role in the academic debate with Minford as a notable exception. Instead, there were two major influences. First, French-speaking economists Malinvaud and Drèze led the disequilibrium approach. Second, the English economists such as Layard and Nickell developed an explanation of unemployment persistence within models of wage- and price-setting behaviour under the rubric of the 'battle between mark-ups'. The latter view, with the NAIRU construct and all its attendant policy implications at centre stage, became dominant in the European macroeconomic policy debate.

1.2.1 Disequilibrium Economics

The seeds for the quantity rationing approach were planted by Patinkin, Clower and Leijonhufvud. Barro and Grossman (1971, p. 84) extended 'the Patinkin and Clower analysis of a depressed economy ... to develop a generalised analysis of both booms and depressions as disequilibrium phenomena'.

Although their analysis attracted a lot of attention, it did not gain any substantial foothold in the American economic debate. The main reason follows from the almost universal recognition of the *ad hoc* assumption of price rigidities. Howitt (1977, pp. 124–5) offers the following insight:

> The substantive shortcomings ... are generally those of the state of knowledge itself ... First the treatment of wage and price dynamics is deficient ... [Second, the analysis] does not present a satisfactory account of the process of exchange.

In reaction to that critique, US economists, sympathetic with the notion of involuntary unemployment, sought to provide a rationale for price rigidities that was consistent with maximizing microeconomic postulates. This approach became known as the New Keynesian paradigm.

It was left to some European economists to pick up the baton. The disequilibrium tradition was strongly advocated by Malinvaud and many, mainly French speaking, economists followed his lead (see de Vroey, 2004, part IV).

In his first book, Malinvaud (1977) introduces the famous distinction between three regimes, with the polar cases of Classical and Keynesian unemployment as the most relevant for our analysis. He notes that Keynes uses the word 'classical' in two different meanings, which induces Malinvaud to distinguish between a Walrasian equilibrium, where all markets clear, and a Classical view, in which a reduction in the wage rate could reduce unemployment. He emphasizes that the latter often relies on a partial equilibrium on the labour market. However, as he states in his opening sentence (1977, p. 1):

... the term *involuntary* unemployment makes it obvious from the start that the labour market is one in which supply exceeds demand. Suppliers are therefore rationed in the sense that some of them do not find jobs. Hence unemployment theory must be closely connected with the theory of rationing.

In spite of refinements to his initial model, Malinvaud's (1980, 1984) theory never gained wide acceptance among the profession at any level. Efforts to incorporate his approach in the European research project, the European Unemployment Program, coordinated by Drèze and Bean had very limited success. In that programme, financed by the EC, participants from ten European countries met to agree on a common theoretical specification of a model to explain unemployment and to estimate that model for their own countries. The central model is quite eclectic, and some authors interpreted it quite liberally when applying it to their own country (see the results presented in Drèze and Bean, 1990).[2]

Drèze and Bean (1990, pp. 59) summarize the (interesting) conclusions of the programme as:

The main and perhaps singular determinant of output growth in the 1980s in Europe has been effective demand. The growth of demand is linked to growth of such exogenous elements as government expenditures and world trade ... [and the goal of full employment] ... will be easier to reach if medium-run expected wage growth is strictly contained. We do not know whether, and how, that condition can be met. Under that condition, the fear that faster output growth would rekindle inflation is probably misplaced ... And the expansion would require cooperation among several European countries if national current account problems are to remain manageable ...[3] [Two concluding remarks are:]
1. Public deficits are more tolerable ... if they correspond to public investments.
2. ... a reduction in labour taxes should be targeted toward the low end of the wage scale.

These two conclusions are also reflected in the proposal by Drèze and Malinvaud for a two-handed policy to combat unemployment in Europe. It includes 'two medium term programs: a drastic reduction of the indirect cost of unskilled labour and an ambitious stimulation of targeted investments'(Drèze & Malinvaud, 1994, abstract). This proposal was widely circulated and was publicly supported by Belgian and French leading economists. These proposals are also reflected in the European Union 1993 'White Paper on Growth, Competitiveness, and Employment'. However, it did not have a strong impact on European economic policy. According to Dostal (2004, p. 441):

The White Paper ... represented a flotation of potential policy options, many of which – such as the seemingly 'Euro-Keynesian' demand for investment in 'Trans-European Networks' – were never properly pursued.

1.2.2   The NAIRU Approach

Layard and Nickell's work pushed the NAIRU framework into the European academic spotlight and the culmination, Layard et al. (1991) (hereafter LNJ), became the path-setting work that continues to influence European policy-making. It was the 'brains' behind the OECD (1994) Jobs Study which set the policy agenda for most European and other OECD countries until today (Dostal, 2004, section 2). As a consequence, it has also had a powerful effect on the EU's European Employment Strategy (Goetschy, 1999; López-Santana, 2003). Finally, it has had a lasting impact on academic research and teaching in Europe.

It is unfortunate that such a flimsy theoretical basis has commanded such uniformity in adherence. Following Friedman (1968), LNJ construct unemployment as arising from the consequences of the battle between mark-ups on wages and prices:

> Only if the real wage desired by wage-setters is the same as that desired by price-setters will inflation be stable. *And the variable which brings about this consistency is the level of unemployment* ... Thus, unemployment is the mechanism which ensures that the claims on national output are compatible ... [thus] ... [t]here is indeed a long-run equilibrium at which both unemployment and inflation will be stable. We call this the long-run NAIRU ... (LNJ, 1991, pp. 12–13)

Although they apparently wish to avoid the conclusion that the NAIRU is an inevitable outcome of the economic process, they cannot but help describe it as 'the state to which the system will return after a disturbance' (LNJ, 1991, p. 9). Moreover, '[i]n the long run, unemployment is entirely determined by long-run supply factors and equals the NAIRU' (LNJ, 1991, p. 16).

LNJ (1991, p. 21) seem to suggest that the fundamental results obtained from the New Classical Lucas supply curve is imposed on them – almost against their will: 'Although our interpretation of the structural model differs so sharply from the new-classical model, it remains true that the reduced forms are indistinguishable.' Notwithstanding this, they then conclude, somewhat relieved, that 'the policy implications of the two approaches are so different'. However, Minford (1993, p. 1055) in his review of the book comments: 'As for policy, it might amaze them, but it is a fact, that there is an overwhelming agreement between at least this New Classical economist and LNJ – for example the need for tougher benefit testing, and for measures to restrict monopoly power'. Ultimately, the policies are not fundamentally different and reflect a construction of the unemployment problem that excludes macroeconomic demand failure and a rigid belief in the NAIRU concept as the 'attractor' which is deemed to be invariant to aggregate demand manipulation.

The equilibrium rate of unemployment is influenced by three kinds of factors: (1) anything that shifts the Beveridge curve, in particular search effectiveness; (2) factors which place upward pressure on wages other than unemployment; and (3) any factor which raises prices at a given level of demand. Search effectiveness is central to their analysis through its impact on the notion of voluntary unemployment. LNJ (1991, p. 11) note:

> Even when unemployment is high, there are no queues for all vacancies. There is a secondary sector in the labour market that does more or less clear ... If people are unemployed, it is generally because they have decided against these jobs. They are however willing to work in a range of 'good' primary sector jobs, but they cannot get them. In this sense unemployment is both voluntary and involuntary. [4]

LNJ (1991, p. 34) also stress that the unemployed should be vigorous in their search activity so that 'firms can get workers more easily and disemployed people face fiercer competition for jobs. Thus if unemployed seek harder, there need be fewer of them in order to restrain wage pressure.' This leads LNJ to conclude that it is the 'effective' unemployed that is the relevant discipline on wage bargaining rather than the actual number of unemployed.

Another implication of their reasoning is that rising long-term unemployment (and reduced search effectiveness) reduces the impact of overall unemployment on wage outcomes. As a consequence LNJ (1991, p. 10) say: '[t]here is however some "short-run NAIRU", which *would* be consistent with stable inflation, and which of course depends on last year's unemployment'. Thus hysteresis may play a role. LNJ (1991, p. 18) say the short-run NAIRU 'lies between last period's unemployment and the long-run NAIRU'. This also implies that 'in the short run, unemployment is determined by the interaction of aggregate demand and short-run aggregate supply ... [but as LNJ hasten to add] ... In the long run, unemployment is entirely determined by long-run supply factors and equals the NAIRU' (LNJ, 1991, p. 16).

LNJ have a confused view on the impact of economic policy on unemployment. On the one hand, as noted by Nickell and van Ours (2000, p. 140), a reasonable interpretation of LNJ is that:

> The equilibrium rate of unemployment cannot be changed with fiscal, monetary or exchange rate policy. What these policies can do is change the way actual unemployment fluctuates around the equilibrium rate.

However, LNJ (1991, p. 13) also observe that 'if financial policy ensures that inflation *is* stable, then unemployment will adjust to its equilibrium level'. The latter observation is reinforced in Nickell and van Ours (2000, p. 142) when they ask: 'Why do we have unemployment?' Basically their answer is that authorities are afraid of generating inflation. A similar divergence in possibilities is observed by Tobin (1996, p. 326): 'What leads to such [equilibrium]? Some economists would stress the ultimate natural equilibration of markets. Other would stress the response of macro policy makers.' Apparently LNJ alternate between both views.

1.3   THE DEFICIENCIES IN THE NAIRU APPROACH

In section 1.3.1, we identify three distinct lines of attack against the notion and use of the NAIRU. In section 1.3.2, we illustrate some of these conceptual flaws using empirical data for the Netherlands.

1.3.1   Three Lines of Attack

In Mitchell and Muysken (2004) we distinguish three broad lines of attack on the concept of the NAIRU. First, the NAIRU is attacked along theoretical lines, although this literature often uses empirical work to consolidate the argument. Blanchard (1997), Phelps (1994) and Phelps and Zoega (1998) amend the NAIRU model to include costs of capital which enables them to implicate high real interest rates for the European unemployment in the 1980s. Rowthorn (1999) also analyses the impact of productivity shocks. Modigliani (2000) and Sawyer (2002) emphasize the role of aggregate demand in determining the NAIRU (essentially through real interest rate effects). Numerous studies look at the impact of hysteresis (Ball, 1999). Finally Akerlof et al. (2000) argue that 'near-rational behaviour', which allows for money illusion, causes a trade-off between unemployment and inflation at relatively low rates of inflation, even in the long run. Mitchell and Muysken (2003, p. 7) conclude in a literature summary: 'once deconstructed it is little wonder that the concept of equilibrium unemployment loses its original "structural" meaning and becomes indistinguishable in dynamics from actual unemployment'.

   Second, a growing literature has documented the empirical failings of NAIRU models. Campbell and Mankiw (1987, 1989) find non-linearities in the reaction of unemployment to shocks. These findings run contrary to the NAIRU approach which is built on smooth linear functions. Chang (1997) and Fair (2000) demonstrate that inflation dynamics do not seem to accord with those specified in the NAIRU hypothesis. There is no clear correlation between changes in the inflation rate and the level of unemployment, such that inflation rises and falls at many different unemployment rates without system. The time-varying NAIRU approach which replaced the discredited constant NAIRU depiction has been similarly tainted by lack of economic and empirical content (Gordon, 1997). Staiger et al. (1997) find large standard errors for NAIRU estimates which render the concept relatively useless for policy analysis (see below). Baker et al. (2002) are highly critical of the NAIRU approach after forensically examining a large number of NAIRU studies. Similar results are obtained from the meta-study of Stanley (2004) on hysteresis. Ball (1999) and Modigliani (2000) demonstrate that close relationships exist between employment and vacancies growth and the inverse of the unemployment rate, and between investment to GDP ratios and the unemployment rate across many countries. They are difficult to interpret as being driven from the supply side.

Third, the usefulness of the NAIRU for policy purposes is also questioned. As a criticism, Galbraith (1997, p. 106) establishes the primacy of the NAIRU in the neo-liberal policy framework:

> One of the serious unintended consequences of economists' preoccupation with the NAIRU has been to convey a message to political leaders that they need not feel responsibility in this area, that the inflation–unemployment trade-off can be fine-tuned with interest rates by the FED.

In assessing whether the NAIRU should have this status, Chang (1997, p. 12) concludes that:

> In practice, the concept of a non-accelerating inflation rate of unemployment is not useful for policy purposes. First, the NAIRU moves around. Second, uncertainty about where the NAIRU is at any point of time is considerable. Third, even if we knew where the NAIRU were, it would be suboptimal to predict inflation solely on the basis of the comparison of unemployment against the NAIRU. A policy of raising the fed funds rate when unemployment falls below the NAIRU may be ineffective ... even if the NAIRU were constant, its location were known and all shocks to the economy were to come from the demand side. Implementing such policy would likely induce changes in the expectations and behaviour of the private sector, an important additional reason to be sceptical about using the NAIRU for policy.

Solow and Taylor (1998) emphasize the dangers inherent in following a NAIRU strategy to control inflation. While there may be stability between inflation and unemployment for a period, a sudden shock, especially from the supply side (as in 1974, for example), can exacerbate the costs of unemployment resulting from a deflationary strategy (which attempts to exploit a given Phillips curve). Evidence from the OECD experience over the last 25 years suggests that this policy is effective in bringing inflation down (Mitchell, 1998; Cornwall, 1983). But rarely are the costs of such a strategy computed or addressed despite the overwhelming evidence that the costs of sustained high unemployment are enormous (Watts and Mitchell, 2000). This is precisely why the Brussels–Frankfurt Consensus is an answer to the wrong question.

1.3.2   The Implausibility of the Dutch NAIRU?

The CPB has recently started to publish data on equilibrium unemployment, which is based on their conception and operationalization of the NAIRU approach. Figure 1.3 presents CPB's recent data. The behaviour of the NAIRU time series recalls Gordon's (1997, p. 28) conclusion that:[5]

> wild gyrations of the estimated NAIRU over a range too wide to be explained by microeconomic changes in market structure and institutions would lead to scepticism about the NAIRU concept ... When applied to Europe ... fluctuations in the NAIRU seem too large to be plausible and seem mainly to mimic movements in the actual unemployment rate.

The equilibrium unemployment data are consistent with those estimated in Broer et al. (2000). Mitchell and Muysken (2003) present strong and diverse criticisms of their approach. First, Broer et al. concentrate on supply-side variables thus ignoring the impact of the demand side on unemployment. We return to that theme below. Second, we show that many of the alleged supply-side variables are strongly influenced by cyclical movements. An illustration is given in Table 1.1 (see also Mitchell and Muysken, 2003, Table 3).

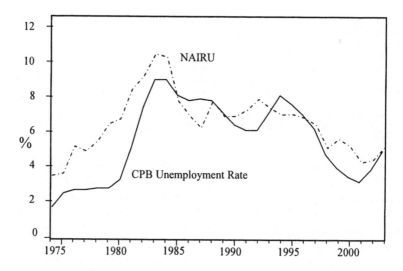

Source: Verbruggen (2003), Figure 4.

Figure 1.3   Actual and equilibrium unemployment, The Netherlands, 1974–2003

Table 1.1   Testing wedge and replacement rate variables for cyclical influence[a]

| | Replacement Rate | | Wedge | |
	Broer[d]	CPB[e]	Broer	CPB
dvar(-1)[b]	0.02	0.18	0.20	0.26
	(0.21)	(1.07)	(1.04)	(1.55)
dlog(CU)[c]	-0.23	-0.23	0.10	-0.01
	(3.05)	(2.97)	(0.57)	(0.06)
dlog (CU(-1))[c]	-0.18	-0.14	-0.39	-0.23
	(2.26)	(1.64)	(2.19)	(1.96)
R^2	0.37	0.39	0.19	0.19
Years	1970-1997	1972-2003	1970-1997	1972-2003

Notes:
[a] Constant not reported. Dependent variables were in change of log form. t-statistics are in parentheses.
[b] dvar(-1) is the lagged dependent variable.
[c] CU is the rate of capacity utilisation.
[d] Broer *et al* (2000).
[e] current official data from the CPB.

The table reports estimates of the wedge (an attempt to measure differences between gross wage costs (borne by employers) and net wage income (received by workers) and the replacement rate (which purports to measure average social security outlays as a percentage of the average wage). Mitchell and Muysken (2003) show that the data used for these and other variables differ, sometimes considerably, over the various studies used (even amongst CPB-related authors). This affects both the estimation results and policy conclusions.

From Table 1.1, it is clear that the 'structural' variables used by Broer et al. (2000) and the official CPB measures vary counter-cyclically with capacity utilization which is consistent with *a priori* reasoning. In the upturn falling unemployment means that lower social security premiums are needed to cover expenses and the wedge will be lower. The replacement rate rises as unemployment rises because there is increasing pressure to increase social security in a downturn. As a consequence of the counter-cyclical behaviour of these so-called 'structural' variables the NAIRU will tend to track the actual unemployment rate in line with demand changes rendering it void of any meaningful independent content.

Our contention that the NAIRU is strongly driven by cyclical movements is also illustrated in Figure 1.4.[6] Two comments should be made here. First, one should be aware that hysteresis (tracking of the actual unemployment rate by the estimated NAIRU) plays an important role in explaining the NAIRU, as illustrated in Figure 1.5. That is, the NAIRU (which may include structural parameters) is dependent on unemployment in the previous period which suggests that structural imbalance is cyclically sensitive. Interestingly, this effect is not modelled by Broer et al. (2000, Equation 17) although their results show that hysteresis does occur.

Second, given the output gap plays no role in the analysis of Broer et al. (2000), we conclude they see no connection between it and the NAIRU. However, Figure 1.4 shows that when we correct for hysteresis in a very simple way (by subtracting lagged unemployment from the estimated NAIRU) there is a clear relationship between the remaining component of the equilibrium unemployment and capacity utilization, which implies that cyclical variation plays an important role. This also links the NAIRU to fluctuations in aggregate demand.

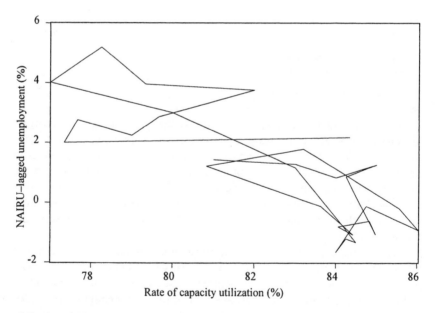

Source: Verbruggen (2003).

Figure 1.4   The NAIRU and capacity utilization, 1974–2003

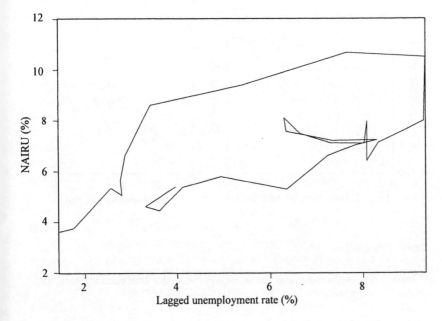

Source: Verbruggen (2003).

Figure 1.5   Dutch hysteresis, 1974–2003

Given these results it is also not surprising that Mitchell and Muysken (2003) find that the Dutch labour market responds positively to strong GDP growth driving strong employment growth. Thus aggregate demand variations rather than labour force (supply) changes dominate employment changes. Moreover, variations in unemployment appear to be strongly associated with movements in labour demand. This is consistent with Modigliani (2000, p. 5) who claims that 'everywhere unemployment has risen because of a large shrinkage in the number of positions needed to satisfy existing demand'.

To analyse the nature of unemployment further, Mitchell and Muysken (2003) present phase diagrams for the unemployment rate and the vacancy rate in the Netherlands (Ormerod, 1994; Mitchell, 2001a). In Figure 1.6 the current values of the series are plotted on the *y*-axis against the lagged value of the same series on the *x*-axis. The OECD consensus interprets the outward unemployment shift in Figure 1.6a as a decline in labour market efficiency.

But the inward shift in Figure 1.6b, using the same logic, would be interpreted as increasing matching efficiency. Clearly, both states cannot hold. A consistent interpretation can be found in the view that the Dutch economy was demand-constrained in the mid-1970s as a result of the collapse of

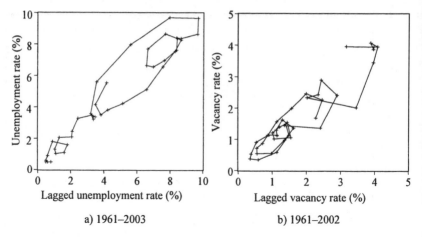

Source: CPB (2003)

Figure 1.6   Phase diagrams for unemployment rate and vacancy rate, 1961–2003

collapse of world trade. The rapid rise in unemployment in 1974 was so large that subsequent (low) growth with ongoing labour force and productivity growth could not reverse the stockpile of unemployed (see Mitchell, 2001b for a similar Australian analysis).

Two conclusions can be drawn from the phase diagrams. First, negative shifts in attractors coincide with recessions. Second, the economy tends to oscillate around these attractors once they are established. This implies that adverse demand shocks have a strong negative impact on unemployment through hysteresis. Thus demand shocks have an adverse impact on unemployment through the direct effects on job creation, as highlighted in the previous section, and indirectly, through hysteresis.

All these observations serve to cast serious doubts on the notion implied by the Brussels–Frankfurt Consensus that combating unemployment should be separated from macroeconomic policy.

1.4   THE OECD JOBS STUDY AND THE EES: TWO SIDES OF THE SAME COIN

Stiglitz (2002, p. 42) gives a fascinating account of how the IMF has dominated thinking about economic policy in both developed and developing countries. Not only does he strongly criticize the 'one-size-fits-all' nature of the IMF policy prescriptions, but he also observes that:

The IMF is like so many bureaucracies; it has repeatedly sought to extend what it does, beyond the objectives originally assigned to it. As IMF's mission creep brought it outside its core area of competency in macroeconomics, into structural issues such as privatisation, labour markets, pension reforms and so forth ...

Stiglitz (2002) argues that the combination of the IMF's fierce promotion of the current dominant ideology in economics, its simplistic yet well-defined policy framework and its good political contacts in the Western world, renders it a very powerful institution, which often overrides the World Bank in its dealing with poor countries. (Stiglitz is of course also critical of the World Bank.)

Although he does not refer to Stiglitz's experiences, Dostal's (2004) account of how the OECD framed EU welfare and labour market policies reveals striking similarities. Dostal (2004, p. 441) describes persuasively how the OECD deliberately used the Jobs Study to position itself in the policy debate and was highly successful therein. An important observation is that:

...[the] preparation for the economic and monetary union separated macroeconomic policy making from the agenda of employment policy [in Europe]. ... Instead, liberal labour market theorists explained unemployment as a structural issue arising from over-regulation of the wage labour relationship and over-generous wage replacement payments ...

This is entirely consistent with the NAIRU approach sketched above (see also Casey, 2004; Watt, 2004).

While the OECD (1994) Jobs Study strategy dominates the European Employment Strategy (EES), there are still differences in the two approaches. Dostal (2004) is correct when he points out that many elements of the Jobs Study have been fully absorbed within the EES, as reflected in the latter's four pillars: employability, entrepreneurship, adaptability and gender equality. Casey (2004) presents a detailed overview of the similarities between the recommendations of both strategies. Casey (2004, p. 5) points out that the recommendations reflect a 'structural' interpretation of unemployment, 'symptomatic of an insufficient ability to adapt to change ... [implying] ... a focus on policies concerned with labour.'

Other authors prefer to stress the differences between the Jobs Study and the EES, which lie not so much in the underlying analysis, but in the implementation of the recommendations. It is widely recognized that the OECD recommendations are framed by NAIRU-based beliefs which provide a unified form of discourse,[7] while the European Union approach is much more eclectic, balancing between various interest groups (Noaksson and Jacobsson, 2003; Dostal, 2004; Casey, 2004). This also is reflected in the so-called open coordination method which is an integral part of the EES, and was introduced at the outset of the Luxembourg process (Goetschy, 1999).

Mosher and Trubeck (2003, p. 83) argue that the open coordination method 'has been touted as a third way in EU governance to be used when harmonisation is unworkable but mutual recognition and the resulting regulatory competition may have unwelcome consequences'. Key elements of this method include the use of best-practice techniques to encourage learning between units within the EU, benchmarking, consultation, and action plans; the latter of which are defined in terms of concrete targets, but with no attendant punishments for non-achievement. Consistent with the 'Third Way' approach, Mosher and Trubeck (2003, p. 64) observe:

> Where some see a creative breakthrough that will solve problems up till now considered intractable, others see another threat to Europe's generous social policies. For the optimists, the EES is not only a methodological breakthrough for the Union, but also an innovation with superior capacity to solve the many social problems Europe faces ... Others, however, fear that by moving away from efforts to mandate uniform and social standards, the Union might contribute to the gradual erosion of social programmes and policies.

These differences in approach between the OECD and the EU lead Casey (2004, p. 19) to conclude that there is 'one view of the labour market, but two views of the welfare state'.

Finally, it is interesting to observe that both the OECD Jobs Strategy and the EES are under revision (OECD, 2004; Watt, 2004). But our expectations of a fundamental change towards a job creation approach are not high. As Watt (2004. p. 135) observes: 'In the wider context of employment policy as a whole, however, the changes ... [in the EES] ... pale into insignificance compared to the short-term threats to employment posed by both by global economic developments and risks, and the inability to reach agreement ... to promote output stability and growth that are needed to bring about a sustained raise in employment.' This observation brings us to the Stability and Growth Pact (hereafter the SGP).

1.5   THE STABILITY AND GROWTH PACT: NEITHER STABILITY NOR GROWTH

According to the Maastricht Treaty in 1992, countries that wanted to be included in the Euro Area had to fulfil amongst other things the following two requirements: (1) a debt-to-GDP ratio below 60 per cent, or converging towards it; and (2) a budget deficit below 3 per cent of GDP. It is now widely recognized that these figures are highly arbitrary without any solid theoretical foundation or internal consistency, although they were consistent with some key empirical situations prevailing at that time. The rationale to control government debt and budget deficits were consistent with the rising neo-liberal orthodoxy that promoted inflation control to be the macroeconomic policy priority and asserted the primacy of monetary policy (a narrow conception notwithstanding) over fiscal policy. Indeed, fiscal policy was forced by this 'inflation-first' ideology to become a passive actor on the macroeconomic stage. Many countries have taken this route in the 1990s including Canada, Australia, New Zealand, the UK, and to a lesser extent, the US.

The limitations of this approach, in the sense that it renders the unemployment rate a policy instrument rather than a target, are aggravated for Europe because the ECB cannot differentiate its monetary policy between European member states. While fiscal policy remains a national affair, the aim was to put it into a straitjacket and hence neuter its effectiveness. The underlying logic of this policy framework, which to us is a nonsensically restricted approach to macroeconomic policy (more about this later), was the perceived danger, articulated in particular by Germany at the inception, that some runaway member states might follow a reckless spending policy, which in its turn would force the ECB to increase its interest rates. Such a policy shift may damage, unjustifiably, the other 'compliant' countries. As a consequence, fiscal constraints should be in place to prevent countries like Italy and Spain from 'spoiling the party' for the rest of the euro countries. Some party it has turned out to be!

Aided by the growth period following the 1991 recession, the fiscal constraints were met by all aspiring member states. Emboldened by this success, and more alert because the date for the euro introduction was approaching, the euro countries decided in the 1997 Amsterdam Treaty that the rules should be sharpened. The deficit should be either zero or in surplus, and when it threatened to reach 3 per cent of GDP, countries should take appropriate measures. This requirement, formalized in the SGP, was criticized by many economists.

Even economists operating from within the relatively orthodox 'deficit dove' paradigm, such as de Grauwe (2003), forcefully argue that there is no rationale for a zero government debt, which a zero deficit should imply in the long run. It is also easy to show that a constant ratio of debt to GDP is sustainable as long as GDP growth exceeds the real interest rate: in that case the deficit can equal the difference between both. That observation illustrates that from this perspective it is much more fruitful to concentrate on stimulating economic growth, than on anxiously guarding government deficits (Fitoussi and Saraceno, 2004). From the 'deficit dove' viewpoint, public borrowing is constructed as a very normal way to 'finance' capital expenditures. Since government invests a lot in infrastructure and other public works, those investments at least should allow for a deficit. This was already recognized by the classical economists as a 'golden rule' of public finance – for a modern variant see Buiter and Grafe (2002). In the next section we will criticize the SGP from the perspective of the functional finance paradigm.

Any economist with even the simplest understanding of the way in which automatic stabilizers operate will see the lack of wisdom in the SGP rule. A sharp negative demand shock which causes an economic downturn will reduce tax receipts and increase benefits, which together automatically increases the deficit. Reducing government expenditures in that situation to meet the 'rule' will worsen (prolong) the recession, which will then in all likelihood involve the country in further SGP rule violations. The vicious circle of spending cuts implied is unsustainable and fiscal lunacy. In other words, fiscal policy becomes pro-cyclical under the SGP rule, violating any sensible ambitions that are the ambit of responsible fiscal management. This is the major reason that France and Germany have refused to comply with the 3 per cent rule over the last few fiscal years.

Another problem relates to the bias in the way fiscal adjustment is conceived – it is automatically assumed that discretionary actions to reduce the budget deficit will involve spending cuts rather than increasing taxes. We cannot help but have the impression that some politicians are not primarily concerned about the size of the budget deficit, but covet the 3 per cent rule as a welcome excuse to force their preferences for 'small government'. In other words, the ideological bias against public activity, particularly in the social security sphere, is dressed up as 'prudential economic management'.

This obsession is even more problematic when one considers that monetary policy is in the hands of the ECB, which is not politically responsible for its actions: it is independent, and its sole aim is to control inflation. The fundamental democratic principle that the citizens have the ability to cast judgement on the policies of their representatives at regular intervals has been abandoned in this set-up.

Stiglitz (2002, p. 45) is highly critical of the EU model:

> There is a wide-spread feeling that Europe's independent Central Bank exacerbated Europe's economic slowdown in 2001, as, like a child, it responded peevishly to the natural political concerns over growing unemployment. Just to show that it was independent, it refused to allow the interest rates to fall, and there was nothing anyone could do about it. The problems partly arose because the European Central Bank has a mandate to focus on inflation, a policy ... that can stifle growth or exacerbate an economic down turn.

The straitjacket that the ECB has voluntarily placed itself in suggests that countries have to use fiscal policy to react to economic shocks which affect the real economy. However, the SGP has imposed an inflexibility on this discretion and stagnant economic outcomes have been the norm (see also Bofinger, 2003; Arestis and Sawyer, 2004).

It is often said that the European economies are 'sclerotic', which is usually taken to mean they have too much labour market protection and overly generous welfare systems. However, the real European sclerosis is found in the inflexible macroeconomic policy regime that the euro countries have voluntarily contrived. The rigid monetary arrangements conducted by the 'undemocratic' ECB and the irrational fiscal constraints that are required if the SGP is to be adhered to, render the nation states within the Euro Area incapable of achieving low levels of unemployment and increasing income growth. These observations then lead to our more embracing criticism of the Brussels–Frankfurt Consensus from the perspective of the functional finance paradigm.

1.6   THE BRUSSELS–FRANKFURT CONSENSUS AND FUNCTIONAL FINANCE

The European economies are in meltdown because their leaders have misunderstood the options open to them under conditions of sovereign currency. The principles of functional finance (Mitchell, 1998; Wray, 1998; Mitchell and Mosler, 2002) describe these options and prescribe how macroeconomic policy instruments should be used to achieve them. In this section, we provide a brief introduction.

There has been a lot of concern in recent years about the strong euro relative to the US dollar. The answer is illustrative of what is wrong with the European economies. National accounting tells us that government deficits are equal to non-governmental savings, which in this context are defined as euro-denominated financial assets. Without loss of generality, the non-governmental sector is comprised of the private domestic sector and the foreign sector. As a matter of accounting, government deficits are the sum of domestic savings plus foreign savings. The private sector savings can be sourced from the public deficit or from the foreign sector. In our view, in recent years there has been a shortage of euros in the foreign sector and a lack of desire by foreigners to take on euro-denominated debt. Thus, for the private domestic sector to accumulate euro savings, the government sector has to be ready to provide the funds. Unfortunately, by design, the sovereign governments in Europe have voluntarily constrained their ability to run discretionary deficits which are essential to meet desired domestic savings targets.

The link between the fact that private domestic participants in Europe are unable to achieve their desired net savings of euro-denominated financial assets and the persistent unemployment and wasteful excess capacity is clear. To resolve the impasse there has to be more euro-denominated spending to challenge inventories and provide incentives for European producers to expand production and employment. The malaise occurs because, in an attempt to net save when there is insufficient public deficit injection, the private sector cuts back spending. The dilemma is the classic macroeconomic compositional fallacy (the so-called paradox of saving) – by trying to save when there is insufficient public spending, the private sector merely exacerbates the problem and achieves lower actual savings.

The persistent weakness of European labour markets is symptomatic of their slack product markets and policy-makers have constructed this malaise in exactly the wrong way. Given the overwhelming dominance of the neo-liberal disdain for fiscal activism, there has been a major shift in the aggregate policy mix towards the centrality of monetary policy under the guise of 'fight-inflation'. The imagery that comes to mind is of a pugilist who goes into fight with one hand tied behind his or her back. Not a clever strategy. It appears that European policy-makers think that lower interest rates (given the monetary policy emphasis) is the only acceptable aggregate policy response to the economic meltdown.

They should think again. If the problem truly is that the private sector is being squeezed relative to its desire to accumulate net savings in euro-denominated financial assets, then interest rates do nothing for this. Only net government spending will provide the 'vertical' liquidity injection to achieve underpinning of the desired private credit structure.

The policy-makers clearly are hoping that lower interest rates will stifle the desire to save and hence consumers and investors will be induced to increase their leverage levels which would underpin a spending recovery. This is a fraught strategy. First, the ECB has artificially constrained itself to CPI rules although it is debated whether the CPI measures anything that is relevant for reflecting price pressure. These constraints are just neo-liberal dogma with little economic content to justify them. If deficits were inflationary, how do the European economists who support the current system explain the situation in Japan or in the US?

Second, the Japanese situation is worth reflecting on. It is unclear that lower interest rates will stimulate demand. It relies on a number of dubious distributional assumptions that have not been substantiated by any credible research. Japan has been running excess reserves in its banking system for years as a result of the public net injection not being fully 'drained' by Bank of Japan bond sales. The result of this deliberate practice has been interest rates of around 0.001 per cent for over a decade. There has been very little spending reaction to the low rates and further the yen remains strong.

The solution to the high unemployment in Europe that we advocate in this chapter is, however, rejected by ill-informed policy-makers. The attack on the unemployment problem should be on two broad fronts. First, the artificial and damaging constraints on fiscal policy under the GSP have to be abandoned and governments should increase their deficit spending to be at least within the range of 5 per cent of GDP until recovery ensures. This level of net spending will underpin the desire to save and create solid demand for inventories which in turn will promote employment growth. It is hard to see this as an inflationary act given the massive excess labour and capital resources that abound right across Europe.[8] The defiant trend demonstrated by Germany and France in recent fiscal years should be generalized. As part of this generalized liquidity expansion, European governments should also introduce an unconditional job offer to any person who is unable to find work. This offer should not chase market wages but should instead be at the minimum living wage. This policy approach – termed a Job Guarantee by Mitchell (1998) – will secure full employment without invoking demand pressures. Indeed as Mitchell and Wray (2005) argue, it could be introduced at a time of demand contraction and still ensure full employment existed. There is simply no economic reason why workers who are being supported in the public sector on welfare should not be provided with an opportunity to productively contribute to their societies by working. The only thing preventing this is the will of European governments to provide these jobs. For a full recent exposition of the Job Guarantee see Mitchell and Wray (2005). Whatever else the governments do by way of spending, they should always have this 'buffer stock' of jobs available. From a resource usage and social benefit perspective, it is far better to fight inflation with a buffer stock of jobs, than it is to use a buffer stock of unemployment (zero output) which is the NAIRU and hence the Consensus approach.

The second policy front that should be opened is to return to the strategy that made Germany one of the world powerhouse economies in the past. At the same time that domestic labour and capital resources have been underutilized, European export growth, which previously was the 'backbone' of the various economies, has stalled. A major part in this slowdown has been the rise in the value of the euro rather than soft world product markets. So what has been the problem? Take the German case before the monetary union was formalized. During that period the Bundesbank always bought enough US dollars to keep the mark from appreciating to such a level that the German exporters would be damaged. The German consumer thus, in part, 'cross-subsidized' the strong GDP growth and fully employed labour force.

If the European governments are intent on maintaining unreasonably tight fiscal policies, then their export markets will have to provide the engine of growth. Even with a modest recovery in world product markets the ECB has to start purchasing large quantities of foreign currency to underpin the export sector. The problem is not only that there has been a concentration on monetary policy at the expense of the fiscal activism, but that the concept of monetary intervention has also been redefined by the neo-liberal ideologues. It is an essential part of a sophisticated monetary policy for the central bank to intervene directly in currency markets and in this case for the ECB to start accumulating US dollars reserves.

The conduct of the Bank of Japan is again illustrative. It is a large purchaser of US dollars which allows it to net spend in terms of the yen. The same applies to the ECB. By purchasing US dollars on foreign currency markets it net spends in the euro and drives up the net euro-denominated savings of the non-government sector. It should be noted that we consider the treasury and the central bank operations to be consolidated when we talk about the public or government deficit relative to the non-government balance.

The other advantage of this strategy would be that it would allow the ECB to maintain euro parity at rates supportive of the European exporters.[9] The ECB would clearly consider such a strategy unacceptable because it would appear that the US dollar was being employed as the reserve currency for the euro. Given the history of the euro and the bellicose intentions of the European central banking mandarins that the new currency should rival the US dollar as the world's reserve currency, this appearance would strike horror.

But the current position is not sustainable. An export growth strategy not supported by central bank currency market interventions means that the export profits find their way into euros which drives the parity higher and undermines the export strategy.

The only strategy left open to European firms facing slowing demand for their export products as a result of this insane policy environment is to cut costs in general to restore profit targets.[10] The casualties are the workers who enter the labour queues and the multiplier effects then generate further income losses and softening domestic product market conditions.

It should be noted that if the ECB wants to promote the euro as a 'rival reserve currency' to the US dollar, there is one essential precondition: Foreigners must be able to 'net save' in euro-denominated financial assets. But due to inadequate export levels emanating from Europe and a failure of the ECB to use all of its monetary policy instruments, this precondition is absent. The solution for European governments is to introduce policies that will stimulate import demand which allows foreigners to accumulate euro-denominated savings. The increased net public spending would certainly help in that regard.

1.7 CONCLUSION

In our view the obsession with low inflation, as reflected in the Brussels–Frankfurt Consensus, is an answer to the wrong question because it ignores the huge economic and social costs imposed on European countries by persistently high unemployment. Unfortunately, this malaise is not considered by EU politics to be a major issue that needs to be solved with the highest priority. Sadly, it is the other way around: unemployment, at best, is seen as an unfortunate consequence of the need to maintain a low-inflation environment and is a symptom of rigidities which hamper a proper functioning of the economy. At worst, it is seen as a voluntary state where individuals choose life paths emphasizing leisure. Never is it constructed as the systematic macroeconomic failure of governments to ensure that there are enough jobs created in their economies.

We have argued that the NAIRU approach and the Brussels–Frankfurt Consensus, which underlie this policy position, gained their influence on European policy through the OECD Jobs Study, the European Employment Study, the Maastricht criteria and the Stability and Growth Pact. However, the approach is not based on a correct interpretation of the options facing sovereign governments with monopolies in currency issues. Further, the empirical evidence suggests that the NAIRU concept is a degenerative paradigm and as such, provides a poor guide to employment policy. Similar arguments are presented against the Brussels–Frankfurt Consensus, where we pay special attention to the Stability and Growth Pact. Using insights from functional finance, we argue that the pact essentially results in neither stability nor growth and is, ultimately, unsustainable.

NOTES

1. In both cases we use unweighted averages.
2. In his sympathetic but critical review of the various efforts in the same volume Blanchard (1990, p. 66) says: 'I am afraid that the research programme may have been overambitious. ... Although much is learned, the very richness of the model makes it harder to see how the model can ... explain what I see as the crucial issue, the persistence of high unemployment.'
3. In this context the role of responsible unions is emphasized. Drèze and Bean (1990, p. 22) note that: 'in contrast to the United States, wage formation in Europe today is dominated by unions who are greatly concerned about distributional fairness'. As a consequence Drèze and Bean (1990, p. 38) argue that 'the mechanism through which unemployment

could be self-correcting is weak. We should not be surprised that in Europe unemployment has been persistent'.

4.   Interestingly enough LNJ (1991, p. 44) abandon this line of thought in the next sentence, stating: 'But in order to understand how the economy changes over time, it may be good enough to proceed as though there were only one sector, whose wages and employment are determined by the kinds of mechanisms discussed in [the battle between mark-ups].' Moreover, if one considers for one moment the high incidence of unemployment amongst the disadvantaged groups, it is obvious that this primary–secondary story does not hold for them. LNJ (1991, p. 44) also add: 'It is however extremely difficult to distinguish between the primary and the secondary sector in the official statistics. The secondary sector is also a fairly small part of the manual labour market.'

5.   Although they do not refer to this statement, Broer et al. (2000, p. 364) respond to the broad point of a fluctuating NAIRU: 'The equilibrium rate is only stable insofar as its underlying determinants are stable. Indeed, the concept of a slowly-moving NAIRU, that forms the backbone of much recent work on inflation forecasting in the US (see e.g. Gordon (1997)), is void of empirical content in times of rapid changes in the structural determinants of equilibrium unemployment.'

6.   The CPB conclusion that 'because of the persistent low GDP-growth, the output gap ... has widened sharply in the last few years ... The main reason why the current output gap is even worse than during the early 1980s recession is that at present the unemployment rate exceeds the estimated non-accelerating rate of inflation rate of unemployment (NAIRU), while it did not so in the early 1980s ... In structural terms the labour market is in much better shape now' (Verbruggen, 2003, p. 11) seems rather bizarre to us. The causality obviously is the other way around.

7.   In this context we cannot resist the following citation, where Stiglitz (2002, p. 24) critiques the IMF: 'One should not see unemployment just as a statistic, an economic "body count", the unintended causalities in the fight against inflation ... The unemployed are people, with families whose lives are affected – sometimes devastated – by the economic policies that outsiders recommend ... [or] ...effectively impose. Modern high-tech warfare is designed to remove physical contact: dropping bombs from 50000 feet ensures that one does not "feel" what one does. Modern economic management is similar: from one's luxury hotel, one can callously impose policies about which one would think twice if one knew the people whose lives one was destroying.'

8.   This excess capacity is also observed in the most recent economic outlook of the OECD, released November 2005, where they predict that the recovery which seemed to be 'just around the corner' will be delayed by one year. See also note 7 above for the case of the Netherlands.

9.   This is the reason why de Grauwe has also advocated this strategy the *Financial Times* of 30 November 2005.

10. Essentially this is also the policy followed by the Dutch Central Bank in the mid-1980s when it tied the Dutch guilder to the Deutschmark, essentially enforcing wage moderation. On the one hand this explains the enormous employment growth, the so-called Dutch miracle. However, one of the prices that have been paid for this success was the high incidence of allegedly disabled workers, who have now become an entrenched problem and constitute about 10 per cent of the workforce (Muysken, 2003).

REFERENCES

Akerlof, G.E., W.T. Dickens and G.L. Perry (2000), 'Near-rational wage and price setting and the long-run', *Brookings Papers on Economic Activity*, 1, 1–61.

Arestis, P. and M. Sawyer (2004), 'Alternatives for the policy framework of the Euro', Presented at the 2nd Workshop of the Centre of Full Employment and Equity Europe, Maastricht, 2004, November 12–13.

Baker, D., A. Glyn, D. Howell and J. Schmitt (2002), 'Labor market institutions and unemployment: a critical assessment of the cross-country evidence', *CEPA Working Paper*, 2002-17.

Ball, L. (1999), 'Aggregate demand and long-run unemployment', *Brookings Papers on Economic Activity*, **2**, 189–251.

Barro, R.J. and H.I. Grossman (1971), 'A general disequilibrium model of income and employment', *American Economic Review*, **61** (1), March, 82–93.

Blanchard, O.J. (1990), 'Unemployment: Getting the Questions Right—and some of the Answers', in J.H. Drèze and C.R. Bean (eds) (1990), *Europe's Unemployment Problem*, Cambridge, MA, US: MIT Press, pp. 66–89.

Blanchard, O.J. (1997), 'The medium run (business cycles and development in Europe and North America)', *Brookings Papers on Economic Activity*, **2**, 89–158.

Bofinger, P. (2003), 'The Stability and Growth Pact neglects the policy mix between fiscal and monetary policy', *Intereconomics*, (Jan/Feb), 1–7.

Broer, D.P., D.A.G Draper and F.H. Huizinga (2000), 'The equilibrium rate of unemployment in the Netherlands', *De Economist*, **148** (3), 345–371.

Buiter, W.H. and C. Grafe (2002), 'Patching up the Pact: some suggestions for enhancing fiscal sustainability and macroeconomic stability in an enlarged European Union', *CEPR Discussion Papers*, 3496.

Campbell, J.Y. and N.G. Mankiw (1987), 'Are fluctuations transitory?', *Quarterly Journal of Economics*, **102**, 875–80.

Campbell, J.Y. and N.G. Mankiw (1989), 'The persistence of economic fluctuations', *Journal of Monetary Economics*, **23**, 319–333.

Casey, B.H. (2004), 'The OECD Jobs Strategy and the European Employment Strategy: two views of the labour market and of the welfare state', *European Journal of Industrial Relations*, **10** (3), 329–352.

Chang, R. (1997), 'Is low unemployment inflationary?', *Federal Reserve Bank of Atlanta Economic Review*, (First Quarter).

Cornwall, J. (1983), *The Conditions for Economic Recovery*, Oxford: Martin Robertson.

CPB (2003), *Centraal Economisch Plan*, The Hague, The Netherlands: CPB.

Dostal, J.M. (2004), 'Campaigning on expertise: how the OECD framed EU welfare and labour market policies – and why success could trigger failure', *Journal of European Public Policy*, **11** (3) (June), 440–460.

Drèze, J.H. and C.R. Bean (eds) (1990), *Europe's Unemployment Problem*, Cambridge, MA, US: MIT Press.

Drèze, J.H. and E. Malinvaud (1994), 'Growth and employment: the scope of a European initiative', *European Economic Review*, **38** (3–4) (April), 489–504.

European Union (1993), *On Growth, Competitiveness, and Employment: The challenges and ways forward into the 21st century – White paper*, COM (93) 700, available online at: http://europa.eu.int/en/record/white/c93700/contents.html.

Fair, R. (2000), 'Testing the NAIRU model for the United States', *Review of Economics and Statistics*, (February), 64–71.

Fitoussi, J.P. and F. Saraceno (2004), 'The Brussels–Frankfurt–Washington Consensus: old and new tradeoffs in economics', in S. Spiegel and J.E. Stiglitz (eds), *Initiative for Policy Dialogue Macroeconomics Companion Volume*, forthcoming.

Friedman, M. (1968), 'The role of monetary policy', *American Economic Review*, **58** (March), 1–17.

Galbraith, J.K. (1997), 'Time to ditch the NAIRU', *Journal of Economic Perspectives*, **11** (1) (Winter), 93–108.

30   *Monetary Policy, Fiscal Policy and the Stability and Growth Pact*

Goetschy, J. (1999), 'The European employment strategy: genesis and development', *European Journal of Industrial Relations*, **5** (2), 117–137.
Gordon, R.J. (1997), 'The time-varying NAIRU and its implications for economic policy', *Journal of Economic Perspectives*, **11** (1) (Winter), 11–32.
Grauwe, P. de (2003), *The Stability and Growth Pact in need of reform*, Brussels: Center for European Policy Studies (CEPS).
Howitt, P. (1977), 'Barro and Grossman: money, employment and inflation', Book review, *Journal of Money, Credit and Banking*, **9** (1), 122–127
Layard, R., S. Nickell and R. Jackman (1991), *Unemployment, Macroeconomic Performance and the Labour Market*, Oxford: Oxford University Press.
López-Santana, M. (2003), 'The 'Pressure from Europe: the European employment strategy and national change', Presented at the European Union Studies Association 8th Biennale International Conference.
Malinvaud, E. (1977), *Theory of Unemployment Reconsidered*, Oxford: Blackwell,
Malinvaud, E. (1980), *Profitability and Unemployment*, Cambridge: Cambridge University Press.
Malinvaud, E. (1984), *Mass Unemployment*, Oxford: Blackwell.
Minford, P. (1993), 'Has labour market economics achieved a synthesis?', *The Economic Journal*, **103** (July), 1050–1056.
Mitchell, W.F. (1998), 'The buffer stock employment model: Full employment without a NAIRU', *Journal of Economic Issues*, **32** (2), 547–55.
Mitchell, W.F. (2001a), 'Measuring persistence in unemployment rates', *Working Paper*, (01-04) (June), Centre of Full Employment and Equity, University of Newcastle.
Mitchell, W.F. (2001b), 'The unemployed cannot find jobs that are not there!', *Working Paper*, (01-07) (May), Centre of Full Employment and Equity, University of Newcastle.
Mitchell, W.F. and W. Mosler (2002), 'The imperative of fiscal policy for full employment', *Australian Journal of Labour Economics*, **5** (2), 243–259.
Mitchell, W.F. and L.R. Wray, (2005), 'In Defence of Employer of Last Resort: a response to Malcolm Sawyer', *Journal of Economic Issues*, **39** (1), 235–244.
Mitchell, W.F. and J. Muysken (2003), 'Misrepresentation and fudge: the OECD NAIRU consensus', *Working Paper*, (03-11) (November), Centre of Full Employment and Equity, University of Newcastle.
Mitchell, W.F. and J. Muysken (2004), 'Involuntary unemployment at the heart of the problem', *Working Paper*, (04-09) (October), Centre of Full Employment and Equity, University of Newcastle.
Modigliani, F. (2000), 'Europe's economic problems', *Carpe Oeconomiam Papers in Economics*, 3rd Monetary and Finance Lecture, April, Freiburg.
Modigliani, F. and Papademos, L. (1975), 'Targets for monetary policy in the coming year', *Brookings Papers on Economic Activity*, **1**, 141–163.
Mosher, J.S. and D.M. Trubeck (2003), 'Alternative approaches to governance in the EU: EU social policy and the European Employment Strategy', *Journal of Common Market Studies*, **41** (1), 63–88.
Muysken, J. (2003), 'Job Growth and Social Harmony: a Dutch Miracle?', in H. Hagemann and S. Seiter (eds), *Growth Theory and Growth Policy*, 226–247, London: Routledge.
Nickell, S.J. and J.C. van Ours (2000), 'Falling unemployment; the Dutch and British cases', *Economic Policy*, **30**, 137–180.

Noaksson, N. and K. Jacobsson (2003), 'The production of ideas and expert knowledge in OECD: the OECD Jobs Strategy in contrast with the EU employment strategy', *SCORE Report*, 2003 (7).

OECD (1994), *Jobs Study*, Paris: OECD.

OECD (2004), 'Editorial: Reassessing the OECD Jobs Strategy', *Employment Outlook*, 11–15, Paris: OECD.

OECD (2005), *OECD Economic Outlook*, **2005/2** (78), November, Paris: OECD Publication Service.

OECD, *Main Economic Indicators*, database available online at http://www.sourceoecd.org

Ormerod, P. (1994), *The Death of Economics*, London: Faber & Faber.

Phelps, E.S. (1994), 'Structural slumps: The modern equilibrium theory of unemployment, interest, and assets', Cambridge and London: Harvard University Press.

Phelps, E.S. and G. Zoega (1998), 'Natural-rate theory and OECD unemployment', *Economic Journal*, **108** (448) (May), 782–801.

Rowthorn, R. (1999), 'Unemployment, wage bargaining and capital–labour substitution', *Cambridge Journal of Economics*, **23** (4) (July), 413–426.

Sapir, A., P. Aghion, G. Bertola, M. Hellwig, J. Pisani-Ferry, D. Rosati, J. Vinals and H. Wallace (2004), *An Agenda for a Growing Europe: The Sapir Report*, Oxford: Oxford University Press.

Sawyer, M. (2002), 'The NAIRU, aggregate demand and investment', *Metroeconomica*, **53** (1), 66–94.

Solow, R.M. and J.B. Taylor (1998), *Inflation, Unemployment, and Monetary Policy*, ed. and with an introduction by B.M. Friedman, Cambridge, MA: MIT Press.

Staiger, D., J.H. Stock and M.W. Watson (1997), 'How precise are estimates of the natural rate of unemployment? Reducing inflation, motivation and strategy', in: C.D. Romer and D.H. Romer (eds), *NBER Studies in Business Cycles*, (30), Chicago: University of Chicago Press.

Stanley, T.D. (2004), 'Does unemployment hysteresis falsify the natural rate hypothesis? A meta-regression analysis', *Journal of Economic Surveys*, **18** (4), 589–612.

Stiglitz, J.E. (2002), *Globalization and its discontents*, London: Penguin.

Tobin, J. (1996), 'Edmond Malinvaud: diagnosing unemployment', Book review, *Journal of Evolutionary Economics*, (6), 325–333.

Verbruggen, J. (2003),'The Dutch economy', *CPB Report 2003-04*, 10–18.

Vroey, M. de (2004), *Involuntary Unemployment*, London: Routledge.

Watt, A. (2004), 'Reform of the European Employment Strategy after five years: a change of course or merely of presentation?', *European Journal of Industrial Relations*, **10** (2), 117–137.

Watts, M.J. and W.F. Mitchell (2000), 'The costs of unemployment in Australia', *The Economic and Labour Relations Review*, **11** (2) (December), 180–197.

Wray, L.R. (1998), *Understanding Modern Money*, Cheltenham, UK and Northampton, MA, US: Edward Elgar.

2. Whither Stability Pact? An Assessment of Reform Proposals

Paola Monperrus-Veroni and Francesco Saraceno

2.1 INTRODUCTION

Theo Waigel, then German finance minister, was in 1995 the first to stress the need for a set of rules aimed at permanently guaranteeing the soundness of fiscal policy for the countries joining the euro. In fact, the criteria set by the Maastricht Treaty only represented a requirement for entry into the EMU, and nothing in principle prevented countries from abandoning fiscal discipline once admitted to the single currency club. The Amsterdam Treaty (1997), better known as the Stability and Growth Pact (SGP), complements the Maastricht Treaty in that its main objective is to make the requirements for public finance soundness permanent, and to increase transparency.

The long slowdown that began in 2001 has strengthened the debate on whether the SGP is an appropriate framework for fiscal policy in the European Union. Reform proposals aimed at avoiding some shortcomings of the current setting flourished. Since Germany and France took a common position on the need for a more flexible implementation of the Pact, in October 2004, the issue has come to the foreground in the political debate. The reform of the current setting is one of the main items in the agenda of the Spring 2005 Council meeting.

The present chapter avoids entering into the debate on whether a stability pact is necessary – this is discussed by Arestis and Sawyer in this volume – and focuses on the reform proposals that are currently under consideration. Our aim is to give a quantitative assessment of the effects on growth (for the three largest Euro Area countries), had the proposed rules been followed in the past. To make such an assessment, we perform a dynamic simulation exercise in the spirit of Eichengreen and Wyplosz (1998; hereafter EW). We first estimate a reduced form VAR model, and then use the coefficients to simulate output gap figures resulting from the use of different rules. Finally we rank the rules according to their impact on growth.

This counterfactual analysis has of course to be evaluated with caution, being subject to some methodological weaknesses. Nevertheless, it allows a uniform comparison across rules and across countries. Furthermore, the main results of the analysis emerge quite robustly: on one side the nominal golden rule would be the most beneficial both using individual countries' criteria and global criteria; and on the other the *status quo*, the Maastricht rule, is less restrictive than most currently debated alternatives and turns out to be amongst the preferred rules for the three countries as a whole.

The next section briefly reviews the institutional features of the Stability and Growth Pact, and summarizes the main criticisms that have been raised against it. Then, it describes the main reform proposals that are under consideration. Section 2.3 describes the counterfactual example we perform in this chapter which we borrow from Eichengreen and Wyplosz (1998); this section also addresses some criticisms of this methodology, and describes the dataset used. Section 2.4 presents the results of our simulation exercise, detailing for each country the effects of alternative fiscal regimes. Section 2.5 discusses the ranking of the different rules that emerges taking a global perspective; we also draw the political economy implications of such a ranking. Finally, section 2.6 ranks the rules according to an alternative measure of welfare, unemployment performance; the rankings obtained using the two measures are quite similar, as the golden rule emerges as the more beneficial for growth; we can thus conclude in favour of the robustness of our results.

2.2 THE FLAWS OF THE PACT AND A DISCUSSION OF REFORM PROPOSALS

The Stability and Growth Pact consists of EU Council regulations 1466/97 and 1467/97, and of a protocol annexed to the Amsterdam Treaty, signed in June 1997. According to the SGP, each year member countries must present a Stability and Convergence Programme, to be examined by the European Commission and the Council. The programmes provide a medium-term objective for achieving the budgetary position of 'close to balance or in surplus', together with the adjustment path towards the objective. The latter include the main assumptions about expected economic developments together with description of budgetary and other economic policy measures being taken and/or proposed to achieve the objectives.

The centrepiece of the fiscal discipline mechanism is the Excessive Deficit Procedure (EDP). The EDP states which deviations from the 3 per cent budget deficit ceiling are acceptable, and gives the Council sanctioning power (by qualified majority) where necessary. The Amsterdam Treaty also stipulates that gross government debt should be maintained below 60 per cent of GDP or, if higher, should be 'decreasing at a satisfactory pace'. Notwithstanding some very minor changes, the Constitutional treaty signed in Rome in October 2004 has left this setting unaltered.

In November 2003, it became apparent that the sanctioning mechanism was malfunctioning since the Council dropped the Commission's proposal to start an Excessive Deficit Procedure against France and Germany. The Commission sought a judgment from the European Court of Justice, which ruled against the Council in July 2004. In the spring of 2004 the EDP was also invoked for the Netherlands, Greece and a number of newly admitted countries.

Facing on one side the increasing deterioration of budgetary positions in a number of countries, and on the other the problems involved in implementation of the current set of rules, the European Commission (2004) put forward a proposal to shift the focus to long-term sustainability, in order to increase flexibility and enforceability. First, it proposes explicitly to consider debt sustainability in the assessment of budgetary positions, by taking into account implicit liabilities that may influence the long-run dynamics of the debt. Second, the Commission agrees to consider country-specific circumstances when defining medium-term objectives of 'close to balance or in surplus'. Finally, it agrees to make more flexible the Excessive Deficit Procedure, by considering the budgetary impact of periods 'of exceptionally weak economic growth' both when it identifies an excessive deficit and when it emits the recommendations and deadlines for correcting it. On the other hand, the Commission maintains the importance of the 3 per cent limit for the nominal deficit, and the requirement of a constant reduction of the structural deficit (0.5 per cent per year) until the close-to-balance position is reached (European Commission, 2002).

While agreeing that exceptional swings in public finances may cause serious problem in a currency union (imposing costs on other countries of the area through excessive interest rates and/or inflationary pressures), economists are divided on the generalization of this principle to normal conditions and hence on the need for fiscal rules to control individual countries' behaviour. The debate is far from settled, if we consider that in a monetary union fiscal policy represents the only instrument left in the hands of governments to pursue their objectives.[1] We choose not to discuss the broader issue of the desirability of discretionary policy[2] because our objective is simply to give a quantitative assessment of the different reform proposals; and on the need of reforming the Pact, the vast majority of economists agree, regardless of their positions.

2.2.1 The Flaws of the Stability and Growth Pact

The first set of problems with the Pact concern its rigidity. The most serious shortcoming is the one-size-fits-all feature of the SGP. This comes not only from the institutional design that requires the 3 per cent limit for the nominal deficit (and the medium-run close-to-balance position) to be observed by all countries, but also from the fact that other important variables, such as the stock of public debt, the need for infrastructure or the population age structure, which vary greatly across countries, have been overlooked in the design of the criteria used to assess the soundness of fiscal positions. Any sensible evaluation of the sustainability of a public deficit should consider these parameters, and hence support the use of different constraints (see for example Arestis and Sawyer in this volume).

Furthermore, many items of public expenditure have an intertemporal character. These range from the multi-annual characters of investment expenditures, to the smoothing over time of the adjustment costs linked to a downturn, or even to future benefits of current expenditure (for example education). The SGP focus on annual accounting prevents any intertemporal smoothing of fiscal policy. This may even be harmful in a supply-side perspective, as it may force governments to postpone structural reforms (for example of the pension system) that would yield benefits only in the medium to long run, while imposing a short-term burden on public finances (for example cuts in public pension system contributions in order to allow financing of private pension schemes; Blanchard and Giavazzi, 2002).

The second shortcoming is the inconsistency of the SGP. Actual practice has until now completely ignored the few references to debt that were present in the treaties. Though arbitrary, the Maastricht 60 per cent debt-to-GDP ratio serves as a basis for the deficit target via the steady-state debt accumulation equation.[3] The SGP fails to take into account this link, neglecting to design sanctions and to define explicitly a numerical rule for the 'satisfactory pace' of reduction in the debt ratio. In fact, the SGP does more than simply neglect the debt criterion. By changing the average deficit target from 3 per cent to 0 per cent, it also implicitly redefines the long-term debt target: a 60 per cent debt-to-GDP ratio would be obtained with an average 3 per cent deficit. The average balanced deficit imposed by the SGP would yield a debt-to-GDP ratio converging to zero (de Grauwe, 2003).

The neglect of long-term sustainability issues is the source of another major problem of the Pact, namely the lack of credibility. Since the winter of 2003, French and German interest rates and public sector bond ratings did not react negatively to the breaking of the debt-to-GDP ratio limit by those countries, nor to the dispute with the Commission that followed, we infer that markets base their judgement on long-term sustainability issues, and that the respect of the Pact is not a major issue. Credibility is further hampered by the limited enforceability of the SGP, as sanctions are too tough (up to 0.5 per cent of GDP) and too tardy (imposed at best three years after the infringement). Furthermore, sanctions are decided by the Council, a body in which political motivation and technical assessments are inextricably linked, since the participants are both judge and defendant.

The Pact may also force pro-cyclical policies in downturns (see Mitchell and Muysken in this volume). Germany, struggling to reduce expenditure and to raise taxes on the brink of a recession early 2001, is a good case in point. In theory, the SGP was designed to provide flexibility, that is, to provide the room for automatic stabilizers to act. That theory was problematic for at least two reasons. First, during the transition to the 'close-to-balance' position, countries would not be able to stabilize their economies if hit by a negative shock (Eichengreen and Wyplosz, 1998). The downturn which began in 2001 proved this point. The second and even more serious problem is the assumption that only automatic stabilization would be required and desirable. In fact, even when countries are operating within the structures of the Pact, it would limit any discretionary fiscal policy, thus potentially depriving democratically elected governments of the only tool left for carrying out their contract with the electorate (Fitoussi, 2002). Thus, in spite of the initial intentions, the SGP has constrained Euro Area countries to neutral, when not explicitly pro-cyclical, fiscal policies. This has had a number of side-effects that further weakened the credibility of the system: the blossoming of creative accounting practices; the bias against politically 'invisible' but crucial expenditures (like education, basic research and investment), in favour of unproductive but politically sensitive items.

Finally, the design of the pact is asymmetric, and contains no incentive for countries to behave properly in good times: 'the problem, with the Pact as presently framed is that it is all stick and no carrot; rewarding good fiscal behaviour in booms rather than, or in addition to, punishing bad behaviour in slumps, would surely make better sense' (Bean, 1998, p. 106). Indeed, nothing in the SGP prevents countries from running pro-cyclical fiscal policies when experiencing above-trend growth (Buti and Giudice, 2002). Buti and Sapir (2002) show that the largest countries of the Euro Area (France, Germany, Italy) did not use the slack given by the expansion of 1997–2000 to consolidate their respective budgets. This finding may be seen as a proof that 'the problem does not lie with the Pact' (Buti and Sapir, 2002), but rather in the inappropriate policies of governments. These misdemeanours nevertheless were predictable, and should have been foreseen when designing an architecture the main objective of which was precisely to avoid them.

To sum up, in its current formulation the SGP lacks the flexibility required to respond to specific shocks; it is asymmetric, providing no incentive to reduce expenses or to increase revenues during strong growth; it has excessive uniformity of rules for all countries, regardless of the rate and variability of growth, of investment needs, of contingent liabilities and of sustainability of public finances; it disregards the growth (and public investment) intertemporal features; finally, it appears to neglect the long-term sustainability of public finances, since it imposes in practice a common and theoretically unwarranted rule of dramatic public debt reduction.

2.2.2 The Reform Proposals

SGP reform proposals have multiplied at the same pace as criticisms of the present framework. In this section we briefly review the proposals that will be subject to numerical evaluation in the remaining of the chapter. We will examine how alternative fiscal rules address the main criticisms that have been levelled at the present SGP settings; and we will also assess these rules according to the criteria for a 'good' fiscal rule (Kopits and Symansky, 1998): operational simplicity, flexibility, consistency and enforceability.

The balanced structural budget
In 2002, the European Commission (2002) acknowledged that the objective of a balanced budget in 2004 was no longer attainable, and postponed it to 2006. Nevertheless this short-term relief was coupled with a more restrictive definition of the fiscal objective which was redefined as a balanced structural budget and as a yearly reduction of 0.5 percentage points in the cyclically adjusted balance until 2006 for countries with structural budget deficits in 2002. As a matter of fact the European Commission claimed that the main reason for higher deficits in the Euro Area in 2001 and 2002 was the deterioration in the structural deficit; the cyclical component of the budget only played a marginal role in the increase of the deficits.

The main advantage of a shift to structural deficit rules would be the increased flexibility in dealing with cyclical stabilization. In particular such a rule would never prevent automatic stabilizers from operating. On the other hand, the operational simplicity would be reduced by the reference to controversial magnitudes of the variables used in calculating the structural budget balance, such as the output gap and the NAIRU.

To assess the Commission's proposal, we will first simulate the output effects of a balanced structural budget rule: $s_s \geq 0$, where s_s is the cyclically adjusted balance-over-GDP ratio; and then the structural deficit reduction at a constant rate of 0.5 percentage points of GDP: $s_s(t) = s_s(t-1) + 0.05$ if $s_s(t-1) < 0$. We also experiment with a different rule, allowing structural deficit convergence from the level of 1990 to balance in 1998, the pre-accession year: s_s $(t) = s_s$ $(t\text{-}1) + x$, where x is the yearly average reduction rate of structural deficit (that depends on the initial level).

The golden rule

The reform proposal that is more popular in political circles[4] is the 'golden rule', according to which the budget is split into a balanced current account and a deficit-financed capital account. Such a rule has the intent of removing the bias against capital spending, thus shifting attention from a mere quantitative target to the quality of public finance. Since a higher public investment is supposed to increase the potential growth rate of the economy, notably for less mature countries, the golden rule is more compatible with country-specific factors than the present SGP setting. It also emphasizes the long-term sustainability requirement, by allowing countries to spread the cost of durables over all the financial years in which they will be in use, and the burden of capital over the generations of taxpayers benefiting from it.[5] Moreover, by implying convergence of the debt-to-GDP ratio to the ratio of public capital to GDP, this rule avoids the inconsistency intrinsic in the convergence to the 0 per cent level (Blanchard and Giavazzi, 2004).

Those opposing the rule claim that there is no clear-cut evidence that the SGP and fiscal consolidation had a crowding-out effect on public investment. The average rate of growth of gross public investment in the Euro Area during the 1990s (2.8 per cent) is only slightly lower than the average recorded in the previous three decades (3.5 per cent), and the reduction cannot be blamed on the treaty, as it was a general phenomenon across OECD countries (Gali and Perotti, 2003). It is further argued that the rule may provide the incentive to an overevaluation of the investment needs, and hence favour projects that are not necessarily profitable or worthwhile. Thus, an infrastructure need would be dealt with more efficiently at the supranational level through the common budget; in the present situation, though, this latter argument appears to be unrealistic. Buti et al. (2003) argue that from an intergenerational point of view it would be more efficient to leave future generations endowed with a lower stock of public capital, and reduced liabilities, because this would allow them to react to their future needs more appropriately. The most serious criticism concerns the possibility of agreeing on a definition of public investment necessary to avoid 'creative accounting' aimed at classifying some current expenditure as investment spending (Balassone and Franco, 2001). Furthermore, some current expenditures that are at least as productive and growth-friendly as investment (education, health, human capital in general) would be penalized by the golden rule. Fitoussi (2002) argues nevertheless that precisely this ambiguity could be an important factor in shaping a common economic policy for

Europe. The Council or the European Parliament could be given the right to define periodically the items to be excluded from deficit figures, in order to pursue specific long-term objectives (for example the Lisbon strategy). This would constitute a powerful instrument of policy coordination 'from the top'.

Finally, the golden rule implies that the rate of borrowing for investment is independent of the inflation rate and of the rate of growth of the economy (Buiter and Grafe, 2004). Creel (2003) argues nevertheless that the risk of a bias towards excessive capital spending is prevented by built-in discipline mechanisms: the interest payment expansion generated by public capital accumulation would impose a constraint to current expenditure growth, and hence at a certain point prevent further capital accumulation.

To examine the applicability of the golden rule, we will use the following for the counterfactual analysis: $s + (I - \delta k_0) \geq -0.03$, where I is the gross public investment–GDP ratio and k_0 is the public capital stock–GDP ratio at the end of the previous period that is assumed to depreciate at a rate δ. As the golden rule may present the major shortcoming of being as cyclically inflexible as the present framework, we will also investigate the effects of a structural version, similar to the one currently in place in the United Kingdom: $s_s + (I - \delta k_0) \geq 0$.

The debt criterion

Shifting the focus from deficit to debt addresses both the issue of long-term sustainability and that of the excessive uniformity of rules. Higher growth and inflation rates in catching-up countries allow higher deficits to be run without jeopardizing the sustainability of public finances. Among mature countries, those with sound public finances may be in a better position for stabilization, exceeding that allowed by automatic stabilizers in order to face asymmetric shocks. Most of the proposals to take into account debt require abandoning numerical rules in favour of discretionary general assessments of the soundness of public finance (Wyplosz, 2002a; Pisani-Ferry, 2002; Coeuré and Pisani-Ferry, 2003). Since our aim is to give a quantitative assessment in terms of growth, we will not deal with these 'qualitative' proposals that are discussed at length in Saraceno and Monperrus-Veroni (2004).

An alternative proposal, put forth by Calmfors and Corsetti (2003) and Calmfors et al. (2003) is to impose a ladder of different deficit targets for different debt intervals (as shown in Table 2.1). The asymmetric bias of the SGP is reduced by these proposals, since discipline and fiscal restraint are rewarded by increased room for manoeuvre and hence scope for stabilization in downturns. However this ladder, where increases in the deficit ceiling for low-debt countries are matched by a reduction for high-debt countries, does not appear to be easily enforceable and therefore politically realistic.

Table 2.1   Possible ways of conditioning the deficit ceiling on the debt ratio

| Calmfors and Corsetti (2003) | | Economic Advisory Group (2003) | | |
Debt ratio	Deficit ceiling	Debt ratio	Deficit ceiling	Countries in the range (debt)
>55	3.0	>105	0.5	Italy (106.2)
		95–105	1.0	Greece (103) Belgium (100.5)
		85–95	1.5	
		75–85	2.0	
		65–75	2.5	Austria (65)
		55–65	3.0	Germany (64.2) France (63) Portugal (59.4)
45–55	3.5	45–55	3.5	Netherlands (54.8) Sweden (51.8) Spain (50.8) Finland (45.3)
35–45	4.0	35–45	4.0	Denmark (45) UK (39.8)
25–35	4.5	25–35	4.5	Ireland (32)
<25	5.0	<25	5.0	Luxembourg (4.9)

Note: All figures in percentage of GDP.

Source: Public Finances in the EMU-2003.

Furthermore, the proposed thresholds further introduce arbitrariness and complexity in the design of the rule.

If debt has to be taken into account, it is possible to design a simple and automatic rule that reduces the risks of arbitrariness and is symmetric (Saraceno and Monperrus-Veroni, 2004). We have suggested weighing the deficit target with 'relative debt', that is, the ratio between the 60 per cent Maastricht debt parameter and the country's actual gross debt in term of GDP.

The deficit target would thus be computed as $d^i{}_t = \frac{0.6}{b^i{}_{t-1}} d_t$ where d^i and b^i are deficit and debt of country i respectively, and d is the union-wide target. Table 2.2 shows what the target would have to be, at the 2003 debt levels, in

Table 2.2 Deficit ceilings weighed by relative debt ratios

	Debt (2003)	Weighted deficit	
		(a)[1]	(b)[2]
Luxembourg	4.9	36.7	65.3
Ireland	32	5.6	10.0
United Kingdom	39.8	4.5	8.0
Denmark	45	4.0	7.1
Finland	45.3	4.0	7.1
Spain	50.8	3.5	6.3
Sweden	51.8	3.5	6.2
Netherlands	54.8	3.3	5.8
Portugal	59.4	3.0	5.4
France	63	2.9	5.1
Germany	64.2	2.8	5.0
Austria	65	2.8	4.9
Belgium	100.5	1.8	3.2
Greece	103	1.7	3.1
Italy	106.2	1.7	3.0

Note:
All figures in percentage of GDP
1.   Takes union-wide deficit target of 3%.
2.   Takes a union-wide deficit target of 4% (and coherently, a debt ratio target of 80%).

Source: Saraceno and Monperrus-Veroni (2004).

the two cases of a union-wide target of 3 per cent and 4 per cent. In the counterfactual analysis below, we will simulate the effects of such a rule.

The advantage of this proposal lies in its operational simplicity, in the total absence of discretion (once we take the Maastricht parameters as given) in setting the deficit ceiling and in the creation of rewards for fiscal discipline. Virtue is encouraged in good times, in order to gain leeway for stabilization in bad times. Thus our proposal, while yielding similar dynamics as other rules (see Saraceno and Monperrus-Veroni, 2004), has more appealing properties. However it may not be easily enforceable because of the political opposition which may come from high-debt countries.[6]

A more drastic way to take debt into account would be to imagine a path to bring its level down to the 60 per cent level in a predefined period. We will try to assess the effects of such a rule, simulating the output gap path corresponding to the cyclically adjusted budget–GDP ratio, allowing for gross debt convergence to remain at that level afterwards. The nominal primary balance–GDP ratio is computed as $s_p - d_0 (r - g) = \sigma$, where σ is the yearly debt reduction in percentage of GDP, necessary for the debt ratio to decrease from its level in 1990 to the Maastricht limit of 60 per cent in 1998. Of course such a rule will be simulated for Italy only, as France and Germany in 1990 had levels below the 60 per cent threshold.

The Maastricht rule
Finally, we will try to assess the effects of the Maastricht rule, had the three per cent limit to the nominal budget deficit been operational over the entire period 1990–2002, that is: $s \geq -0.03$ where s is the nominal budget balance–GDP ratio.

2.3 THE EFFECTS ON OUTPUT OF FISCAL RULES: A COUNTERFACTUAL EXERCISE

To give a quantitative assessment of the reform proposals described above we follow the approach of Eichengreen and Wyplosz (1998). They develop a counterfactual exercise, asking what consequences the SGP would have had, in terms of growth, had it been applied since the early 1960s. Such an exercise has many shortcomings, acknowledged by the authors themselves. The main one is that it is typically susceptible to the Lucas' Critique: had the pact been applied in the past, agents would have embedded its consequences in their behaviour, which would, as a consequence, have been different. Actual data thus have limited explanatory power when trying to quantify the effects of alternative policies or, as in this case, alternative institutions. The paper by Eichengreen and Wyplosz (1998) is of significant interest because it provides a measure of the magnitude of costs and benefits of the Pact. Furthermore, in our framework the Critique could be less problematic because we are interested in the relative performance of the different rules rather than in the absolute figures. Eichengreen and Wyplosz (1998) do the following. (1) They estimate the reduced form of a standard model, specifically a two-equations VAR with output gap and inflation changes as endogenous. Among the exogenous variables, they introduce the fiscal impulse (that they define as the change in the structural deficit). (2) They use the estimated coefficients and an artificial series for the fiscal impulse (derived by capping total deficit at 3 per cent for each period in which it surpassed the threshold) to build the simulated series for output gap and inflation. (3) They compare the simulated output gap series with the actual one, to compute the difference in output.

We use a similar procedure to rank the different reform proposals that have been discussed. This is done by simulating fiscal adjustment strategies that would result from the enforcement of each of the fiscal rules that have been described above.

The data used are from the OECD Economic Outlook (2003). Our analysis focuses on the three largest countries of continental Europe, which, by joining the monetary union, fully accepted the institutional set-up designed by the Maastricht and Amsterdam treaties. The first year commonly available for the three countries is 1973. We use the output gap calculated by the OECD according to the production function approach; inflation is obtained as a change in the Consumer Price Index; nominal budget balances are calculated as government net lending net of UMTS receipts; and net investment is computed by using the government consumption of public capital as depreciation. The structural deficit (surplus), consistent with an output gap calculated with the production function approach, is provided by the OECD.

The following section presents the results of our simulation exercise. We begin by estimating, for our dataset, the same reduced form estimated by EW. Then, we use the estimated coefficients to simulate the path of output and inflation corresponding to the fiscal adjustment paths consistent with the different rules. Each artificial fiscal impulse series is the change in the cyclically adjusted deficit that we would observe were the rule followed.

The artificial fiscal impulse series used in our counterfactual exercise is the simulated change in the cyclically adjusted deficit corresponding to the fiscal adjustment paths consistent with the different rules to be tested. Thus, for rules constraining nominal balances, such as the Maastricht rule, the nominal golden rule and the relative debt rule rules, we have to compute the corresponding change in cyclically adjusted terms. We start from the hypothesis that a change in the fiscal adjustment path in *t-1* influences growth and the output gap in *t* and that this change in the output gap has an effect only on the cyclical component of the budget balance without affecting its structural component in the short term. We then calculate the new nominal budget balance in *t* adding the new cyclical component to the original, unchanged structural budget balance. The new cyclical component in *t* is obtained by applying the government budget elasticity to cyclical variations in economic activity calculated by the OECD (van den Noord, 2000) to the simulated output gap in *t-1*, consistent with the fiscal adjustment strategy implemented. The nominal budget balance, thus obtained, is then constrained according to the rule and adjusted for the cycle.

For fiscal adjustment strategies that result from rules constraining structural deficit, such as the structural balanced budget, structural balance convergence, the half-point structural deficit reduction, the structural balance allowing for debt convergence and the structural golden rule, the original structural deficit is directly constrained.

With our procedure the output gap is endogenously determined by the implementation of different rules; in so doing, we respond to some of the criticisms that have been addressed to the EW paper (for example Bean, 1998).

A further manipulation was necessary for the two golden rule exercises. To avoid taking into account the possible effects of consolidation on investment in the 1990s (that the rule would have made unnecessary), we took, as a measure of public capital accumulation (*I* in the formula above), the average value of net investment in the three previous decades. Thus, the artificial deficit series is obtained by summing the actual current balance capped at 3 per cent (or the structural balance capped at 0 per cent) and the past average investment expenditure.

For each rule we compared the results with those of the same simulation, obtained by using the actual values of the fiscal impulse (our 'benchmark'). We could have used the actual values of the output gap and inflation, but then the difference with the simulated series would have also captured all the noise coming from the imperfect fit of the regression. By using simulated series as a benchmark, we gain in coherence and consistency of the results.

2.4   THE RESULTS

2.4.1   The Reduced Form Estimation

Table 2.3 shows the results of the reduced form estimation corresponding with Table 8 in EW. In spite of revised figures for the output gap and the structural adjusted budget, our dataset yields the same qualitative behaviour.

The effect of the fiscal impulse on the output gap is in all cases lower than in EW,[7] but only for France remarkably so. The coefficients for inflation are in line with those of EW, but as in their work, the explanatory power of the regression is quite low.[8]

Table 2.3   Reduced form estimates[a]

	France		Germany		Italy	
	Output Gap	Δ Inflation	Output Gap	Δ Inflation	Output Gap	Δ Inflation
Output Gap (-1)[b]	0.952 (8.71)	0.688 (3.16)	0.828 (10.6)	0.113 (1.40)	0.672 (6.52)	0.758 (1.62)
Δ Inflation (-1)[b]	-0.175 (-2.11)	-0.308 (-1.87)	-0.270 (-1.92)	-0.324 (-1.96)	-0.01 (0.44)	-0.377 (-2.37)
Fiscal Impulse[bc]	-0.382 (-1.31)	0.935 (1.61)	-0.446 (-1.92)	0.029 (0.122)	-0.318 (-2.40)	-0.73 (-1.23)
R^2	0.720	0.495	0.794	0.14	0.646	0.194
Obs	24	-	32	-	38	-

Notes:
[a] Following EW, we also used country specific dummies to improve the estimation fit. The coefficients are not reported.
[b] t-statistics in parentheses.
[c] Fiscal impulse is defined as the change in the cyclically adjusted total budget deficit. For France and Italy it is lagged one period.

Source: OECD, Economic Outlook, December 2003.

The detailed results on the longer period (1973–2002) and the discussion of the effects of each rule are reported in Monperrus-Veroni and Saraceno (2005), where we also briefly deal with effects on inflation. Here we limit our analysis to the output performance of each country during the 'Maastricht decade' (1990–2002). Following that, in the next section, we will take a global perspective.

2.4.2   France

Table 2.4 reports the differences between the average output gap corresponding to each rule, and the output gap of the benchmark simulation. It can be seen that the fiscal stance permitted by the golden rule is substantially more expansionary than the benchmark, showing that public investment would have provided an important slack to fiscal policy. The

Table 2.4   France: Ranking of rules (1990–2002)

	Gap[a]
Nominal golden rule	0.64
Relative debt	0.51
Structural golden rule	0.16
Structural deficit convergence	0.02
Maastricht	-0.40
½ point structural deficit reduction	-0.58
Balanced structural budget	-1.01

Note:
[a]   Difference with the benchmark in average yearly values.

structural golden rule would also have been good for growth, but it would have allowed a lower structural deficit than its nominal counterpart. The simulation shows that the relative debt rule would have been quiteadvantageous as well, and this is explained by the low starting debt to GDP ratio, that allowed a high deficit ceiling (3.1 per cent on average).

The structural deficit convergence (for France we have $x = 0.003$ in the formula above, given an initial level of 2.8 per cent) would have yielded an output gap analogous to the benchmark. The Maastricht rule would have been more restrictive, a result that is not surprising given that France's deficit was maintained above 3 per cent on average during the decade under consideration. Last in the ranking come two rules that would have required strong reduction in the structural deficit. In particular, the balanced structural deficit would have yielded one point of GDP per year less than the benchmark and the half-point deficit reduction would have entailed an even more restrictive stance than the structural deficit convergence.

2.4.3   Germany

The rankings for Germany are reported in Table 2.5. The first thing to notice is that the golden rule, either in its nominal or in its structural version, would also be the preferred choice for Germany. As was the case for France, and will be shown below for Italy, the nominal version of the rule is more

Table 2.5   Germany: Ranking of rules (1990–2002)

	Gap^a
Nominal golden rule	0.45
Maastricht	0.13
Structural golden rule	0.05
Relative debt	-0.08
Balanced structural budget	-0.36
Structural deficit convergence	-0.38
½ point structural deficit reduction	-0.39

Note:
[a]   Difference with the benchmark in yearly values.

expansionary than the structural one, because in fact it would have allowed about 1.5 points of GDP of structural deficit every year.

Contrary to France, for Germany the Maastricht rule would have yielded a better outcome than the benchmark, preventing the building up of the deficit in 1991 and 1995 and thus the subsequent fiscal restriction in the years 1997–99. Relative debt would not have an impact significantly different from the benchmark, since the 2.6 per cent average deficit ceiling allowed almost coincides with the effective fiscal stance. All the other structural rules, with the exception of the golden rule, are at the bottom of the ranking, with a yearly loss of almost 0.4 points of GDP. In Germany, as in the other two countries, the actual structural deficit and the one allowed by the 3 per cent ceiling, were in 2002 still above the 0 per cent limit, thus it is not surprising that in all cases the Maastricht rule proves less restrictive than the balanced structural budget. Structural deficit convergence ($x = 0.004$), or the half-point reduction of the Commission proposal are almost equivalent, and are at the bottom of the ranking, since Germany started the decade with a larger structural deficit than France.

2.4.4   Italy

The ranking for Italy shows one striking result (Table 2.6). The proposal that would be more expansionary, with respect to the benchmark, is the Commission's proposal of half a point of structural deficit reduction. In fact,

Table 2.6   Italy: Ranking of rules (1990–2002)

	Gap[a]
½ point structural deficit reduction	0.34
Nominal golden rule	0.25
Structural golden rule	0.07
Relative debt	-0.07
Debt convergence	-0.12
Maastricht	-0.13
Structural deficit convergence	-0.17
Balanced structural budget	-0.31

Note:
[a]   Difference with the benchmark in yearly values.

in Italy the consolidation process, especially in earlier years of the decade, has been much stronger than that which would have been required by the Commission rule (that, if followed since 1990, would have still allowed a 6 per cent structural deficit in 2002).

On the other hand, the structural deficit convergence (that would have required a yearly reduction of 1.6 per cent of GDP), would have been extremely costly for Italy (that started at a level of 12.4 per cent in 1990). Similarly, the initial tremendous effort to bring the structural deficit to balance since 1990 would have yielded a larger output loss than the output loss effectively cumulated over the whole period.

The exceptional size of consolidation in Italy also explains why, in spite of the high stock of liabilities, the country would not have suffered too much from the debt-related rules, which, while more costly than for the other two countries, turn out to be only slightly more restrictive than the benchmark. The application of the Maastricht rule since 1990, on the other hand, would have prevented the deficit build-up of the early 1990s and its positive effects on income. Moreover the consolidation required during the first year of implementation of the Maastricht rule in our simulation would have been significant, thus having negative effects on output.

The golden rule, especially in its nominal version, would have yielded a significantly higher output than the benchmark. Imposing a golden rule since the beginning of the 1990s would have avoided further building up of the deficit and consequently severe consolidation at the eve of the EMU.

2.5   THE RANKING OF ALTERNATIVE REFORM PROPOSALS

We saw in the preceding section that for most of the rules the differences from the benchmark are quite significant, indicating that the choice of the fiscal regime would not have been neutral. In the following section, we ask whether a counterfactual exercise allows the ranking of the different fiscal rule proposals and hence the drawing of policy implications for the debate on SGP reform.

2.5.1   A Summary of Individual Country Rankings

Table 2.7 summarizes the findings of the previous section, in terms of the different rules as compared with the benchmark. A general result is the surprisingly large number of cases in which the simulated rules would have yielded a better outcome than the benchmark (positive differences). This maybe explained of course by the deficit reduction efforts undertaken by all countries in the run-up to the euro, during the years under consideration.

The second feature of our exercise is that rules constraining structural deficit are mostly towards the lower end of the ranking, especially for France and Germany. This suggests that the consolidations that countries undertook overlooked this aspect, focusing instead on the nominal balance required by the Maastricht Treaty. In Italy the consolidation implied a significant reduction of structural deficit, from its peak in 1990, and this explains why the Commission's proposal turns out to be expansionary with respect to the other proposals (and to the benchmark). Notwithstanding this, and precisely because of the very large initial deficit, consolidations requiring overly strong initial reductions would have resulted in significant output loss. Interestingly, debt-related rules do not penalize Italy as much as might be expected, once again because of the important consolidation effort of the 1990s.

2.5.2   Social Choice

Ranking alternative rules by country constitutes little more than a *curiosum*, an intellectual exercise, given the present institutional situation in Europe. That is, the rules of the game are decided at the Union level and need a consensus among governments. Thus, we need to evaluate the rules at a global level.

Table 2.7   Differences between rules' simulations and benchmark (1990–2002)

	France		Germany		Italy[a]	
	Gap[b]	Rank	Gap[b]	Rank	Gap[b]	Rank
Maastricht	-0.40	5	0.13	2	-0.13	6 (5)
Balanced structural budget	-1.01	7	-0.36	5	-0.31	8 (7)
Structural deficit convergence	0.02	4	-0.38	6	-0.17	7 (6)
½ point structural deficit reduction	-0.58	6	-0.39	7	0.34	1
Nominal golden rule	0.64	1	0.45	1	0.25	2
Structural golden rule	0.160	3	0.05	3	0.07	3
Debt convergence	-	-	-	-	-0.12	5
Relative debt	0.514	2	-0.08	4	-0.07	4

Notes:
[a]   The parentheses denote the ranking were the debt convergence rule was not taken into account.
[b]   Difference from the benchmark in average yearly values.

A global welfare approach

First, we can ask what kind of rule maximizes the average welfare of the three countries. Table 2.8 reports the rules ranked according to two different but related criteria. The first is simply the average individual rank in the three countries. The second is the weighted average of the output gap differences reported in Table 2.7.[9]

Table 2.8   Global welfare maximizing approach

	Average rank[a]	Average output gap difference[b]
Nominal golden rule	1.33	0.47
Structural golden rule	3.00	0.09
Relative debt	3.33	0.11
Maastricht	4.33	-0.09
½ point structural deficit reduction	4.67	-0.29
Structural deficit convergence	5.67	-0.21
Balanced structural budget	6.67	-0.56

Notes:
[a]   The rank is a simple average.
[b]   The output gap difference is weighted by GDP.

Table 2.9   Consensus approach

	Min. Rank	Countries blocking
Nominal golden rule	2	Italy
Structural golden rule	3	France, Germany, Italy
Relative debt	4	Germany, Italy
Maastricht	6	Italy
Structural deficit convergence	6	Germany, Italy
½ point structural deficit reduction	7	Germany
Balanced structural budget	7	France, Italy

As would be expected from the single country cases, the global welfare maximizing rule is the nominal golden rule (which was first for France and Germany and second for Italy). Second and third respectively are the structural golden rule and the relative debt rule. The *status quo*, Maastricht, comes only in the fourth position, entailing an average loss in output. The half-point deficit reduction and structural deficit convergence precedes in ranking the last option: aiming at balancing the structural budget.

A consensus approach

The European decision-making procedure, based on consensus and on veto power, makes another ranking interesting. In Table 2.9 we adopted a sort of 'max-min' approach whereby rules were ordered by the lowest individual ranking. Such a procedure is the best fit to reflect the consensus spirit (such that a proposal preferred by all countries, except one that strongly opposes it, has lower chances of being adopted than a proposal that is second-best for everyone).

The result of this 'consensus approach' is very similar to the welfare-maximizing one. The nominal golden rule, first choice for Germany and France, and second choice for Italy, comes first by far. The Maastricht rule which comes second in Germany's preferences would be vetoed by the two other countries. The half-point structural deficit reduction, which is first in Italy's ranking, would be vetoed by the two other countries.

2.6 ROBUSTNESS: AN ALTERNATIVE MEASURE OF WELFARE

The conclusion of the previous section, namely the superiority of the golden rule over the other reform proposals, emerged quite clearly from the analysis. Nevertheless, the weak explanatory power of the VAR regression of Table 2.3 requires results to be taken cautiously, unless their robustness is somehow tested. Given the limited data availability, we were unable to work on improving the fit of our base equations, so a different approach has been used. We undertook the same analysis as in sections 2.4 and 2.5, but the dependent variable in the VAR was unemployment rather than the output gap. We then ran the same simulations as above and considered the ranking using cumulated unemployment as a measure of welfare.[10] Table 2.10 summarizes our findings.

It can be seen that the superiority of the golden rule is confirmed in this different setting, even if in its structural rather than nominal form. The latter is penalized by its bad effect on the German economy, which affects only marginally its average ranking, but would seriously undermine its possibilities of being implemented in a consensus approach. The other difference is that the *status quo*, represented by the Maastricht rule, comes immediately after the two golden rules in terms of average ranking, and would even be the second preferred reform, if we used the consensus ranking.

Table 2.10   Rules ranked according to unemployment criterion (1990–2002)

	Country ranking			Global Welfare	Consensus
	France	Germany	Italy	Average. Rank	Minimum rank
Structural golden rule	2	2	3	2.33	3
Nominal golden rule	1	5	2	2.67	5
Maastricht	4	1	4	3.00	4
½ point structural deficit reduction	7	4	1	4.00	7
Relative debt	3	6	5	4.67	6
Balanced structural budget	5	2	7	4.67	7

2.7   CONCLUSION

In spite of the shortcomings of the method used, we can highlight two results that emerge from our simulation exercises:

1. The first is that the golden rule emerges as that which is less restrictive. This is true in the individual countries' preferences and when using global criteria; in the global welfare case, as in the consensus case. If as a measure of welfare we use unemployment instead of the output gap, the preference is for the structural rather than the nominal version of the rule, but nevertheless, the main message remains unchanged. This result is even more interesting if we notice that our exercise focuses on the short-term effects of the rules, as we make no assumption in our simulations on how the potential of the economy evolves. If we were to consider the effects of public investment on potential growth, the conclusion in favour of the golden rule would probably be strengthened.

2. The picture is less clear-cut as far as the existing framework, the Maastricht rule, is concerned. If we refer to the output gap, the *status quo* does not perform too brilliantly when compared to most of the alternatives currently being debated. For Germany individually, it is the second preferred alternative, but it ranks at best fifth for the two other countries. On the other hand, this result is not confirmed by our robustness test: when referring to unemployment, the Maastricht rule is second only to the structural golden rule.

A major lesson that we draw from our exercise is that if any reform proposal has a chance of being implemented in the near future, this might be some form of golden rule, since, as our simulations show quite robustly, it is the one more likely to catalyse consensus among the three large countries of the Euro Area.

NOTES

1. For arguments against constraining fiscal policies, see Arestis and Sawyer in this volume, or Fitoussi and Saraceno (2002).
2. A good starting point, to look into the debate, is Brunila et al. (2001). Two good taxonomies of the shortcomings of the Pact may be found in Wyplosz (2002b) and Buti et al. (2003).
3. The 3 per cent target had been set on the basis of a rough calculation as the figure stabilizing the debt ratio at the 60 per cent level, assuming a 5 per cent increase in nominal GDP (3 per cent of potential growth and 2 per cent of inflation); if the GDP elasticity of deficit is 0.5 (the average EU value as calculated by the Commission), the limit would allow a 6 per cent deviation from potential growth starting from a balanced structural budget.
4. The two heavyweights of the European Union, France and Germany, recently joined the group of those calling for the exclusion of investment from deficit figures ('Paris and Berlin seek relaxation of fiscal rules', *Financial Times*, 27 October 2004).
5. In this spirit, the rule must apply to net investment and capital depreciation must be accounted for as current spending.
6. In fact the 4 per cent case would ensure political feasibility as the highest debt country, Italy, would have a deficit target of 3 per cent, equivalent to the current one.
7. The EW coefficients for fiscal impulse, in the output gap equation, are: -0.68 (France), -0.58 (Germany) and -0.43 (Italy). We thank C. Wyplosz who provided us with his dataset and helped us to carry out the comparison between our dataset and his own.
8. Notice that in these reduced-form estimates we consider each country in isolation. In particular, we overlook spillover effects of fiscal impulses. In fact, we chose to focus on the simplest possible reduced forms (as EW do) in order to highlight the direct effects of fiscal impulses
9. The weights are given by the relative GDP in 2004, that is 0.21 for Italy, 0.32 for France and 0.47 for Germany (OECD, 2004).
10. The detailed results of the VAR estimation and of the simulations for each country are not reported for reasons of space, but are available upon request.

REFERENCES

Balassone, F. and D. Franco (2001), 'The SGP and the Golden Rule', in A. Brunila, M. Buti and D. Franco (eds), *The Stability and Growth Pact: The Architecture of Fiscal Policy in EMU*, New York: Palgrave.

Bean, C. (1998), Discussion of B. Eichengreen and C. Wyplosz 'The Stability Pact: More Than a Minor Nuisance?', *Economic Policy: A European Forum*, **13** (26), 104–07.

Blanchard, O.J. and F. Giavazzi (2002), 'La Crisi Della Germania E Le Riforme Del Patto Di Stabilità', *La Voce - Opinioni* November, 26. http://www.lavoce.info.

Blanchard, O.J. and F. Giavazzi (2004), 'Improving the SGP through a Proper Accounting of Public Investment', *C.E.P.R. Discussion Papers*, (4220) February.

Brunila, A., M. Buti and D. Franco (eds) (2001), *The Stability and Growth Pact: The Architecture of Fiscal Policy in EMU*. New York: Palgrave.

Buiter, W.H. and C. Grafe (2004), 'Patching up the Pact: suggestions for enhancing fiscal sustainability and macroeconomic stability in an enlarged European Union', *Economics of Transition*, **12** (1), 67–102.

Buti, M., S.C.W. Eijffinger and D. Franco (2003), 'Revisiting the Stability and Growth Pact: Grand Design or Internal Adjustment?' *CEPR Discussion Papers*, (3692) January.

Buti, M. and G. Giudice (2002), 'Maastricht's fiscal rules at ten: an assessment', *Journal of Common Market Studies*, **40** (5), 823–48.

Buti, M. and A. Sapir (2002), 'EMU in the Early Years: Differences and Credibility', in M. Buti and A. Sapir (eds), *EMU and Economic Policy in Europe: The Challenge of the Early Years*, Cheltenham, UK and Northampton, MA, US: Edward Elgar.

Calmfors, L. and G. Corsetti (2003), 'How to reform Europe's fiscal policy framework', Mimeo, Stockholm, Rome, January.

Calmfors, L., G. Corsetti, J. Flemming, S. Honkapohja, J. Kay, W. Leibfritz, G. Saint-Paul, H.-W. Sinn and X. Vives (2003), *EEAG Report on the European Economy 2003*, Munich: IFO Institute for Economic Research.

Coeuré, B. and J. Pisani-Ferry (2003), 'A Sustainability Pact for the Eurozone', Mimeo, Paris, February.

Creel, J. (2003), 'Ranking fiscal policy rules: the Golden Rule of public finance Vs. The Stability and Growth Pact', *Observatoire Français des Conjonctures Économiques Document de Travail*, 2003–04.

Eichengreen, B. and C. Wyplosz (1998), 'The Stability Pact: more than a minor nuisance?' *Economic Policy: A European Forum*, **26**, 65–104.

European Commission (2002), 'Strengthening the co-ordination of budgetary policies', *Communication to the Council and the European Parliament*, 27 November.

European Commission (2004), 'Strengthening economic governance and clarifying the implementation of the Stability and Growth Pact', *Communication to the Council and the European Parliament*, 3 September.

Fitoussi, J.-P. (2002), *La Règle Et Le Choix*. Paris, La république des idées, Seuil.

Fitoussi, J.-P. and F. Saraceno (2002), 'A theory of social custom of which soft growth may be one consequence: tales of the European Stability Pact', *Observatoire Français des Conjonctures Économiques Document de Travail*, 2002–07, October.

Gali, J. and R. Perotti (2003), 'Fiscal policy and monetary integration in Europe', *Economic Policy*, **37**, 533–64.

Grauwe, P. de (2003), 'The Stability and Growth Pact in need of reform', Mimeo, University of Leuven.

Kopits, G. and S. Symansky (1998), 'Fiscal policy rules', *IMF Occasional Papers*, 162.

Monperrus-Veroni, P. and F. Saraceno (2005), 'Reform of the Stability and Growth Pact: reducing or increasing the nuisance?' *Observatoire Francais des Conjonctures Economiques (OFCE) Documents de travail*, January.

Noord, P. van den (2000), 'The size and role of automatic fiscal stabilizers in the 1990s and beyond' *OECD working paper*, ECO/WKP 2000 (3).

OECD (2003), *OECD Economic Outlook*, **2003/2** (74), December, Paris: OECD Publication Service.

OECD (2004), *Main Economic Indicators*, **2004/12**, Paris: OECD Publication Service.

Pisani-Ferry, J. (2002), 'Fiscal discipline and policy coordination in the Eurozone: assessment and proposals', Mimeo, Université Paris-Dauphine, Paris, May.

Saraceno, F. and P. Monperrus-Veroni (2004), 'A simple proposal for a debt-sensitive Stability Pact', *Vierteljahrshefte zur Wirtschaftsforschung – Quarterly Journal of Economic Research*, **73** (3), 471–80.

Wyplosz, C. (2002a), 'Fiscal discipline in EMU: rules or institutions?' Paper prepared for the April 16, 2002 meeting of the Group of Economic Analysis of the European Commission, April.

Wyplosz, C. (2002b), 'The Stability Pact Meets Its Fate', Paper prepared for the 'Euro 50 Group' Meeting, 27 November.

3. Alternatives for the Policy Framework of the Euro

Philip Arestis and Malcolm Sawyer

3.1 INTRODUCTION

The establishment of the Economic and Monetary Union (EMU) and the introduction of the euro have clearly been major steps in the project of economic integration by European Union member countries (albeit only applying to 12 out of the 25 current members). The immediate build-up to the EMU began in 1992 with the adoption of the convergence criteria (under the Maastricht Treaty) for a country to adopt the euro. These convergence criteria related to nominal convergence (inflation, interest rates, stability of exchange rates) and did not make any mention of real convergence (whether of unemployment levels, business cycles or income per capita). Further, the convergence criteria also included fiscal variables (budget deficit less than 3 per cent of GDP, government debt less than 60 per cent of GDP) and the independence of the national central banks.

Most countries which subsequently joined the euro did not actually meet the convergence criteria (Arestis et al., 2001), setting a precedent of rules being broken subsequently with respect to the Stability and Growth Pact (SGP). The criteria concerning fiscal variables and the independence of the central bank did, though, mark out a neo-liberal agenda, which was subsequently embodied in the SGP. It is this policy framework which is the centre of our attention in this chapter where we present a critique of it before moving on to suggest some alternative policies.

3.2 THE CURRENT POLICY FRAMEWORK AND ITS PROBLEMS

The EMU is a major experiment in the use of a pre-Keynesian, or indeed a new Keynesian variety, macroeconomic policy. The present policy and institutional framework for the Euro Area can be readily summarized. The

European Central Bank (ECB), which is 'independent' of the political authorities in the European Commission and national governments and of the European Parliament, is entrusted with using monetary policy to pursue 'price stability' which it has interpreted as inflation below, but near to, 2 per cent per annum. It is also required to 'support general economic policies in the Union in order to contribute to the achievement of the Union's objectives' (ECB, 2004c). The monetary policy instrument is the use of interest rates and the ECB foregoes forms of monetary policy such as credit controls.

There is a requirement for the EU budget to be balanced each year and hence no fiscal policy is exercised at the EU level (and the EU budget is itself rather small at just over 1 per cent of EU GDP). The fiscal policy of national governments is, in principle, subject to conformity with the SGP. The SGP imposes an upper limit of 3 per cent of GDP on budget deficits, with the view that budgets will be broadly in balance or with a small surplus over the business cycle. Automatic exemption was in place for falls of GDP of more than 2 per cent. Discretionary exemptions were possible for falls in output of between 0.75 per cent and 2 per cent. Both situations would represent very major recessions. A system of non-interest bearing deposits, which could turn into fines, was also in place, but it has not been invoked despite a number of budget deficits exceeding 3 per cent (in the face of economic slowdown but not of declining output).

The European Central Bank (ECB) is the only federal economic agency, but its remit is the control of inflation, which has been persistently above the target level. The ECB appears to have been slow to recognize the beginnings of the slowdown in economic activity, and when it did so, it did not cut interest rates in an aggressive manner on a par with the US Federal Reserve System. However, the ECB has been faced with inflation at or above its target level alongside an economic slowdown: attention to its mandate and to establish 'credibility' with the financial markets pushed it towards maintaining a tight monetary policy.

We have argued elsewhere (Arestis and Sawyer, 2003) that the macroeconomic policy of the EMU can be understood as the application of the 'new consensus in macroeconomics'. The significant aspects of this 'new consensus' include the ideas that:

1. The level of output moves around a supply-side determined equilibrium (which can be described as corresponding to the 'natural rate of unemployment'). This equilibrium level of output (and the corresponding level of employment) is seen as unaffected by the level and time path of aggregate demand.

2. At this 'natural' level of output, inflation would be constant. Output above the 'natural rate' would involve 'overheating' of the economy and a tendency for inflation to rise.
3. Monetary policy, in the form of interest rates, is to be used to target the rate of inflation, where inflation is viewed as a demand-pull (and not cost-push), such that variations in the interest rate influence the level of demand which in turn influences the rate of inflation. Monetary policy is viewed as an effective instrument for the control of inflation. The workings of monetary policy are enhanced by it being placed in the hands of an 'independent' central bank. The credibility of such a central bank and the perception that it is committed to low inflation aids the achievement of low inflation through favourable effects on inflationary expectations.
4. Active fiscal policy is viewed as impotent and unnecessary. There is a recognition that fiscal policy can act as an 'automatic stabilizer', and that the budget position will vary over the course of the business cycle in a way which will dampen down the extent of those fluctuations. But active fiscal policy, whether in the form of a persistent budget deficit or varying tax and expenditure in a counter-cyclical manner is not required, under the presumption that there is sufficient aggregate demand to sustain the 'natural rate' of output. The rate of interest, as set by the central bank, can be aligned with the 'natural rate of interest', in the Wicksellian sense, such that the level of demand corresponds to the 'natural' level of output determined on the supply side as in point 1.

The first three points have led to the position where the ECB is set the sole objective of price stability under the assumptions that an 'independent' central bank will more readily gain a reputation as an 'inflation hawk' and monetary policy does not have long-term effects on the real side of the economy. We have argued elsewhere (Arestis and Sawyer, 2004) that this is unlikely to be the case. Indeed the orthodox argument is that interest rates do affect aggregate demand, which in turn affects the rate of inflation. The component of demand which is supposedly sensitive to interest rates is investment, and the pace of investment settles future productive capacity and the ability of the economy to provide high levels of employment.

Even if it is accepted that the budget should be balanced over the cycle, there is little reason to think that the extent of the swings in the budget position will be similar across countries. What reason is there to think that a swing in the deficit to a maximum of 3 per cent of GDP is relevant for all countries? Countries will differ in the extent to which their GDP varies in the course of a business cycle and in the extent to which the budget position is sensitive to the business cycle. Buti et al. (1997), for example, found that the budget balance is negatively linked to GDP growth, and they estimated that a 1 percentage point change in GDP causes on average a 0.5 percentage point change in the budget deficit at the EU level. At the country level the effect can be more dramatic: for example, the estimates were 0.8 and 0.9 percentage points for the Netherlands and Spain respectively. The notable feature is the differences amongst countries.

The next question is whether there is any reason to think that a (on average) balanced budget is compatible with high levels of employment – indeed whether it is compatible with any level of employment (including the NAIRU). A well-known identity (though generally forgotten by advocates of the SGP) drawn from the national income accounts tells us that: (Private Savings minus Investment) plus (Imports minus Exports) plus (Tax Revenue minus Government Expenditure) equals zero, which is in symbols:

$$(S - I) + (M - X) + (T - G) = 0 \qquad (3.1)$$

Individuals and firms make decisions on savings, investment, imports and exports. For any particular level of employment (and income), there is no reason to think that those decisions will lead to $(S - I) + (M - X)$ being equal to zero. But if they are not equal to zero, then $(G - T)$, the budget deficit, will not be equal to zero, since $(G - T) = (S - I) + (M - X)$. The SGP in effect assumes that any level of output and employment is consistent with a balanced budget $(G - T = 0)$, and hence compatible with a combination of net private savings and the trade position summing to zero. But no satisfactory justification has been given for this view. Two possible arguments could be advanced.

First, it could be argued that budget deficits cannot be run for ever as the government debt-to-income ratio would continuously rise and that would be unsustainable. Hence governments eventually have to run (on average) balanced budgets. However, that depends on whether the post-tax rate of interest (on government bonds) is greater or less than the growth rate, the debt-to-income ratio being unsustainable in the former case but not in the latter case. Further, it relates to the size of the primary deficit, which is the deficit that excludes interest payments. It is the overall budget deficit which is targeted by the SGP, and it can be readily shown that an average 3 per cent budget deficit and a 60 per cent debt ratio are compatible and sustainable, if the rate of growth of nominal GDP is 5 per cent (which is not an unreasonable assumption and could arise from, for example, 2.5 per cent inflation and 2.5 per cent real growth).[1] In general a 3 per cent budget deficit would be compatible with a sustainable debt ratio of $3/g$ where g is nominal growth rate.

Second, some form of Say's Law could be invoked to the effect that intended savings and investment are equal at full employment (or modified for foreign trade, domestic savings plus trade deficit equals investment). Even if Say's Law held (which we would dispute), what is required here would be that the level of private demand could sustain the supply-side equilibrium – that is the non-accelerating inflation rate of unemployment (NAIRU) – and the NAIRU does not correspond to full employment. In particular, there is no reason to think that a balanced budget position is compatible with employment at the level given by the NAIRU.

Further reservations include the separation of the monetary authorities from the fiscal authorities. The decentralization of the fiscal authorities inevitably makes any effective coordination of fiscal and monetary policy difficult. Since the ECB is instructed to focus on inflation while the fiscal authorities will have a broader range of concerns, there will be considerable grounds for conflict. A serious implication of this is that the SGP is in danger of becoming the 'instability' pact. This suggests a need for the evolution of a body which would be charged with the coordination of EMU monetary and fiscal policies. In the absence of such a body, tensions will emerge in the real sector when monetary policy and fiscal policy pull in different directions. The SGP in effect resolves these issues by establishing the dominance of the monetary authorities (ECB) over the fiscal authorities (national governments).

The SGP has sought to impose a 'one size (of straightjacket) fits all' fiscal policy – namely that over the course of the cycle national government budgets should be in balance or slight surplus with a maximum deficit of 3 per cent of GDP. It has never been shown (or even argued) that fiscal policy ought to be uniform across countries. The SGP imposes a fiscal policy, which may in the end fit nobody.

Within the Euro Area there has to be a single central bank discount rate. It is well known that the setting of that single interest rate poses difficulties – the rate which is appropriate for a country experiencing high demand and perhaps inflationary pressures is not appropriate for one facing low demand. Further, what reason is there to think that what is in effect a single fiscal policy (balanced budget over the cycle) is appropriate for all?

A number of reservations may be raised in terms of the efficacy of this monetary policy. There is the problem of the 'one-size-fits-all' monetary policy, a point raised by the Governor of the Bank of England. He argued, in an interview on German television on 20 December 2001, that such policy is risky and that 'The same monetary policy is not necessarily the best for every country at the same time' in such a diverse economic area. The Governor also suggested in an interview on BBC radio on 21 December 2001, that unlike monetary policy in a single country where 'mitigating factors' exist, such as labour migration and fiscal redistribution, these factors 'are not present to any significant degree at the Eurozone level'. There is, thus, no way that a country can offset undesirable effects of a too-high or a too-low rate of interest imposed by the ECB. A further point impinges crucially on the problem of the transmission mechanism of monetary policy in the euro area, since, as Duisenberg (1999, p. 189) concedes, 'Relatively little is known as yet' about it. Consequently, 'One important challenge for the Euro-system is to obtain better knowledge of the structure and functioning of the Euro area economy and the transmission mechanism of monetary policy within it, so that policy actions can be implemented accordingly' (Duisenberg, 1999, p. 189).

This policy arrangement suffers from three major defects. First, if inflation is induced by a demand shock (that is, a higher level of demand pushes up inflation), then a policy to influence aggregate demand, and thereby it is hoped inflation, may have some validity. But such a policy is powerless to deal with cost inflation or supply shock inflation. A supply shock would lower (raise) output whilst raising (lowering) inflation. Further, the extent to which the domestic interest rate can be changed is circumscribed by exchange rate considerations and is likely to take some time to have any impact on aggregate demand (and then the impact may be rather small). Indeed, the British monetary authorities (and others) talk in terms of a two-year lag between the change in interest rates and resulting impact of changes in aggregate demand on the rate of inflation. Interest rates are likely to influence investment expenditure, consumer expenditure, market interest rates and asset prices, expectations and the exchange rate. These changes in turn influence domestic and external demand, and then inflationary pressures. In addition, interest rate changes can also have distributional effects, whether between individuals or between economic regions.

Second, changes in interest rates have only a limited impact on aggregate demand. But further, insofar as interest rates do have an impact, it comes through effects on investment and on the exchange rate. High interest rates have long-term detrimental effects through reducing future productive capacity and through the impact of foreign trade. We have surveyed elsewhere (Arestis and Sawyer, 2004) the results of simulations of the effects of monetary policy using macro-econometric models. The survey is based on work undertaken for the ECB, for the Bank of England and for the central bank of the United States, the FED. The conclusion of that survey is that the effects of interest rate changes on inflation tend to be rather small – typically a 1 percentage point change in interest rates may dampen inflation by 0.2 to 0.3 percentage points after two years.

Third, monetary policy may address the average inflation picture but cannot address differences in inflationary experience across the Euro Area countries. At the time of writing and for the past few years, there is evidence of significant disparities in inflationary experience despite the convergence of inflation that was required by the Maastricht criteria (and indeed a number of countries now would not satisfy the inflation convergence conditions of the Maastricht Treaty). At the time of writing (February 2005) annual inflation rates vary from 0.0 per cent (Finland), 1.5 per cent (Netherlands) and 1.8 per cent (Germany) through to 3.3 per cent (Spain) and 3.2 per cent (Greece). Further, the impact of interest rate changes is likely to differ markedly across countries.

3.3 THE FOCUS ON LABOUR MARKET FLEXIBILITY

Although the ECB has been granted independence with a remit to use monetary policy to target inflation, this has not stopped it from seeking to intervene in a broader range of policies. The ECB may be free of political control but it is subservient to a particular neo-liberal economic doctrine, along the lines sketched above. It has persistently called for a tight fiscal policy. A recent statement illustrates this:

> With respect to the Stability and Growth Pact, discussions now need to be brought to a convincing conclusion with an outcome that safeguards fiscal discipline. The credibility of the excessive deficit procedure needs to be fully preserved. This is not only fundamental for macroeconomic stability and cohesion in the Euro area but also for confidence and growth prospects in all Member States. (ECB, 2005, p. 7)

It has also argued for labour market 'reforms' to increase so-called labour market flexibility on the erroneous basis that aggregate demand and macroeconomic policy are irrelevant for unemployment but that supply-side measures can reduce unemployment:

> In order to decisively overcome the obstacles towards greater employment growth and to reduce the trend or structural level of unemployment, further comprehensive labour market reforms are of the essence .(ECB, 2004b, p. 7)

> Given the signs that the economic recovery will continue, it is particularly important that fiscal policies and structural reforms play their part in improving the economic fundamentals of the Euro area. It is regretful that recent fiscal developments have not been helpful in this respect. A growing number of countries are reporting significant imbalances and fiscal consolidation efforts fall disappointingly short of commitments. In order to strengthen confidence in a sustainable upswing, it is now essential that clarity about the future course of consolidation of fiscal policies is re-established in all countries concerned. This requires credible measures with an emphasis on structural expenditure reform so

that imbalances are redressed, tax/benefit systems become more growth-friendly and social security systems are put on a sound financial footing. These measures, together with a revived momentum towards effectively implementing structural reforms in labour and product markets, would provide very valuable support to the current economic upswing. (ECB 2004a, p. 6)

This advocacy of labour market 'reforms' is consistent with the theoretical framework outlined above in which demand has no long-lasting effects on output, and in which the supply side of the economy is viewed as determining the level of economic activity. It is a stage further to argue that relevant changes in the labour market will lead to changes in the level of unemployment, but a stage which is often followed. However, the evidence that labour market flexibility favourably impacts upon the level of employment is weak. It does not readily fit with the low levels of unemployment experienced in many countries, which were then or have subsequently become members of the EU, and the generally much higher levels of unemployment experienced from the mid-1970s onwards. It also does not fit with the variations in the current unemployment experience: the rate of unemployment in the EU countries currently ranges from 4.4 per cent in Austria to 11.1 per cent in Spain, where the correlation between unemployment and labour market 'rigidity' is not self-evident. The wide range of unemployment within countries, for example Spain where in 2003 it varied from 5.5 per cent in Comunidad Foral de Navarra to 18.6 per cent in Andalucia, cannot be explained in this framework since labour market institutions are similar across the regions.

A study by Baker et al. (2002) provides empirical evidence on labour market regulations and unemployment for 20 OECD countries spanning 40 years, 1960–99. Different time periods are utilized as well as different combinations of variables. The most comprehensive measure of labour market institutions and policies utilized can only account for a minor part of the differences in the evolution of unemployment. The evidence in Baker et al. (2002) provides little or no support for explanations based on labour market rigidity, or labour market institutions in general. An index of the extent of labour market deregulation in the 1990s is constructed, but this variable also showed no meaningful relationship between labour market deregulation and shifts in the NAIRU. The same study poses the question of 'reverse causality' in the studies they discuss, to conclude that 'While clearly not universal, this evidence of reverse causation provides serious grounds for viewing test results showing a correlation between high unemployment and long benefit duration with caution' (Baker et al., 2002, p. 28). Palley (2001), by accounting for micro- and macroeconomic factors and also for cross-country economic spillovers, concludes that unemployment in Europe emanates from 'self-inflicted dysfunctional macroeconomic policy' (p. 3). An

OECD (1999) study is more damning to the 'labour market flexibility' thesis. It covers the period from the late 1980s to the late 1990s and utilizes new and improved data on employment legislation in 27 OECD countries. It employs multiple regression analysis and techniques, so that it is able 'to control for other factors that can influence unemployment' (p. 88). The study demonstrates that employment protection legislation[2] (a measure of labour market flexibility) has little or no impact at all on total unemployment. Consequently, dismantling employment protection would not solve the current unemployment malaise in the 27 countries considered in the study.

These studies do not give support to the view that labour market 'reforms' are needed to reduce unemployment. The current requirements are for a more stimulatory macroeconomic policy including expansionary fiscal policy and lower interest rates, and for the creation of productive capacity especially in regions and countries with high unemployment.

3.4 THE NEW EU CONSTITUTION: A MISSED OPPORTUNITY

The European Convention began its work in early 2002 to draw up what is widely referred to as a European Constitution. The Convention reported in June 2003, and after its proposals were rejected by national governments in the summit held in December 2003, a revised version was accepted by all 25 national governments in June 2004. At the time of writing, the treaty (Treaty establishing a Constitution for Europe: document CIG 86/04 available on the web site of the European Union) awaits ratification, whether through Parliamentary votes and/or national referenda.

The work of the European Convention provided a timely opportunity to fundamentally reform the macroeconomic policy-making frameworks of the Euro Area. The first years of the euro, and indeed the years preceding the launch of the euro, have not seen the most favourable economic performance in the Euro Area countries, and the deflationary climate created by the economic institutions of the Euro Area have been a major factor in this. The slowdown over the years 2001–2004 has clearly shown the major difficulties imposed by the SGP. The work of the European Convention was timely because the strains and problems of the SGP were becoming so clear to all, with many countries having exceeded the 3 per cent GDP budget deficit limit in time of economic slowdown. But the opportunity was spurned. Based on the reports of the working groups of the Convention, there appears to have been no serious consideration of alternatives. The neo-liberal macroeconomic policy frameworks will be locked into a Constitution, which will be difficult to change in the future, requiring agreement of all countries concerned. This had been the previous situation, but the drawing up of the Constitution did provide a 'window of opportunity', which is unlikely to occur again for many years to come.

The European Constitution imposes as a constitutional requirement that national governments balance their budget over the cycle and are subject to the upper 3 per cent limit, even though many countries have broken this limit repeatedly. It would be much more appropriate if the Constitution imposed the objectives of economic policy, including full employment and sustainable economic development. Putting the instruments of economic policy into a constitution is highly restrictive, and limits the development of alternative instruments. Further, the 'independence' of the central bank is a current economic policy fad, and enshrining that in the Constitution will make for unnecessary difficulties when the current fashion changes.

3.5   REQUIRED EMU ECONOMIC POLICY CHANGES

3.5.1   Fiscal Policy

Under the present arrangements, national fiscal policies could be said to be coordinated by the Stability and Growth Pact, though 'subordinated' may be a better word. The rationale for the present form of coordination comes from the notion of spillover effects between national economies and the interests of one country in the effects of other countries' fiscal policy. However, in the approach taken here, the case for coordination of fiscal policies arises from the following considerations:

1.   When the Euro Area (or EU) is impacted upon by shocks (for example general rise in the price of oil) which affects all of the economies (albeit not to the same extent), a coordinated response to such a generalized shock is appropriate.
2.   There are likely to be substantial spillover effects between national economies given the extent of trade between them, and hence a fiscal stimulus in one country will raise demand in neighbouring countries. The setting of fiscal policy is one country then needs to take into account what is happening to fiscal policy in neighbouring countries.
3.   Monetary and fiscal policies both affect the level of aggregate demand, exchange rate and perhaps the rate of inflation, and that points towards a need for coordination between monetary and fiscal policies.

The coordination of national fiscal policies faces many difficulties. A major one arises from the issue of what the aims and effects of the fiscal policies are. Under the present arrangements, it could be said that the aim of a fiscal policy is a balanced budget and that the effects of budget deficits are perceived to be generally negative (for example leading to high interest rates and inflation). It is clearly difficult for two (or more) individuals (or countries) to coordinate their activities if the purpose and effects of co-ordination are matters of dispute amongst the parties concerned. Thus, we would argue, coordination of national fiscal policies needs to be based on a shared set of objectives – and here we would advocate the inclusion of the objectives of high and sustainable levels of demand and economic activity. Coordination would also benefit greatly from shared views on the need for an active fiscal policy and its effects. This requires a sharp change from the prevailing 'conventional wisdom' embedded in the SGP.

A rather more direct form of coordination among fiscal policies would come from the development of an EU fiscal policy. The development of such a policy would require a large increase in the scale of the EU budget and the ability of the EU to operate a budget deficit (or indeed a budget surplus). The requirement for a significant EU budget was acknowledged in the MacDougall Report of 1977 (Commission, 1977, vol. 1, p. 14) which estimated an amount of 7.5 per cent of EU GDP as necessary to manage a monetary union. Goodhart and Smith (1993) and Currie (1997) argue that a rather lower figure for the EU budget, provided that it was well targeted to aid stabilization, would suffice, but their figures of around 2 per cent would still be double the current level of the EU budget. We would favour a somewhat larger figure, say of the order of 5 per cent, which would include measures to enhance investment and economic development in the less prosperous regions. However, the significant point here is the need for an EU budget which is not constrained to be balanced as at present, and which can be utilized for EU-wide stabilization purposes.

It may be argued that the current (March 2005) changes proposed by the European Commission and agreed by the European finance ministers for the EMU countries and those EU countries aspiring to join the EMU,[3] are significant and go a long way to meeting the reservations raised here. Although the strict nominal anchors of the original pact remain in place, namely the 3 per cent deficit-to-GDP ratio and the 60 per cent debt-to-GDP ratio, they are relaxed rules, since 'due consideration' will be given to countries that exceed these ceilings. The factors that will be taken into consideration under such circumstances include international aid, European policy goals and European unity. This will, of course, increase 'creative accounting' in the case of those countries that face an excess deficit procedure. The problems with the SGP since its introduction in 1999 will not simply disappear with the new SGP. In any case, the changes proposed are of little consequence. It is the complete abandonment of the SGP that EMU countries need, so that proper fiscal policy can be put in place that would coordinate with monetary policy with the clear objective of full employment and price stability.

3.5.2 Monetary Policy

Monetary policy inevitably suffers from the 'one size fits all' problem. It is well known that the setting of an interest rate which rules across many economic areas poses difficulties – the rate which is appropriate for a country experiencing high demand and perhaps inflationary pressures is not the same as that appropriate for one facing low demand and perhaps deflation. Indeed, monetary policy may address the average inflation picture but cannot address differences in inflationary experience across the Euro Area countries.

Therefore, the objectives and mode of operation of the ECB need to be changed. The objectives of the ECB should conspicuously include growth and employment variables, and not merely inflation.[4] The reformulated ECB should be required to act as lender of last resort and not merely possess the potential to act as such. Moreover, the ECB should adopt a more proactive stance regarding bank surveillance and supervision. The proposal for the reformulation of objectives readily follows from what has been previously said: the ECB should be charged with setting interest rates in a manner that encourages growth and full employment, rather than merely keep inflation in check. Further, EMU institutional arrangements are required for the operation of an EMU fiscal policy and to ensure that monetary authorities do not dominate economic policy-making; serious coordination of monetary and fiscal policies is paramount, just as the European Convention suggests, but it would have to go hand-in-hand with the other changes to which we have just alluded. These are important institutional changes. In terms of economic policy, further changes are required.

Monetary policy has become virtually synonymous with variations in the interest rate, which have an uncertain effect on the rate of inflation and economic activity. Alternative forms of monetary policy should also be considered (see for example Arestis and Sawyer, 2005). Explicit forms of credit control implemented by the central bank, or other government agencies, could be used to supplement interest rate policy. There are well-known difficulties with the use of credit controls. They can be evaded (legally or otherwise) through switching from regulated to unregulated forms of credit, including the development of products which fall outside the range of regulation and the switch of lending to overseas sources. Strict credit controls may have some effect in restraining credit and thereby expenditure, but the reverse may not be true. Relaxation of credit controls may do little to stimulate expenditure during a downswing.

Credit controls may have a role to play in slowing down the development of asset price bubbles, which may be worthwhile insofar as the extent of the subsequent downturn is a function of the extent of 'irrational exuberance'. These are circumstances which may be better tackled by controls over the volume of credit rather than attempting to prick the bubble through traditional monetary policy measures that use the price mechanism of interest rate increases. Appropriate forms of credit control may be focused on sectors where 'overexuberance' is developing, rather than using the blunt instrument of interest rate changes which has impacts on all sectors of the economy. Credit controls may be implemented in a variety of forms, and those which operate through reserve ratio requirements would appear to be feasible.

The major changes, which are required with respect to monetary policy, are:

1. A reformulation of the objectives of the ECB to include high and sustainable levels of employment and economic growth; and indeed these objectives should also be firmly embedded in the European Constitution.
2. The ECB must be made accountable to the European Parliament, and its statutes changed so that it can clearly be involved in the coordination of fiscal and monetary policies. Indeed, it should ultimately be able to take instructions from other European bodies such as ECOFIN.

There are some other changes which would also be desirable. Any reference to the growth of the money supply should be discarded in recognition that a central bank cannot in any way control the growth of the money supply. The development of alternative instruments of monetary policy should also be considered. The role of the ECB in securing stability in the European financial system should be emphasized and a clear requirement made that the ECB acts as a lender of last resort.

3.5.3 Exchange Rate Policy

The euro has become the second major currency in the world after the US dollar. The euro, of course, replaced another major currency (the German mark) and some other not quite so major currencies such as the French franc. The euro can be viewed as the second currency after the dollar when considered in terms of the size of the Euro Area economy, the use of the euro for international trade and the degree to which other countries have linked their currency to the euro.

The exchange rate between euro and dollar has become particularly important for a large chunk of international trade. The volatility of the euro–dollar exchange rate becomes significant not only for the Euro Area and the

US, but also for those countries who have linked their currency to either the euro or the dollar. The exchange rate has gone through major gyrations – the value of the euro started at $1.18 at its launch, fell to a lowest value of $0.82 (in November 2001) and then rose back to reach a current level of around $1.35 (as of March 2005).

As aforementioned, these swings in the euro–dollar exchange rate do not only impact upon the United States and the Euro Area. Since many countries link their currency with either the dollar or the euro, their own exchange rate position is much affected by the euro–dollar exchange rate oscillations. These large movements in the exchange rate are not conducive for decision-making with regard to participation in trade or to undertaking foreign investment. The volatility of the exchange rates not only discourages trade but also exacerbates the vulnerability of national economies to external events. As the exchange rate fluctuates, imports and exports, and thus the distribution of employment and output between countries, are subject to ups and downs.

The importance of the exchange rates between the dollar, the euro and the yen, and the harmful effects of the volatility of exchange rates, strongly point towards the development of mechanisms which could help to stabilize the trilateral exchange rates. The volatility between the three major currencies affects most international trade since many currencies are linked with one (or more) of those major currencies. The existing volatility, associated with speculative bubbles in the exchange markets, could well be having detrimental effects on trade and foreign direct investment.[5]

Any attempt to stabilize the exchange rate of the euro would necessarily involve the ECB and other central banks, and coordination between them would be particularly important. Interest rate differentials would be used to influence the exchange rates and hence the need to coordinate interest rate decisions in order to arrive at the required interest rate differential. But the reliability of the effect of changes in interest rate differentials on the exchange rate weakens the usefulness of interest rates in this regard. Interest rates are currently used to target the rate of inflation, though much of the effect of interest rates on inflation may come through the exchange rate. The policy indicated here requires a broadening of the remit of central banks clearly to include an exchange rate target. The interest rate instrument is likely to be rather ineffectual in this regard, and hence direct intervention by central banks in the exchange markets would generally be required. The ability of a single central bank to intervene in the exchange markets is limited by its own reserves. The combination of central banks would be in a much stronger position to intervene, in part as they have a greater volume of reserves. However, the main reason is that while a central bank is limited by its own foreign reserves, the central bank of the currency which is not under pressure can buy to an unlimited extent the currency under pressure. Any policy seeking to establish stable exchange rates between the major currencies would require some significant institutional changes within the EU, including changes in the objectives of the ECB to include that of the external value of the currency, and interest rates would have to be set with regard to their effects on the external value of the euro.

Indeed a range of changes would be required for any policy which seeks to achieve a target exchange rate for the euro, whether or not in cooperation with other countries. The target exchange rate would be set and by and the overall responsibility for the pursuit of an exchange rate policy should lie with the Council of Ministers of the Eurogroup, and the ECB would be required to support that policy. International negotiations would be in the hands of that group of ministers, and this could be aided by the creation of a permanent apparatus to support those negotiations and their implementation.

It is very important for the EMU to formulate an official exchange rate policy and abide by it. At the moment, the slightest indication by any of the EMU officials on the exchange rate results in 'brutal' (according to the ECB chairman) gyrations in the euro exchange rate with inevitable and undesirable uncertainties creeping in that hurt an already fragile economy with unacceptably high rates of unemployment (we may note that the annual rate of GDP growth is less than 2 per cent in 2004 and projected to be even lower in 2005, and unemployment is stubbornly at 8.9 per cent and rising). The latest example is the statement by the Dutch finance minister, Gerrit Zalm, who argued that the euro's appreciation was 'evolving within acceptable margins' (*Financial Times*, 28 December 2004). The euro achieved a new high against the dollar as a result (and that happened for the third consecutive session). In the midst of this gloomy picture, the ECB is reluctant to lower interest rates which would help the euro exchange rate to reach a more palatable rate. If anything, though, the ECB is contemplating and leaning towards a rise of the rate of interest.

3.6 SUMMARY AND CONCLUSIONS

The first years of the euro have not been economically successful ones. The inflation target has generally not been achieved, though the extent of the failure is relatively small. The limits on budget deficits laid down by the Stability and Growth Pact have been breached under the impact of the economic slowdown in most EU countries. The operation of the SGP has managed to combine a deflationary bias in the operation of fiscal policy with rules which are not maintained in practice. Even the relaxation of the SGP rules recently agreed upon would not deliver for the very simple reason that the changes are rather cosmetic. If anything, they would produce more problems through creative accounting, as argued in the text. The macroeconomic policies of the Euro Area need a complete overhaul with the re-establishment of high levels of employment as the major objective and the use of fiscal (and other) policies to support the achievement of that objective.

NOTES

1. The general formulation is $d = b/g$ where b is budget ratio, d debt ratio and g the rate of nominal growth.
2. The employment protection legislation is defined broadly and covers all types of employment protection measures resulting from legislation, court rulings, collective bargaining or customary practices. The OECD (1999) study considered a set of 22 indicators, summarized in an overall indicator on the basis of a four-step procedure (pp. 115–18).
3. Presidency Conclusions of the European Council, Brussels, 22 and 23 March 2005, Annex II, Doc 05/1.
4. The question whether the ECB differs from the FED in this respect, is discussed in the contribution of Kool in this volume.
5. One recent review, undertaken for the HM Treasury (2003) in the UK, concluded that 'even from this subset of evidence ... that negative impacts are not very large'. But they go on to say that 'estimates of the maximum gains to trade from the complete elimination of exchange rate volatility are in the region of 15 percent, while the consensus estimate of these studies is typically less than 10 percent' (p. 28).

REFERENCES

Arestis, P., A. Brown and M. Sawyer (2001), *The Euro: Evolution and Prospects*, Cheltenham, UK and Northhampton, MA, US: Edward Elgar.
Arestis, P. and M. Sawyer (2003), 'Macroeconomic policies of the Economic and Monetary Union: theoretical underpinnings and challenges', *International Papers in Political Economy*, **10** (1), 1–54.
Arestis, P. and M. Sawyer (2004), 'Can monetary policy affect the real economy?', *European Review of Economics and Finance*, **3** (3), 9–32.
Arestis, P. and M. Sawyer (2005), 'Aggregate demand, conflict and capacity in the inflationary process', *Cambridge Journal of Economics*, **29** (6), 959–974.
Baker, D., A. Glyn, D. Howell and D. Schmitt (2002), 'Labour market institutions and unemployment: a critical assessment of the cross-country evidence', *CEPA Working Paper*, **17** (8 November), New York: New School University.
Buti, M., D. Franco and H. Ongena (1997), 'Budgetary policies during recessions: retrospective application of the "Stability and Growth Pact" to the post-war Period', *Economic Papers*, (121), Brussels: European Commission.
Commission of the European Communities (1977), 'Report of the study group on the role of public finances in European integration, chaired by Sir Donald MacDougall', *Economic and Financial Series*, **A** (13), Brussels.
Currie, D. (1997), *The Pros and Cons of EMU*, London: HM Treasury.
Duisenberg, W.F. (1999), 'Economic and Monetary Union in Europe: the challenges ahead', in *New Challenges for Monetary Policy, proceedings of A Symposium*

Sponsored by the Federal Reserve Bank of Kansas City, Jackson Hole, Wyoming, August 26–28, 185–194.

ECB (2004a), *Monthly Bulletin*, June.

ECB (2004b), *Monthly Bulletin*, October.

ECB (2004c), *Protocol on the Statute of the European System of Central Banks and of the ECB*, 1 June.

ECB (2005), *Monthly Bulletin*, March.

Goodhart, C.A.E. and S. Smith (1993), 'Stabilization, European economy, reports and studies', *The Economics of Community Public Finance*, (5), 417–455.

HM Treasury (2003), *EMU and Trade*, London: HMSO.

OECD (1999), *OECD Employment Outlook*, (June), Paris: OECD.

Palley, T. (2001), 'The role of institutions and policies in creating high European unemployment: the evidence', *Working Paper Series*, (336), Levy Economics Institute of Bard College (August).

4. What Drives ECB Monetary Policy?

Clemens J.M Kool

4.1 INTRODUCTION

The European Central Bank (ECB) has been in charge of monetary policy for the Euro Area since 1998. The ECB took power under the conditions set by the Maastricht Treaty, which stipulated that 'the primary objective of the ESCB shall be to maintain price stability'. In addition, the treaty stated that 'without prejudice to the objective of price stability, the ECB shall support the Community's general economic policies and its objectives'. A high level of employment and stable economic growth are among these latter objectives. However, the manner in which the ECB would implement monetary policy and how it would weigh its primary objective against other, secondary, considerations was unclear. An additional complication was the fact that the ECB had no proven track record as an inflation fighter at its start. Of course, its creators hoped the ECB could inherit the Bundesbank's reputation in this respect. Nevertheless, common opinion was that being too loose would considerably reduce any inherited credibility the ECB might have. For that reason, many observers expected the ECB to focus on price stability alone. Alesina et al. (2001), for instance, formulate a benchmark interest rate rule for the ECB that only includes the deviation of inflation from its target as a determinant.

Between 1999 and 2004, many academic and popular commentators have commented on ECB policy and criticized its choices. Popular sentiment typically appears to be that ECB policy choices compare unfavourably with those of the Federal Reserve System in the United States. While the chairman of the Board of Governors of the Federal Reserve System (Fed), Alan Greenspan is seen as a fine-tuning expert 'playing' the market with a keen eye for real developments, the ECB – and particularly its past president Wim Duisenberg – do without the glamour and charisma and stubbornly talk about the need to maintain low inflation. Politicians in large countries with low growth – notably Germany, France and Italy – tend frequently to complain about the lack of ECB attention towards economic growth and (un)employment in its monetary policy. The academic literature, on the other hand, generally provides evidence that the ECB does pay attention to both price and output developments in setting monetary policy. Here, however, criticism more often takes the form of the ECB being too loose. A related but separate issue concerns the question whether the ECB exclusively sets interest rate policy on the basis of Euro Area-wide economic developments or whether regional issues (in)appropriately play a role too.

This chapter summarizes and analyses the available evidence on the ECB's performance in the first five years of its existence. Quite naturally, the question arises of whether and to what extent the ECB has been successful in reaching its goals. Moreover, an evaluation of the goals themselves and the strategies to achieve these goals are in order. In my view, it is a natural time to do so for two main reasons. First, in November 2003 Trichet became the second president of the ECB, succeeding Duisenberg and bringing the ECB into a new phase. Second, in 2003 the ECB itself performed an internal evaluation of its monetary policy strategy and implemented a number of changes to this strategy. Note though that even a five-year period may be still quite short for a final verdict.

This chapter will focus on three questions. First, the extent to which the ECB's focus has been on price stability as compared to a broader concern for macroeconomic stability is analysed. Second, an examination is made of the extent to which policy has been set according to Euro Area-wide developments as opposed to regional developments. Third, ECB behaviour is compared with that of the Fed to investigate whether the ECB really has been more hawkish as an inflation fighter and simultaneously less activist in pursuing output goals than the Fed.

The chapter is set up as follows. In section 4.2, a brief overview of the way these issues have been treated in the literature is presented. In section 4.3, the data used for the analysis are described. Here, the focus is on the period from 1999:1 to 2004:2 using quarterly data. In section 4.4, hypothetical interest rate paths are computed using standard Taylor rules to analyse Euro Area policy settings, both for centralized (Euro Area-wide) and decentralized (national) developments. Subsequently, ECB and Fed interest rate policies are compared. Section 4.5 contains a summary and conclusion.

4.2   A REVIEW OF THE ISSUES

4.2.1   The Importance of Real Developments: Words Versus Deeds

In 2003, the ECB presented the outcome of an internal evaluation of its monetary policy strategy (ECB, 2003). In summary, according to the ECB its strict focus on price stability as the core element of its monetary policy strategy remained unchanged. However, the ECB 'clarified' – and slightly adjusted upward – its quantitative definition of price stability. Instead of defining price stability as a positive rate of increase in the HCIP (the Harmonized Index of Consumer Prices) lower than 2 per cent, the ECB reformulated its objective to maintain inflation below but close to 2 per cent. Moreover, it downplayed the role of the second 'monetary' pillar as a determinant of short-run monetary policy. Gali et al. (2004) critically review the ECB's evaluation outcomes. They argue that the ECB in fact has structurally shown concern for the real side of the Euro Area economy and has set monetary policy accordingly. That is, while in words ECB policy is aimed at price stability *per se*, ECB deeds reflect a more balanced concern for both price and output developments. In their view the recent strategy adjustments are a way to gradually reconcile words and deeds of ECB actions. Gali et al. (2004) blame the ECB for not being more explicit and transparent about its goals.

In a chapter entitled 'The Duisenberg Record', Gali et al. (2004) also evaluate the results of ECB policy. Here, they conclude that the ECB has failed to accomplish its own (inflation) goals when measured against the ECB's own yardstick. They quote from Duisenberg's words before the Committee on Economic and Monetary Affairs of the European Parliament on 23 November 2000 as follows:

> At what point would I say that we can talk about a failure? That would be, if, over the medium term future, we were to have domestic inflation of our own making, which would over time, continue to exceed the definition of, at maximum, two percent inflation. Then we would be justified in speaking of a failure, but this is a hypothetical situation which I do not envisage happening at all. (Gali et al. 2004, pp. 49–50)

Given the fact that HCIP inflation in the Euro Area has fluctuated between 2 and 2.5 per cent per year for the complete period 2000–2003, Gali et al. (2004) conclude that even when accounting for all contingencies Duisenberg mentions in the above quote, they 'cannot find convincing evidence that the ECB has worked hard at keeping inflation in check and back in line, when it crept back above the 2% maximum'.

Sapir et al. (2004) more or less arrive at the same conclusion. However, they look at it much more positively. Sapir et al. (2004, p. 54–55) conclude:

> There is a large consensus that the ECB did a good job in an eventful period where it had to operate with less-than-perfect statistical information and knowledge of the functioning of the euro-area economy. Before the euro was launched, observers pointed to the risk of an over-restrictive monetary policy given the need of the newly-created central bank to build up its anti-inflationary reputation. This risk has

not materialised and price stability has been achieved while maintaining a growth-supporting monetary stance.

Empirical work on monetary policy reaction functions largely confirms the hypothesis that the ECB does put a positive non-zero weight on output gaps in its interest rate setting. Most of this work is based on the Taylor rule type of equations.[1] These generally take the following form:

$$i_t = R^* + \pi_t + \alpha (\pi_t - \pi^*) + \beta(y_t - y^*) \qquad (4.1)$$

where i represents the nominal short-term (policy) interest rate, R^* is the equilibrium real interest rate, π and π^* are realized and target inflation respectively and y and y^* are actual and potential output. Consequently, $(y_t - y^*)$ represents the current output gap and $(\pi_t - \pi^*)$ is the deviation of inflation from its target. According to Taylor (1993), a sensible monetary policy rule would be equation (4.1) with coefficients α and β both equal to 0.5. Taylor shows that actual interest rate policy in the United States in the period 1987-1992 closely follows this rule. In empirical work, equation (4.1) is typically reformulated as a regression equation of the following form:

$$i_t = \rho\, i_{t-1} + (1 - \rho)[c_0 + c_1(\pi_t - \pi^*) + c_2(y_t - y^*)] + \varepsilon_t \qquad (4.2)$$

Here, ε_t is the error term of the regression. Note that in this specification values for c_1 and c_2 corresponding to $\alpha = 0.5$ and $\beta = 0.5$ are 1.5 and 0.5 respectively. Different specifications are used in the literature. Sometimes current inflation is replaced by lagged inflation or forward-looking measures, either inflation expectations or future inflation realizations. For the output gap, lagged variables are used as well. Finally, as shown in equation (4.2) a one-period lagged interest rate term is often added to capture possible interest rate smoothing by the central bank.

Hayo and Hofmann (2003) estimate a Taylor rule both for the Bundesbank (1979–98) and the ECB (1999–2003). They find significantly positive coefficients c_1 and c_2 in both regressions. However, they conclude that the (long-run) output weight given by the ECB (c_2 equal to 1) considerably exceeds that by the Bundesbank (c_2 equal to 0.4). In both regressions they find c_1 to equal 1.2, suggesting a lower weight on inflation than in the original Taylor rule. Moreover, they report substantial persistence in interest rates as witnessed by an autoregressive parameter ρ around 0.9. Smant (2002) reports similar estimates for the Bundesbank's policy rule prior to 1999 and claims that the ECB set its interest rate consistent with the Bundesbank's old policy rule from mid-2000 to mid-2001. Gerlach and Schnabel (2000) estimate a hypothetical Taylor rule for the aggregated EMU-11 group of countries over the period 1990–98 with similar results. In addition, they show that the use of forward-looking expected inflation rather than actual inflation reduces the size of the output coefficient. The latter remains significant, though. They suggest that the current output gap is an indicator of future inflation pressures. Results showing that the central bank attaches a positive weight to inflation thus do not necessarily prove that the central bank intends to stimulate output. Alternatively, the central bank may use current output development to stabilize future prices. Nevertheless, the fact that the output coefficient remains significant even with the inclusion of forward-looking inflation measures suggests some output stabilization is still present. Finally, Fourçans and Vranceanu (2004) also provide evidence supporting a positive ECB response to the output gap in setting the interest rate under the Duisenberg presidency, using monthly data from January 1999 to October 2003.

Overall, the literature suggests that the ECB does indeed put a non-zero weight on real developments in setting its policy rate. The potential criticism that the ECB is a rigid inflation hawk with disregard of output losses appears to be unfounded, therefore. Note that most of the empirical work only relates to the first years of the ECB, that is, approximately the period 1999–2001. Relatively scarce empirical studies are available on the second part of the five-year period.

It also appears that little empirical work exists that explicitly compares the Federal Reserve's and ECB's reaction functions. Begg et al. (2002) are the exception. They focus on events in 2001 and find that 'faster reductions in interest rates in the United States in 2001 reflected a more rapid deterioration in economic conditions than in Europe, not any systematic difference in how the ECB and the Fed respond to new information'. In addition, they state that 'a Fed-in-Frankfurt would have replicated ECB behaviour fairly closely'. This suggests that the differences between the Fed and the ECB may reflect presentation rather than content.

4.2.2   The Importance of National versus Aggregate Developments

Most research on the implementation and outcomes of the ECB's monetary policy uses an aggregate approach, focusing on Euro Area-wide information variables. Such approach is consistent with the ECB's mandate to ensure price stability in the Euro Area as a whole, as well as with the ECB's often-repeated position that the 'one-man one-vote system' in the ECB Governing Council neither in theory nor in practice serves to guard national special interests.

However, it is clear that a common – one-size-fits-all – monetary policy may not be optimal in the case where the participating countries (regions) do not form an optimum currency area. In such a case, the existence of asymmetric shocks or asymmetric transmission of common shocks due to differences in economic and financial structure may lead to temporary national inflation differentials – and output growth differentials for that matter – across countries.[2] Arnold and Kool (2004) provide empirical evidence on the magnitude of regional inflation differentials in the United States and their role in economic adjustment processes. They also observe that inflation differentials within the Euro Area have considerably increased since the start of EMU. For each year from 1999 onwards, at least three of the participating countries did not observe the Maastricht Treaty inflation criterion. Sapir et al. (2004) also report that inflation convergence and cross-country inflation correlations significantly decrease after 2000.

Berger and de Haan (2002) and Berger et al. (2003) argue that monetary policy decision-making is relatively decentralized in the EMU compared to the situation in both the United States (the Fed) and the old Bundesbank system. In their view, the current voting system in the ECB makes small countries too powerful in the determination of monetary policy. Heinemann and Hüfner (2002) apply the median voter theory to extend the standard Taylor rule specification. Based on this generalized monetary policy reaction function, they find weak evidence of some regional impact on the ECB's policy choices. On the other hand, von Hagen and Brückner (2001) use empirical Taylor rule results to argue that in its early years, the ECB mainly focused on events in Germany and France in its monetary policy choice and succeeded in overcoming the 'median country's perspective on monetary policy'.

Arnold (2004) provides a theoretical rationale to support a stronger position for the large and relatively closed economies in the EMU. In his view, small and relatively open (peripheral) economies trade more with countries outside the Euro Area. These countries then have automatic stabilizers in the form of real exchange rate changes *vis-à-vis* non Euro Area trading partners that the larger relatively closed EMU economies lack. Consequently, ECB policy then could and should focus more on the latter group's development than on that of the former.

In summary, the evidence on the existence of growing national (regional) disparities – although temporary in character – is quite strong. The extent to which this influences ECB decision-making is inconclusive. Some research suggests ECB policy is more than proportionally directed at Germany and France, the two large and central EMU economies, while other research suggests undue influence of the peripheral countries.

4.3   THE DATA

The focus of the analysis that follows is the period 1999:1–2004:2. Quarterly data are used for the 12 individual European countries participating in EMU, that is, Austria, Belgium, Finland, France, Germany, Greece, Ireland, Italy, Luxembourg, the Netherlands, Portugal and Spain, as well as for the Euro Area as a whole and for the United States.

All data were downloaded from DATASTREAM. For the individual European countries as well as the overall Euro Area harmonized CPI and real GDP were used. For Euro Area real GDP as well as the Spanish real GDP series, the period was 1980:1–2004:2. For all other European countries a real GDP series was available from 1973:1 onward. Subsequently, a Hodrick-Prescott filter was applied to these long real GDP series in order to extract a trend. The output gap (Gap 1 HP) then was defined as the difference (expressed in annual percentages) between observed real GDP and its trend value. Obviously, this derived measure of the output gap is subject to measurement error. One problem is the fact that trend estimates of output are particularly sensitive to actual observations at the first and last observations of the sample. This makes the trend estimates less reliable exactly in the period of most interest, the final years 1999–2004. Possible future data revisions of the final few years of the sample further compound the problem. Overall, these issues suggest that caution is required in the interpretation of the empirical results. To check for the sensitivity of the conclusions with regard to the specification of the output gap, a quarterly output gap measure was also directly downloaded from DATASTREAM that was computed by the OECD (Gap 2 OECD). For Belgium, Luxembourg, Portugal and Spain the OECD does not provide quarterly output gaps, so that these four countries are excluded when the second gap measure is used.

Thus, in the analysis two different output gap measures are used. Inflation is computed as the year-over-year percentage price increase in the HCIP. The nominal interest rate is the Euro Overnight Index Average (EUEONIA), measured as the three-month average of daily rates. For the United States, a similar procedure was applied to real GDP, using data from 1973:1 to 2004:2. For the United States, the CPI excluding food and energy is used. The nominal interest rate is the federal funds rate measured as the three-month average of daily rates.

Figure 4.1 shows actual inflation performance as well as the two output gaps over the period 1999:1–2004:2 for the Euro area as a whole. It confirms that inflation has been slightly above 2 per cent per year for almost the complete period with little downward tendency. The two output gap measures roughly display the same pattern and their correlation coefficient is 0.82. Gaps rose in 1999 and 2000 and subsequently turned negative in early

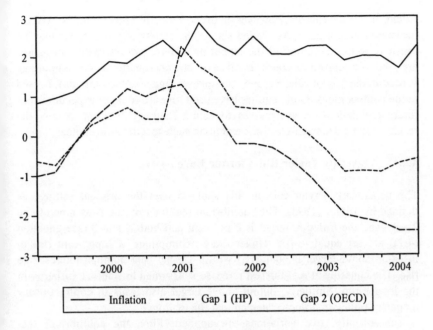

| | Inflation | ------ Gap 1 (HP) | ----- Gap 2 (OECD) |

Figure 4.1   Inflation and output gaps in Europe

2001 in line with the growing impact of the recession. However, from 2001 onward the OECD estimate of the output gap is considerably lower than the HP extracted gap. The difference equals one percentage point in 2001–2002, increasing to almost two percentage points in 2003. In the next section, we will use these series to construct artificial interest rate paths.

4.4   RESULTS

Due to the short sample, no estimations are performed here. Rather we simply construct various hypothetical interest rate paths, based on different assumptions with respect to the specification of the Taylor rule. The advantage of using a number of different assumptions underlying the Taylor rule is that it allows for a robustness analysis in the evaluation of actual ECB policy. Note that here we abstract from the autoregressive component in a Taylor rule; that is, we construct the long-run interest rate path based on assumptions about the equilibrium real interest rate, the inflation target and the sensitivity of the interest rate to inflation deviations from target and to the output gap. Based on the graphical evidence a discussion is then presented concerning which Taylor rule the ECB may have followed and to what extent. A few caveats are, however, in order. First, different methods exist for measuring output gaps. As argued above, the results of the analysis may be sensitive to the definition of the output gap. Here, two alternative measures are used as a robustness check. In all cases, the one-quarter lagged output gap is used in the Taylor rule. Second, one-quarter lagged annual inflation is used in the computations. Other studies have used forward-looking expectations of future realizations as alternatives to actual (lagged) inflation. Again, the results may be dependent to some extent on such specification choices.

4.4.1   Aggregate Taylor Rules for the Euro Area

The benchmark Taylor rule in this analysis uses the original settings as defined by Taylor (1993). The equilibrium real interest rate is assumed to be 2 per cent, the inflation target is 2 per cent and both α and β (see equation (4.1)) are set equal to 0.5. Under these assumptions, a 1 per cent rise in inflation above target is countered with a 1.5 per cent nominal interest rate rise. The consequent real interest rate rise is assumed to stabilize inflation in the longer run. Similarly, output above target also leads to contractionary monetary policy in order to dampen real fluctuations.

Subsequently, two variations are applied. First, the equilibrium real interest rate is raised to 2.5 per cent. Second, the inflation target is lowered to 1.5 per cent to better reflect the ECB's quantitative definition of price stability. Figure 4.2 gives the actual time path of the EUEONIA together with the hypothetical interest rate paths based on the three alternative Taylor rules described here. In Figure 4.2a output gap measure 1 (HP) is used, while in Figure 4.2b output gap 2 (OECD) is used. According to the evidence in Figure 4.2, actual interest rates are reasonably consistent with a standard Taylor rule until early 2001, but have been too low since 2001, regardless of the way the Taylor rule is specified. As could be expected from inspection of the relative values of the two output gaps, the appropriate interest rate according to Taylor rule computations is lower when the OECD output gap is used than for the HP output gap. In the latter case, the actual interest rate is about 1.5 to two percentage points lower than predicted by these three rules since 2001, while for the former case (the OECD gap measure) actual interest rates have been about one percentage point too low with the interest rate gap declining further in 2004. Note that both increasing the equilibrium real interest rate and lowering the value for the ECB's inflation target below 1.5 per cent increase the gap between actual and computed interest rates. Only a very low equilibrium real interest rate would be able to solve the issue.

A second way to investigate the robustness of the results is to vary the value of coefficients α and β from equation (4.1). In Figure 4.3, evidence on the issue is presented for both output gaps. Again, the actual interest rate is shown together with the time paths predicted by three different Taylor rules. In all rules the equilibrium real interest rate is assumed to equal 2 per cent, while the inflation target is set at 1.5 per cent. Given the mandate of the ECB to make price stability its first objective, the first alternative reaction function considered increases the weight on inflation (α) to 1 and reduces the weight of the output gap (β) to 0. This is a pure inflation rule. In the second and third rule, the output coefficient (β) is assumed to equal 1 and 2 respectively.

Clearly, the puzzle remains in the sense that no individual Taylor rule specification is able to roughly replicate actual ECB interest rate policy over the full period. Obviously, pure inflation rules exacerbate the problem as the divergence between actual and predicted interest rates increases. Since inflation has persistently remained above 2 per cent, a strict inflation rule would require nominal interest rates of at least 4 per cent over the whole period.

Here, the use of actual (lagged) inflation rather than more appropriate forward-looking inflation forecasts in the Taylor rule should be noted. One might argue that the ECB has consistently been too optimistic about the future decline of inflation below 2 per cent and has been willing to lower interest rates based on that belief. To the extent that this has played a role in actual policy-making, it may partly explain the observed interest rate gaps in Figures 4.2 and 4.3. However, it simultaneously throws doubt on the ECB's ability to predict future inflation developments. Consistent overshooting of its own forecasts will at some point have negative repercussions on the ECB's reputation and credibility.

The evidence in Figures 4.3a and 4.3b for higher – or even extreme – weights on the output gap is less uniform, though no rule is doing a good job for the whole period. Generally speaking, raising the output gap coefficient to higher values reduces the difference between the predicted and actual interest rates in the later part of the sample (2003 and early 2004) but does so at the expense of even larger discrepancies between the two in the period 2000– 2002. When using output gap 1 (Figure 4.3a), predicted interest rates remain above actual rates even when the output coefficient is raised to a level of 2. It is possible to align predicted and actual interest rates for the last few years when output gap 2 is used and the output gap coefficient is equal to unity. Note that such high policy responsiveness to output developments is vehemently denied by the ECB.

Overall, ECB policy appears to have been overly expansionary since early 2001.[3] This conclusion is based on an analysis that concentrates on aggregate Euro Area developments. These appear to be not very helpful in explaining ECB interest rate policy.

Therefore, we now turn to the possible influence of regional factors. In this respect, it is interesting to refer to earlier literature evaluating ECB

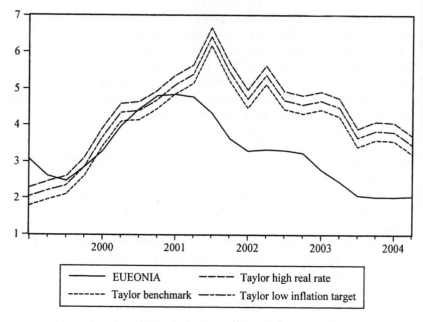

Figure 4.2a   Taylor rule interest rates (Gap 1 HP)

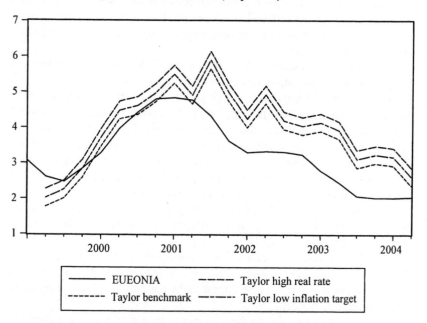

Figure 4.2b   Taylor rule interest rates (Gap 2 OECD)

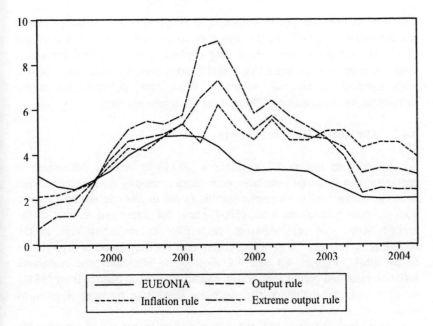

Figure 4.3a   More evidence on Euro Area Taylor rules (Gap 1 HP)

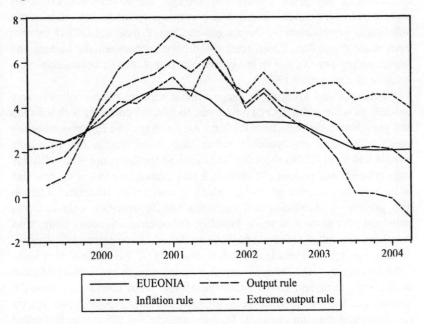

Figure 4.3b   More evidence on Euro Area Taylor rules (Gap 2 OECD)

policy in its first two years. According to von Hagen and Brückner (2001) and Alesina et al. (2001), ECB policy was too expansionary in mid-1999 and 2000.[4] Both sources have a hard time explaining this apparent looseness. Both come up with evidence that actual interest rates are much more in line with standard Taylor rule behaviour when only inflation and output developments in Germany and France are taken into account.

4.4.2   The Role of Regional Factors

As explained in section 4.2, asymmetric shocks as well as differences in economic and financial structures may cause transitory divergences across countries in the EMU. Automatic stabilizers are in place to ensure long-run convergence. Arnold and Kool (2004) show for states and regions in the United States that real exchange rates play an important role in the equilibrating process. To give an indication of the magnitude of divergences in the EMU, Figures 4.4 and 4.5 display the minimum and maximum inflation rates and output gaps across countries for each quarter from 1999:1 to 2004:2. As a benchmark, the aggregate Euro Area measure is given as well.[5]

Clearly, both inflation and output gap dispersion can be of considerable magnitude at any point in time. On average, the difference between the highest and lowest value is about three percentage points for the inflation gap and output gap measure 1. Output gap measure 2 from the OECD exhibits even more dispersion. Sometimes, the difference between the highest and lowest output gap is close to ten percentage points. For inflation, dispersion actually increases after 1999.

Figures 4.4 and 4.5 strongly suggest that a one-size-fits-all policy is very unlikely to achieve the desired objectives. In fact, for countries with inflation and growth very different from the Euro Area average, the common monetary policy may work pro-cyclically rather than stabilizing in the short run. Arnold and Kool (2004) show for the United States that states with relatively high inflation and growth end up with a real interest rate that is too low due to the common interest rate policy which in turn further stimulates inflation and growth. A stabilizing real exchange rate appreciation only becomes dominant after about two years. Possibly, the common monetary policy thus lengthens individual country's business cycles. To some extent, this depends on inflation expectations in individual countries. If the citizens of a high-inflation country – say Ireland – expect Irish inflation to equal EMU inflation in the long term and consequently base their wage claims and financial contracts on the low EMU expected inflation rate, the (expected) real interest rate in Ireland may not decrease. Then the pro-cyclical effect may be limited or even absent. The more that national experience and indicators play a role

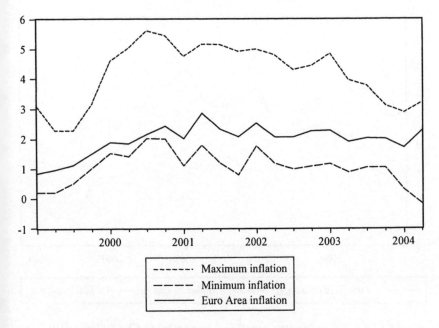

Figure 4.4   Cross-country inflation dispersion in EMU

in the formation of inflation expectations, the more of a problem the common policy is.

A natural consequence of the observed difference in inflation and output developments across EMU countries is a difference in preferred monetary policy. Put differently, countries using the same Taylor rule for their own economies may arrive at quite different optimal interest rate levels. Despite all this, national central bank governors sitting on the Governing Council of the ECB in theory are supposed to only consider the common EMU interest. Section 4.2 above presented literature that questioned this assumption.

In Figure 4.6, the optimal Taylor rules based on individual German, French and Austrian economic conditions are displayed together with the preferred overall EMU Taylor rule (which is identical to the low inflation target rule from Figure 4.2) and the actual EUEONIA. The choice of countries is not random. The three countries typically had low growth and low inflation over (most of) the period and – according to the Taylor rule approach – should have been in favour of low interest rates more than most EMU members. Naturally, they all have preferred interest rates below the optimal EMU rate. More interesting is the comparison between the actual EUEONIA and each country's preferred interest rate. Here, a distinction is again made between the two alternative ways to measure the output gap.

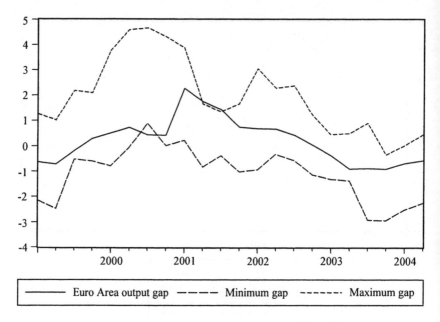

Figure 4.5a   Cross-country output gap dispersion in EMU (Gap 1 HP)

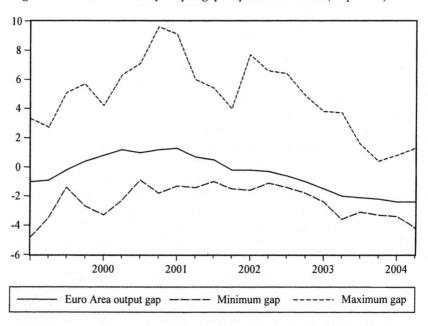

Figure 4.5b   Cross-country output gap dispersion in EMU (Gap 2 OECD)

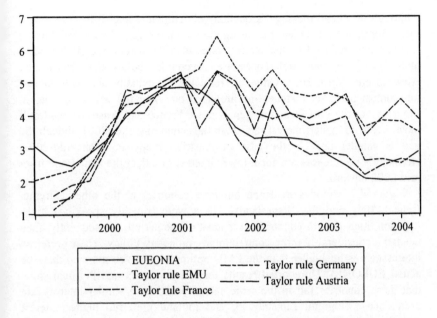

Figure 4.6a   Taylor rules: Low growth and inflation countries (Gap 1 HP)

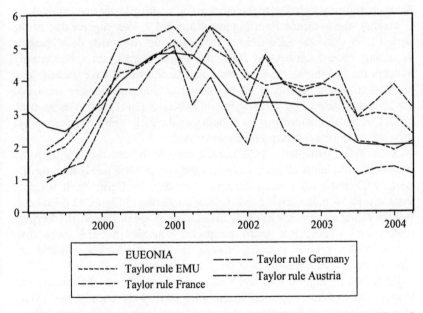

Figure 4.6b   Taylor rules: Low growth and inflation countries (Gap 2 OECD)

Although the broad message is qualitatively similar, some difference exists. From Figure 4.6a it is clear that using the HP output gap, France and Austria would have preferred higher interest rates than the actual rate (EUEONIA) after 2001.[6] German preferences are structurally below the French and Austrian ones since 2001. Only for Germany, the actually observed interest rate almost perfectly matches the preferred one over the whole sample. In Figure 4.6b, the OECD output gap is used. France and Austria would still have preferred higher interest rates than the actual rate after 2001, though the gap is smaller and, in the case of Austria, disappears after mid-2003. Germany's preferences are for a lower interest rate than the actual one from mid-2002 onward.

Figure 4.7 provides evidence on three countries at the other extreme, Ireland, Italy and the Netherlands. These were (roughly speaking) high-inflation, high-growth countries over most of the period. Consequently, they needed a considerably more contractionary monetary policy. Their preferred interest rate is far higher than the EMU optimum and even more so than the actual EUEONIA. Unreported results for Greece, Spain and Portugal show that these countries fall in the same category and have similar interest rate preferences. Belgium, Luxembourg and Finland preferred higher interest rates than the EMU optimum up till 2001 – which puts them in the same group as Ireland, Italy, Spain, Portugal, Greece and the Netherlands – but then subsequently switched to the other group wanting lower interest rates.

Overall, the evidence from Figures 4.6 and 4.7 does suggest that in the period 1999–2004 the ECB did not focus on Euro Area-wide developments in setting interest rates. Until 2001, the actual interest rate approximately matches the rate that Germany, France and Austria would have wanted. This conclusion is not dependent on the actual output gap measure used and supports the findings by von Hagen and Brückner (2001) and Alesina et al. (2001) who also claimed that ECB policy in the early years was (primarily) driven by common German–French preferences.

Since 2001 particularly, ECB interest rates have been too low from the perspective of almost all Euro Area countries. According to Figure 4.6a, the actual EUEONIA has been at the right level only for Germany. It suggests that Germany is in the driving seat. Casual inspection of Figure 4.6b indicates that the actual interest rate has been set as the average of French and German preferences. Claims that small peripheral countries have a more than proportional say in ECB policy-making through the voting schedule are clearly rejected here, regardless of the output gap measure used.

As shown by Figures 4.6a and 4.6b, interest preferences of Germany and France start to diverge to some extent after 2001. Theoretically, that would allow an analysis of the relative weights of these countries in actual interest rate determination. However, casual inspection of these figures shows that

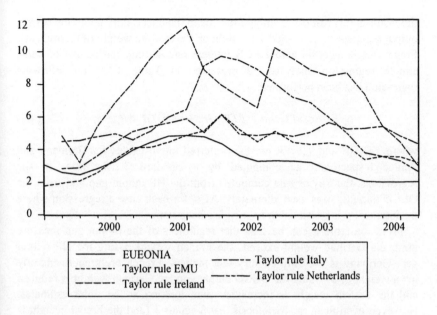

Figure 4.7a Taylor rules: High-growth, high-inflation countries (Gap 1 HP)

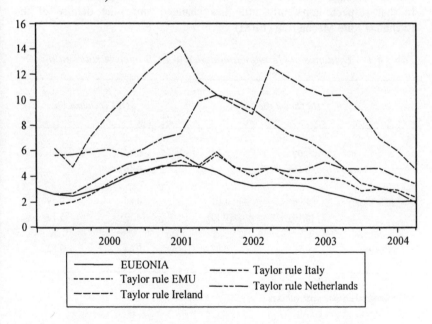

Figure 4.7b High-growth, high-inflation countries (Gap 2 OECD)

the result in this respect is ambiguous due to the uncertainty about the correct output gap measure. To shed some light on the relative weight of German and French preferences in actual ECB interest rate setting, the results of some simple regression analysis are presented in Table 4.1. The following regression has been performed:

$$EUEONIA_t = \alpha + \beta TR\_GE_t + (1-\beta)TR\_FR_t + u_t \qquad (4.3)$$

where TR_GE and TR_FR are the preferred interest rates for Germany and France respectively as computed by a standard Taylor rule. In the regressions, the Taylor rule computed from the HP output gap and from the OECD output gap is used alternately. Also, for each case a regression where the intercept α is restricted to be zero has been run.

From the table it can be seen that regardless of the output gap measure used, the German weight exceeds the French weight. Using the HP output gap, Germany is the only country that matters. French preferences literally get a weight of 0. Using the OECD output gap the German weight is reduced and the French weight is increased when looking at the point estimates. However, even then, the hypothesis that β equals 1 (and the French weight is 0) cannot be rejected when an intercept is included in the regression. Overall, our results suggest that Germany is still the dominant party in the Euro Area. In that respect, apparently little has changed since the demise of the Exchange Rate Mechanism (ERM).

Table 4.1   Evidence of German dominance in ECB interest rate setting

	HP Output gap		OECD Output Gap	
α	0.09	-	0.45	-
	(0.19)		(0.16)	
β	1.05	1.01	0.80	0.59
	(0.19)	(0.13)	(0.12)	(0.10)
R^2 adj	0.55	0.57	0.64	0.52

Note: standard errors in parentheses.

4.4.3 The Fed versus the ECB

Finally, we turn to the comparison between the Fed and the ECB. Figures 4.8 and 4.9 show the observed output and inflation developments in the United States and the associated actual and preferred (Taylor rule) interest rates respectively. In the Taylor rule, the target is taken to be 2 rather than 1.5 per cent to better reflect US attitudes in this respect. From Figure 4.8, it can be seen that the OECD output gap indicates a somewhat deeper recession than the HP output gap from 2001 onwards, and a somewhat stronger boom before. This is comparable with Figure 4.1 for the Euro Area. It is clear that the output gap in the US fell earlier, faster and deeper than in Europe in the period 2000–2001. As a result, the US interest rate reacted before the European rate (see Begg et al., 2002 for a more detailed account of this episode). Apart from that, the behaviour of the federal funds rate compared to the Taylor rule rate for the United States since 2001 according to Figure 4.9 is surprisingly similar to that of the EUEONIA rate compared to the EMU Taylor rule rate as presented in Figure 4.2.

At first sight, therefore, the Fed and the ECB appear to have reduced nominal interest rates significantly below the levels suggested by a standard Taylor rule in a similar way. It is true that the gap between the rates is somewhat higher in the US than in Europe, about two percentage points versus one and a half percentage points respectively. That is, the Fed may indeed have been a little more aggressive than the ECB. Similarly, *ex post* real interest rates in the US have been around -0.5 per cent in the US since mid-2001, whereas in the Euro Area they have been marginally positive until late 2003.

However, the evidence presented in this chapter suggests that the ECB policy appears to have been primarily geared towards the interest rate preferences of Germany and to a lesser extent France. Then, the interpretation of our findings changes. Based on German (and French) preferences, the actual euro interest rate approximately matches the predictions of the Taylor rule. In that case, we need to conclude that indeed the Fed has been much more aggressive than the ECB in fighting the real economic downturn.

In summary, two alternative explanations are feasible which cannot be distinguished on the basis of the current data. The ECB may have been concerned with Euro Area-wide aggregates in setting policy. In that case, the actual interest rate has been set far too low (as compared to a benchmark Taylor rule). Policy then is comparable in content with that of the Fed.[7] Alternatively, the ECB may have focused on the economic situation in Germany (and France) and implicitly reduced the weight of the smaller peripheral countries. This would satisfactorily explain the actual interest rate

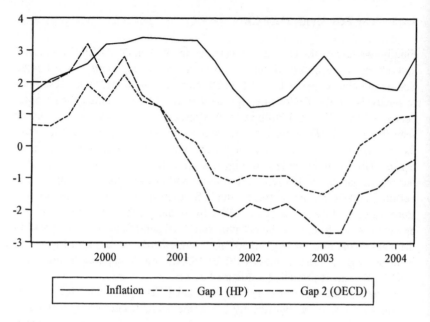

Figure 4.8   Inflation and output gaps in the US

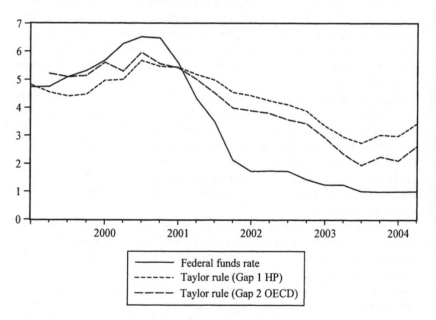

Figure 4.9   Taylor rule interest rates US

setting. It would simultaneously suggest that indeed the Fed has been much more willing to reduce interest rates to fight unemployment and low growth than has been the ECB.

4.5 CONCLUSIONS

This chapter has presented an analysis of ECB interest rate setting in the first five years of its existence. Contrary to popular belief and frequent ECB statements, the ECB has not acted as an obsessed inflation fighter. By any measure, output considerations do play a significant role in the ECB's policy rule. In this respect, the analysis presented here supports earlier work on this issue.

In terms of actual policy, if anything, the ECB has been on the loose side, especially since 2001, when taking economic development in the Euro Area as a whole as the starting point. A wide range of Taylor rule specifications is unable to explain the low interest rates of the past few years. Certainly, according to conventional wisdom, the Euro Area as a whole needed a higher rate. Actual interest rates have been consistent with German (and to a lesser extent French) preferences, however. This suggests that the ECB has put a dominant weight on German economic developments. Claims that small peripheral countries are too powerful within the EMU are clearly rejected by the data. If anything, their interests receive insufficient weight rather than too much weight. When we assume that the ECB does primarily look at the preferences of the core countries of the Euro Area in setting its interest rate, the actual interest rate in fact can be roughly replicated using a standard Taylor rule.

Finally, the answer to the question whether the Fed and the ECB behave more or less similarly in the face of economic developments strongly depends on the view one takes with regard to the ECB's focus. In case the ECB actually focuses on Euro Area-wide developments, its looseness is comparable to that of the Fed. In case ECB policy actually is geared towards Germany's preferences – or perhaps the average German–French preferences – the ECB has been much closer to a standard Taylor rule interest rate setting than the Fed. In that scenario, the Fed indeed has been much more aggressive in the lowering of its interest rates in the face of adverse economic shocks.

NOTES

1. See Taylor (1993) for the original idea and exposition of the Taylor rule. Orphanides (2001) criticizes the use of Taylor rule estimations based on final, possibly revised, data. Since policy-makers only have real-time data as a basis for their decisions, inferences based

on final data may be misleading. However, Adema (2004) concludes that using final data does not lead to more misleading policy descriptions compared with (quasi-) real-time data for the Euro Area over the period 1994–2000.

2. Alberola (2000) provides a more detailed examination of the causes of regional inflation differentials.

3. Growth rates of the M3 monetary aggregate in excess of its reference value support this conclusion as well.

4. The evidence in Figure 4.2 shows that this verdict depends on the assumed level of the equilibrium real interest rate and the inflation target. Alesina et al. (2001) indeed assume the real rate to equal 2.5 per cent. Figure 4.2 shows that the evidence presented here then supports their conclusion.

5. Note that individual and aggregate output gaps by construction are not linearly additive, so that the aggregate gap can occasionally fall outside of the individual gap boundaries.

6. Interest rate preferences until 2001 were almost perfectly aligned across these three countries.

7. The way their respective policies have been sold to the public of course has greatly differed. While the Fed (Greenspan) has had a tendency to move interest rates in small steps relatively frequently with high visibility and the pretence of being able to fine-tune the economy, the ECB has changed rates less often with larger steps and with persistent focus on its task of maintaining price stability.

REFERENCES

Adema, Y. (2004), 'A Taylor Rule for the Euro Area based on quasi-real time data', *DNB Staff Reports 2004*, (no. 114), Amsterdam: De Nederlandsche Bank.

Alberola, E. (2000), 'Interpreting inflation differentials in the Euro Area', *Economic Bulletin*, (April) Banco de Espana.

Alesina, A., O. Blanchard, J. Gali, F. Giavazzi and H. Uhlig (2001), *Defining a Macroeconomic Framework for the Euro Area Monitoring the ECB No. 3*, London: Center of Economic Policy Research.

Arnold, I.J.M. (2004), *Optimal Regional Biases in ECB Interest Rate Setting*, working paper, Nyenrode University, The Netherlands.

Arnold, I.J.M. and C.J.M. Kool (2004), 'The role of inflation differentials in regional adjustment: evidence from the United States', *Kredit und Kapital*, 37 (1), 62–85.

Begg, D., F. Canova, P. de Grauwe, P. Fatás and P. Lane (2002), *Surviving the slowdown Monitoring the ECB No. 4*, London: Center of Economic Policy Research.

Berger, H. and J. de Haan (2002), 'Are small countries too powerful within the ECB?', *Atlantic Economic Journal*, 30 (3), 1–20.

Berger, H., J. de Haan and R. Inklaar (2003), 'Restructuring the ECB', *CESifo Working Paper* (1084).

European Central Bank ECB (2003), 'The Outcome of the ECB's evaluation of its monetary policy strategy', *Monthly Bulletin*, (June).

Fourçans, A. and R. Vranceanu (2004), 'The ECB interest rate rule under the Duisenberg presidency', *European Journal of Political Economy*, 20, 579–595.

Gali, J., S. Gerlach, J. Rotemberg, H. Uhlig and M. Woodford (2004), *The Monetary Policy Strategy of the ECB Reconsidered Monitoring the ECB No. 5*, London: Center of Economic Policy Research.

Gerlach S. and G. Schnabel (2000), 'The Taylor Rule and Interest Rates in the EMU Area', *Economics Letters*, 67 (2), 165–171.

Hagen, J. von and M. Brückner (2001), 'Monetary policy in unknown territory: the European Central Bank in the early years', Zentrum für Europäische Integrationsforschung (ZEI) *Working Paper* (B18).

Hayo, B. and B. Hofmann (2003), 'Monetary policy reaction functions: ECB versus Bundesbank', Zentrum für Europäische Integrationsforschung (ZEI), *Working Paper* (B24).

Heinemann, F. and F.P. Hüfner (2002), 'Is the view from the Eurotower purely European? National divergence and ECB interest rate policy', ZEW *Discussion Paper* (02–69).

Orphanides, A. (2001), 'Monetary policy rules based on real-time data', *American Economic Review*, **91**, 964–998.

Sapir, A., P. Aghion, G. Bertola, M. Hellwig, J. Pisani-Ferry, D. Rosati, J. Vinals and H. Wallace (2004), *An Agenda for a Growing Europe: The Sapir Report*, Oxford: Oxford University Press.

Smant, D. (2002), 'Has the European Central Bank followed a Bundesbank policy? Evidence from the early years', *Kredit und Kapital*, **35** (3), 327–343.

Taylor, J.B. (1993), 'Discretion versus policy rules in practice', *Carnegie-Rochester Conference Series of Public Policy*, **39**, 195–214.

5. Interest Rates, Debt, Counter-Cyclical Policy and Monetary Sovereignty

Jan Kregel

5.1 INTRODUCTION

Since the decline of monetarist influence, mainstream monetary policy has returned to interest rate management, usually with an explicit or implicit inflation target pursued via some sort of Taylor rule.[1] The US Federal Reserve is the only central bank that has disavowed such a policy, favouring what Alan Greenspan, using anticipatory plagiarism, calls 'pre-emptive' policy. The ECB has both an implicit inflation target and a legal commitment to inflation management even though it does not formally follow inflation targeting. Irrespective of the particular policy, these approaches all take a very limited view of the impact of interest rates on the economy, focusing on the link between interest rates and the rate of change in goods prices. This chapter argues that changes in interest rates have a much broader effect on the economy and discusses the question whether the EU-15 can replace government expenditure-led growth with export-led growth. The chapter concludes that a pure export-led growth strategy is not impossible, but it is unsustainable.

5.2 INTEREST RATES AND FINANCIAL STABILITY

There is a long tradition of analysis that considers the impact of interest rates on other aspects of the economy. For example Samuelson (1945) proposed a paradoxical post-war argument that raising interest rates would increase the stability of the financial system. Recall that the US had financed the war at extremely low interest rates, with the long rate below 2 per cent and short rates of around 3/8ths per cent. Thus it was clear that interest rates had to rise, much as in the present period. Samuelson made the very simple point that the negative impact of rises in rates on the value of assets could be avoided if they are foreseen. But even if they are not, he argued that higher rates must be a good thing, since the higher returns on future investments will increase an individual's lifetime wealth and eventually offset any present loss. Further, Samuelson was arguing in the absence of perpetuities, so that long-term bonds, if they don't default, eventually will be redeemed at par, eliminating the capital loss, so that the higher interest receipts on the reinvestment of interest means that lifetime accumulation would be higher.

Samuelson applies this analysis to the impact of higher interest rates on the receipts and payments of a financial institution. He defines an 'average' time period of the sum of the discounted receipts and payments, using the time period in which the payments take place as the weights. He argues that a rise in the rate of interest would benefit any financial institution which had a weighted average of disbursements greater than its receipts, since the latter would be higher due to higher reinvestment rates. The net present value of the stream of payments would thus be higher and the institution more stable.

5.3   INTEREST RATES AND THE DEFINITION OF 'INCOME' IN A DYNAMIC CONTEXT

Samuelson's analysis echoed the prior discussion in Part 2 of Hicks's *Value and Capital* (1939) where he deals with dynamic theory, or better his prelude to dynamic theory in the form of temporary equilibrium in which there are transactions which occur across 'weeks'. One of the points he makes is that income is not an appropriate concept for 'dynamic' theory as he defines it. This is because it is extremely difficult to give a precise definition of income when some of the income is composed of fixed-income securities resulting from long-term borrowing and lending. If income is defined as what an individual can consume without impoverishing himself, there are a number of ways this idea can be expressed. It could be the expenditure that leaves the present value of his future net receipts constant, or it could be the amount that can be spent in perpetuity, either in nominal or in real terms. Hicks asks what happens to income when there is a change in the rate of interest or the rate of inflation.   A rise in the rate of interest increases the future income from current investment, so that future expenditure may rise if capital is being reinvested each 'week'. But, if it is invested for a fixed number of weeks, then possible expenditure can rise by less. Put in simple terms, if the individual's entire portfolio is reinvested each week then the impact of the higher interest is greater than if the capital is committed for a longer period. Thus, comparing two individuals with the same earned income and capital position, the one with the shorter commitment will benefit more from an increase in the rate of interest. As a result, 'income' depends on the portfolio composition of individuals.

To solve this problem Hicks defines what he calls the 'average period' to measure a standard stream of income. He takes the current actually expected income stream based on current portfolio composition, and calculates the net present value of that stream at the current rate of interest (on the standard assumption that the yield curve is flat). He then asks what notional constant income stream would produce the same present value, given the same current rate of interest. He calls this the 'standard stream'. Changes in the rate of interest will change the present value of both the 'actual' and the 'standard' income stream. Hicks then says that 'income' can be said to be higher if the increase in the rate of interest changes the present value of the actual stream by more than it changes the standard or average stream.

As is usual for the period in which he was writing, Hicks looks at the interest elasticity of the two definitions of income and argues in terms of the relative elasticities. If the actual income stream has an interest elasticity which is greater, then a fall in the rate of interest (Hicks in fact works with the discount factor, one over one plus the rate of interest) will increase actual income more than standard income and the individual will be better off as a result of the change in the interest rate.   He defines this elasticity as the 'average period' of the income stream and states that it represents 'the average length of time for which the various payments are deferred from the present, when the times of deferment are weighted by the discounted values of the payments' (p. 186). He can then compare the average periods of the standard and actual income to determine the impact of changes in the rate of interest on income. If the average period of actual income is greater, then a rise in interest rates will decrease 'income'.

5.4   INTEREST RATES, INFLATION AND CAPITAL VALUES

In fact, both Hicks and Samuelson are using analyses first worked out by Keynes and Fisher in their discussion over the validity of the Gibson Paradox. Keynes was interested in arguing that lower interest rates could increase future incomes while Fisher supported the position still dominant in most financial markets that higher interest rates simply offset higher inflation and thus were neutral in their impact on income (remember that Fisher excluded capital gains from his income definition). The end result was the specification of what we now call the 'duration' of an investment, measuring the amount of time that it takes for the fall in capital value due to a rise in interest rates to be offset by the higher reinvestment rates for coupon interest and the appreciation of capital value as the security approaches maturity.

All of these discussions are amplifications of the difficulties of the simultaneous analysis of stocks and flows on the behaviour of individuals and of the aggregate economy. The reason for this is that for confidently expected future payments, the present value of these payments is determined by discounting them at the current rate of interest. This is tantamount to assuming that interest rates will remain unchanged over the life of the investment. However, if interest rates change over time, the original present values will no longer be correct and adjustments will have to be made. For fixed interest obligations, an increase in interest rates represents a reduction in the present value and is accounted as a capital loss. However, future income from the investment will increase as a result of the higher interest that will be earned on the reinvestment of subsequent interest payments. Thus, at some future date the accumulated higher interest receipts will offset the capital loss and a break-even point, called the duration of the income stream, will leave the net position of the investor unchanged.

Discussion of the impact of interest rates on income has resurfaced more recently in analysis of the impact of the Japanese Central Bank's interest rate policy with some, such as Stephanie Bell and Warren Mosler (and a number of Japanese politicians) arguing that higher interest rates would support recovery by increasing personal incomes. This would seem to echo Hicks's analysis if Japanese households have portfolios with short average periods.

5.5   INTEREST RATES AND THE BURDEN OF THE DEBT AND INTERNATIONAL STABILITY

In addition to these analyses of the impact of higher interest rates on national income and financial stability that depend on the portfolio composition of households and banks, there are others that deal with the financial condition of the government. Domar (1944) sought to counter the argument that government borrowing to finance public investment expenditures required to keep the economy at full employment would lead to an ever-increasing government debt or an ever-increasing increase in tax rates. He notes that if government borrows a fixed share of national income this result could occur only if public expenditure has no impact on national income or if income only grows by a fixed amount. However, when national income grows at a constant rate, since the deficit will be a fixed share of the increased income, the accumulated deficit which is the debt will grow at the same rate. He thus argues that the ratio of debt to income will eventually reach a constant value, or alternatively the tax rate necessary to keep a given ratio of debt to income will be stable. As a result, he concludes that the burden of the debt is directly proportional to the government deficit as a share of national income and the rate of interest and inverse to the rate of growth, so that the problem of the debt burden is a problem of an expanding national income. From this analysis eventually emerged the golden rule that the rate of interest on debt cannot exceed the rate of real income growth.[2] Here, lower rates of interest are clearly positive for both the ratio of debt to national income and for the stability of income distribution and prices.

Another set of arguments deals with the stability of a country's international accounts. Again, Domar (1950) provided the analysis by noting that international investment is very similar in nature to domestic investment. The discussion turned around a problem similar to that raised in objection to debt finance. The question was whether a trade surplus in the US could provide the means to permanent full employment, substituting exports for government expenditure. Since this would require foreign lending, some argued that a permanent trade surplus would require ever-increasing foreign loans that would soon produce an ever-increasing reflow of interest payments that would eventually eliminate the surplus.

Domar, recognizing the similarity with his earlier argument on the sustainability of debt-financed public investment, provided the answer. As long as capital outflows increased at a rate that was equal to the rate of interest received from the outstanding loans to the rest of the world, the inflows created on the factor service account by the interest and profit payments would just be offset, so there would be no net impact on the trade balance. On the other hand, if interest rates were higher than the rate of increase in foreign lending, the policy would become self-defeating and the trade balance eventually become negative to offset the rising net capital service inflows. Eventually the continually rising factor service flows would turn the trade balance negative.

5.6   INTEREST RATES AND DEVELOPMENT STRATEGY

At the time, the discussion was not concerned with the impact of the US policy on the rest of the world – the idea was to find a way to full employment that did not require domestic borrowing. Foreign lending seemed clearly favourable to domestic borrowing on both political and economic grounds. Few recognized that this policy was precisely what would be required if the developed world were to provide the finance for the developing world – positive net resource flows from developed to developing countries – that has been the basis of development policy in the post-war period. Reversing Domar's analysis allows analysis of this problem, but now from the point of view of a developing country as the recipient of the foreign lending. This analysis has been presented elsewhere as follows (Kregel, 2004).

Since foreign capital is required to finance the excess of imports of necessary consumption goods and capital goods over exports, a development strategy based on external financing implies a trade deficit balanced by foreign capital inflows. But the obverse of the argument for a developed country says that the deficit on goods trade will soon generate debt service payment outflows that cause the current account deficit to increase unless the trade deficit is reduced to accommodate a fixed level of capital inflows. Alternatively, capital inflows would have to rise to accommodate the rising current account deficit caused by the increased payments on the capital factor services account for any given goods account deficit. Following Domar's argument for developed countries, it is only possible to maintain a development strategy based on net imports financed by foreign capital inflows if the interest rate on the foreign borrowing is equal to the rate of increase of foreign borrowing. If the interest rate is higher than the rate of increase of inflows, just as in the case of a developed country seeking to preserve full employment through a permanent trade surplus, the policy will eventually and automatically become self-reversing as the current account becomes dominated by interest and profit remittances that exceed capital inflows.

It is important to note that increased exports will do little to eliminate this problem. For example, in the case of a fixed level of capital inflows a rise in exports to offset the rising debt service will reduce the net trade deficit and thus the net resource inflow available to finance development. The same will be true if exports rise to meet the excess of capital remittances over increasing capital inflows, for this will also lead to a reduced deficit on the goods account.

With respect to the stability of the financial system, it is interesting to note that the Domar conditions for a sustained long-term development strategy based on external financing, and on sustained positive net resource transfers, are the precise equivalent of the conditions required for a successful Ponzi financing scheme. As long as the rate of increase in inflows from new investors in a pyramid or Ponzi scheme is equal or greater than the rate of interest paid to existing investors in the scheme, there is no difficulty in maintaining the scheme. However, no such scheme in history has ever been successful – they are bound to fail, eventually, by the increasing size of the net debt stock of the operator of the scheme. In actual practice it is highly likely that capital inflows will start to fall off as the current account deficit increases beyond some threshold level, currently considered to be around 4 per cent of GDP, and quickly create crisis conditions in which official support is necessary in the form of an official financing. The resolution of the crisis caused by the breakdown of the Ponzi financing scheme is the generation of a negative flow of real resources that is sufficient to generate the external surpluses necessary to resume debt servicing on its private debt and to repay the official lending.

Just as a permanent current account surplus financed by a permanent increase in foreign lending at interest rates higher than the rate of interest on the lending did not provide the US with a permanent full employment policy, so external financing cannot provide developing countries with a permanent development strategy unless the rate of increase of export earnings is equal to the rate of interest on the outstanding debt.

5.7   INTEREST RATES AND EXPORT-LED GROWTH WITH BALANCED BUDGETS

Now, the argument that needs to be made in the current European context is that the EU-15 looks very much like the US in the 1950s in its attempt to replace government expenditure-led growth with export-led growth. If we look at the golden rule condition, currently, policy interest rates of 2 per cent come out in real terms at roughly zero, which gives the possibility that any positive growth rate makes debt sustainable. On the other hand, in order to keep exports at a constant share of area GDP, the rate of capital outflow from Europe would have to be increasing at or above the rate that is being earned on foreign investments. We can simplify this by looking at the world as if it were composed of only the US and the EU, with the EU exporting goods and capital to the US. For the EU to keep a constant export demand the Domar condition would require that EU investments in the US increase at a rate that is at least equal to the rate of interest earned on those investments in the US. Given that US policy rates have been extremely low, rates on short government bonds have been in the range of 2 per cent, but the Fed funds rate is now 2 per cent so the medium rates are edging upwards. On the other hand, the majority of EU investment has been in direct investments, which have rates of return that are much higher. While it is difficult to calculate the average rate, it is probably more in the range of 15 per cent, a figure that is most likely higher than the rate of increase of EU capital outflows to the US. This means that not even the Domar–Ponzi conditions are currently being met, so that factor service receipts in the EU are greater than outflows, leading to an offset of the export balance.

On the other hand, the return on US assets to the EU can be reduced by currency adjustment and it is the exchange rate adjusted rate of return on foreign assets that is relevant for the EU external payments accounts. Dollar depreciation between 2002 and 2004 has been in the range of 10 to 15 per cent, which largely offsets the impact of the net factor service payments. However, it also goes to offset the competitiveness of EU exports, so that what is gained on the financing side is lost on the price side. Of course, the point of the Domar analysis is that even when the stability conditions are being met, it is an unstable Ponzi policy. But when it is not met and factor service inflows are greater than capital account outflows, the pressure that is exerted on the exchange rate that acts to restore the condition has a negative impact on exports due to loss of competitiveness. A pure export-led growth strategy is not impossible, but it is unsustainable. This is just as true of the EU policy based on external lending as it is of the development strategies based on external borrowing.

5.8 CONCLUDING REMARKS

So far, the impact of a government deficit on domestic demand within the Euro Area context has not been discussed. The creation of the EU has notionally eliminated the external accounts of each nation in the Union. The creation of the euro has eliminated the possibility for national governments to operate their own monetary policy or finance their deficits through the issue of currency. From the point of view of any individual EU government the euro is much like a foreign currency. This means that EU governments are much like independent countries in relation to their budget financing since the financing has to be covered by acquiring euros from private domestic residents, from other EU residents, or by borrowing in foreign currency from non-residents. If it is done by borrowing from private domestic residents the impact of the deficit on demand is neutralized. If it is borrowed from other EU residents there will still be an impact on government interest service so that if the primary budget position is to be kept at a constant share of GDP the government will have to increase borrowing at a rate equal to the rate of interest on its debt. A rising overall deficit to GDP ratio will then be required to keep the demand impact constant. If the overall deficit is to be kept constant, then the primary balance will have to be decreasing, and eventually it will disappear as interest costs take up the entire budget deficit.

NOTES

1. In this volume, Kool elaborates on the use of Taylor rules by the FED and the ECB.
2. See also the contribution of Arestis and Sawyer in this volume.

REFERENCES

Domar, E.D. (1944), 'The "burden of the debt" and the national income', *American Economic Review*, **34** (4), 798–827.

Domar, E.D. (1950), 'The effect of foreign investment on the balance of payments', *American Economic Review*, **40** (5), 805–826.

Hicks, J.R. (1939), *Value and Capital: An Inquiry into some Fundamental Principles of Economic Theory*, Oxford: Clarendon.

Kregel, J. (2004), 'External financing for development and international financial instability', *G24 Discussion Paper Series* No. 32, Geneva: UNCTAD.

Samuelson, P., (1945), 'The effect of interest rate increases on the banking system', *American Economic Review*, **35** (1), 16–27.

PART TWO

Labour Markets and Labour Market Policies

Labour Market and Labour Market Policies

6. Institutions and the Labour Market: Examining the Benefits

Tom van Veen

6.1 INTRODUCTION[1]

The relationship between labour market institutions and labour market performance has attracted a lot of attention from both researchers and policy-makers. The idea is that differences in labour market institutions can account for the difference in the development of unemployment between the US and Europe since the 1980s. It has been argued that various labour market institutions have made the European labour market more rigid (in terms of the capability for adjustment) than the US labour market and therefore labour market performance in the US has outperformed labour market performance in Europe. Using panel data techniques, the relationship between labour market institutions and labour market performance has been researched. In addition to labour market institutions, macroeconomic shocks have been modelled and interactions between the two have also been modelled and investigated (Blanchard and Wolfers, 1999).

Most analyses result in policy recommendations in which are suggested the breaking down of labour market institutions that, it is argued, hamper the proper functioning of the labour market. Although this may appear logical at first examination, labour market problems are in fact more complicated. Labour market institutions reflect more than just an arbitrary set of rules that can be changed in any direction. Most institutions are the result of long struggles between the government, employers' organizations and employees' organizations and reflect values such as consensus building, decent treatment of employees and so forth. These values may differ by country although, strangely, in the research on labour market institutions and labour market performance, relatively little attention is paid to the analysis of country-specific variables.[2] Alternatively, if the research shows that there is a positive relationship between employment protection and unemployment, then the policy recommendation has been to decrease employment protection in order to decrease unemployment. Because of the lack of country-specific variables, it is then frequently suggested that this conclusion will hold for all countries in the sample. Hence, the conclusions of much research suggest that a one-size-fits-all approach is appropriate for solving unemployment problems.

In our view, such a one-size-fits-all approach is, however, not as appropriate as its proponents assert. Although most OECD countries have similar labour market institutions, the structure of these institutions differs. For example, the average benefit replacement rate was 70 per cent in the Netherlands and 20 per cent in Italy over the period 1989–94. On the other hand, the Netherlands is ranked 9th (out of 20, with 1 being weak employment protection) and Italy is ranked 20th on the list of employment protection (Nickell, 1997, Table 4).

Institutions thus differ to a large extent in the various OECD countries which raises the question of why there is so much difference. Baker et al. (2002) suggest the beginnings of an answer by proposing that institutions reflect a long process of struggle by citizens and the labour movement (Baker et al., p. 56). Labour market institutions have not developed rapidly and in many countries it has taken several years or even decades to build the current systems of labour market relations. Why did it take so long? In our view, one part of the answer is that institutions incorporate the cultural values of a society. To quote Krueger (2000, p. 132): 'Every country's labour market operates with some rules and institutions. Despite popular opinion in Europe, even the US is a long way from unbridled cowboy capitalism. The labour compact in many European countries is extraordinarily generous to workers, *probably reflecting values and norms*' (Krueger, 2000, p. 132, emphasis added). And 'When in doubt,' writes Josef Joffe (*New York Times*, 12 October 1999), 'the English speakers will go for liberty and the market while the Europeans will opt for equality and paternalism'. For example the famous Dutch *polder* model is based on cooperation between employers, employees and the government. This cooperative attitude stems from the view that employers and employees are not natural opponents but natural partners with more or less similar interests. The same holds for the type of labour market relations observed in Scandinavian countries. On the other hand, Anglo-Saxon labour market relations seem to be based more on the 'opponents view'. Labour market institutions thus appear to incorporate cultural values of a society and therefore the relation between labour market institutions and labour market performance differs between countries. Alternatively, it is argued that there is a cost of labour market institutions in terms of relatively slow adjustment of wages and employment to shocks in an economy, but there are benefits as well, for example in terms of materializing the values of a society. This implies that a one-size-fits all policy prescription is not the best solution for solving the current labour market problems in Europe. It could be expected, furthermore, that the cost–benefit ratio differs per country even though, so far, the focus has only been on the costs of labour market institutions. This chapter focuses on the benefits of labour market institutions. We will argue that labour market institutions reflect cultural differences and that changing one or a few elements of the system is no guarantee of better functioning labour markets. We start in section 6.2 with a short overview of the research into labour market institutions and labour market performance to benchmark the discussion and to make clear how our analysis links up with existing research. Section 6.3 discusses various types of labour market models in Europe and in section 6.4 we discuss the benefits that labour market institutions generate. Section 6.5 relates labour market institutions to cultural values, while section 6.6 discusses the policy implications of our analyses. Concluding remarks are presented in section 6.7.

6.2   LABOUR MARKET INSTITUTIONS AND LABOUR MARKET PERFORMANCE : RESEARCH RESULTS

First it is appropriate to specify what exactly is investigated in this relationship. Concerning labour market performance, long-term and/or short-term unemployment is typically used to measure relative labour market performance. This is somewhat obvious given the levels of unemployment in Europe, although one could also use the employment-to-population ratio as a measure of labour market performance. Note, however, that these measures lead to different interpretations of the performance of labour markets (Baker et al., 2002). Given this, a relevant question then becomes whether employment or unemployment is to be explained and whether the choice matters. This will depend of course on the problem that is to be solved, but interestingly in the 2004 OECD Employment Outlook, the focus has changed from strategies to decrease unemployment to strategies to increase employment (OECD, 2004). Further to this, the Lisbon agenda also focuses on employment strategies rather than on strategies to reduce unemployment. Given these perspectives, the explanation of employment might be the better alternative for evaluating labour market performance.

Concerning labour market institutions, they can be considered as encompassing all sorts of agreements that govern labour market relations. To quote North: 'Institutions are the rules of the game in a society or, more formally, are the humanly devised constraints that shape human interaction. In consequence, they structure incentives in human exchange, whether political, social, or economic' (North, 1990, p. 3). Institutions that govern labour market relations include, for instance, laws concerning dismissal of employees. It must also be recognized that the labour market itself is also an institution. Based on the definition of North it is obvious why institutions are essential in an economy. They make transactions easier and in addition they 'reduce uncertainty by providing a structure to everyday life' (North, 1990, p. 3).

If the labour market were a free market where perfect competition prevailed, involuntary unemployment would not occur. Hence, in this view, market imperfections cause unemployment (Keynes, 1939). In turn, labour market institutions cause these imperfections because they are responsible for labour market rigidities (Blanchard and Wolfers, 1999). Hence the relevant institutional factors include the role of union power, wage bargaining systems, unemployment benefits, replacement rates and legal aspects such as employee protection laws. Although it is difficult to measure the extent of these institutional factors and their influence on unemployment, Nickell (1997) and Blanchard and Wolfers (1999) have investigated this point. Their research is based on the database on institutions as developed by Nickell (1997), and Table 6.1 shows the various labour market institutions and the way in which the impact of these institutions is measured for empirical purposes.

Table 6.1 summarizes the research results of Nickell (1997) and Blanchard and Wolfers (1999). These results can be considered representative for the research in this field (see also Baker et al., 2002).[3]

In the most basic research, labour market institutions have been related to the labour market performance indicator by way of multiple regression analysis techniques. In addition, to multiply the data points, panel techniques have been used. The results then indicate how the labour market performance indicator changes if the level of the institution changes and the coefficient is interpreted as a common effect over the countries that are taken into account. The results of Nickell (1997) are based on this type of research. Blanchard and Wolfers (1999) have extended this approach by including macro-economic shocks such as productivity shocks, demand shocks and real interest rate shocks. In addition they focus on the interaction between macro-economic shocks and labour market institutions. This enables them to examine whether the labour market effects of macroeconomic shocks are related to the level of the labour market institutions. So do the effects of a demand shock differ between countries with different levels of unemployment benefits? The evidence that Blanchard and Wolfers show confirms this conjecture and they conclude: 'we believe that the results so far suggest that an account of the evolution of unemployment based on the interaction of shocks and institutions can do a good job of fitting the evolution of European unemployment, both over time and across countries' (p. 32).

Table 6.1   *Variables that have been used in the research on the relation between labour markets institutions and labour market performance*

Indicator	Definition	Effects on[a]			
		TU[b]	LTU[c]	STU[d]	E[e]
Employment protection	Strength of legal framework governing hiring and firing (ranking)	No effect +	+	-	-
Unemployment benefits	Replacement rate	+ +	No effect	+	No effect
Duration of benefits	Months/years of duration	No effect +	+	+	-
Active labour market policies	Active labour market spending per unemployed person as a % of GDP per member of the labour force	- +	-	No effect	No effect
Taxes	Payroll tax rate / Total tax rate	+ +	No effect	+	-
Union power	Union density, proportion of union members as % of wage earners / Union coverage (index)	+ No effect	No effect/+[f]	No effect	No effect
Coordination in wage setting	Index of co-ordination between unions / Index of co-ordination between employers	- +	-	-	+

Notes:
[a] A '+' or a '-' sign denotes a significant (at 10%) positive or negative influence. Upper line is for Nickell, below is for Blanchard and Wolfers. The coefficients of Blanchard and Wolfers measures the interaction effects while Nickell measures the effects of the institutions as such.
[b] Total unemployment.
[c] Long-term unemployment.
[d] Short-term unemployment.
[e] Employment/Total population.
[f] No effect for union density, positive for union coverage.

Sources: Baker et al. (2002); Blanchard and Wolfers (1999); Nickell (1997).

Note that the relationship between unemployment and these institutions is not unambiguous at first sight: Ireland, Spain and Italy have above average unemployment rates but their institutions differ markedly. The results of the empirical research by Nickell (1997) and Blanchard and Wolfers (1999) help to explain this result: not all institutions have a significant influence on unemployment. Nickell (1997) concludes that generous unemployment benefits and high unionization without coordination in wage bargaining are the most significant institutional factors that positively contribute to total unemployment. Employment legislation was not a significant variable in this respect. In addition, Nickell concludes that it is not the level of unemployment benefits *per se*, but the incentives to take a job that are included in the benefit system as well as 'resources to raise the ability/willingness of the unemployed to take jobs' (p. 72) that determine the relationship between the benefit system and unemployment. Finally, Nickell concludes that high unionization in combination with coordination in wage bargaining has no significant negative effect on unemployment. The analyses by Calmfors and Driffill (1988) and Blanchard and Wolfers (1999) support Nickell's findings.

What does this relatively new research direction tell us about institutions and the labour market? There is an interrelationship between the level of unemployment and labour market institutions. Those institutional factors that cause rigidities on the labour market also cause persistence in the level of unemployment. In this context, adverse shocks might explain the level of unemployment and a decrease in aggregate demand might be such an adverse shock. This interaction between labour market institutions and the employment level might explain why unemployment in Europe has not developed in a similar way as in the US despite the fact that these countries have faced the same shocks.

What are the policy implications of this research? Do the results suggest that reform of labour market institutions is a necessary prerequisite to solving unemployment problems in Europe? A number of issues suggest that firm policy conclusions cannot yet be drawn from this research. First, the results are far too ambiguous. Second, many studies have used panel data analysis, one disadvantage of which is that country-specific effects are lost in the analysis. Hence, results are averaged out over the panel members. Third, these panel data analyses suggest one-size-fits-all solutions, while in fact it can readily be argued that labour market institutions do not necessarily need to be similar among countries. The remaining part of the chapter examines the latter points.

6.3 LABOUR MARKET MODELS IN EUROPE

One drawback of existing research is that it does not take differences between countries into account. As Boeri (2002) argues, within the OECD area it is possible to distinguish between various types of labour markets models: the Nordic, the Anglo-Saxon countries, continental European countries and the Mediterranean countries. Similarly Adnett (1996) identifies a number of distinctions in relation to European labour markets. Table 6.2 lists the features of these models and identifies the various countries that they are characteristic of. The allocation of the countries is based on Boeri (2002), Adnett (1996) and assessment by the present author.

It can be seen from Table 6.2 that there are important differences. There are two extremes: the Nordic social democratic model and the Anglo-Saxon liberal model. While in the latter model, labour market outcomes are largely determined by market forces with a relatively low level of institutional influence, the former model heavily relies on labour market institutions to govern labour market relations. The corporatist model is the main model in

Table 6.2   Four labour market models for the OECD countries

Name	Characteristics	Countries
Nordic or social democratic model	Centralization in wage bargaining; relatively high level of employment protection and high levels of social security benefits. Social security systems developed for redistribution purposes as well.	Denmark, Finland, Norway, Sweden.
Continental European or conservative corporatist model	Institutions aim to prevent class-conflicts. Social security developed for safety net purposes.	Austria, France, Germany, The Netherlands
Mediterranean model or traditional rudimentary model	Little labour market regulations and little social security benefits systems. Church and family ties substitute for labour market institutions.	Greece, Italy, Portugal, Spain
Anglo-Saxon model or liberalist-individualistic model	Decentralized wage bargaining systems; relatively low level of employment protection and social security benefits.	Canada, United Kingdom, United States, Australia, New Zealand

Source: after Boeri (2002), Adnett (1996) and author assessment.

Labour Markets and Labour Market Policies

Table 6.3   *Labour market institutions in selected countries (1989-1994)*

		Employment protection[a]	Labour standards[b]	Benefit replace-ment rate (%)[c]	Benefit duration (years)	Active labour market policies[d]	Tax rates[e]
Nordic or	Denmark	5	2	90	2.5	10.3	46.3
social	Finland	101	5	63	2	16.4	65.9
democratic	Norway	13	5	65	1.5	14.7	48.6
model	Sweden		7	80	1.2	59.3	70.7
Continental	Austria	16	5	50	2	8.3	53.7
European or	France	14	6	57	3	8.8	63.8
conservative	Germany	15	6	63	4	25.7	53.0
corporatist model	Netherlands	9	5	70	2	6.9	56.5
Anglo-Saxon model or	Canada	3	2	59	1	5.9	42.7
liberalist-individualistic	United Kingdom	7	0	38	4	6.4	40.8
model	United States	1	0	50	0.5	3.0	43.8
	Australia	4	3	36	4	3.2	28.7
	New Zealand	2	3	30	4	6.8	34.8

Notes:

a Employment protection measures measure the strength of the legal framework for hiring and firing. The ranking ranges from 1 to 20, with 20 being the most strictly regulated
b Labour standards refer to the strength of the legislation of the labour market. The index ranges from 0 to 10, with 10 having the most strict legislation.
c The replacement rate shows the share of income that is replaced by unemployment benefits.
d Active labour market policies is active labour market spending per unemployed person as a percentage of GDP per member of the labour force.
e Tax rates are total tax rate (payroll taxes plus income and consumption taxes) respectively.

Source: Nickell (1997).

between, and is based on cooperation between employers, employees and the government. The Mediterranean model is a separate model because it is based on more 'personal' types of relations, such as the family and the church. In the following we will focus on the Nordic model, the continental European model and the Anglo-Saxon model.[4] Finally, concerning the classification of the countries, there is not much disagreement in the literature.[5]

How do the labour market institutions differ between the models identified above? Table 6.3 shows in more detail the differences in labour market institutions. It shows that there are clear differences between the labour market institutions among European countries. The Nordic countries have a higher level of employment protection, more strict regulation, higher benefit replacement rates and a larger part of GDP per member of the labour force spent on active labour market programmes. In addition, tax rates have been higher in the Nordic countries. Note that the major difference is between the Nordic countries and the Anglo-Saxon countries. Remarkably, there is not much difference in the benefit duration between the various models, and if there is any difference, the duration in the Nordic countries is shorter than in the Anglo-Saxon countries. This is remarkable because according to Nickell, in explaining the importance of labour market institutions, benefit duration matters more that the replacement rate.[6]

It is also relevant to examine the labour market performance of the various models. Table 6.4 shows unemployment rates for various decades, under the different labour market regimes. Importantly, there seems to be no clear-cut relationship between the type of labour market model and unemployment, and hence between institutions and unemployment. In the period 1955–89 Nordic unemployment was below unemployment in the Anglo-Saxon countries and in particular the UK and the US, and unemployment rates in the Nordic countries have long been below the OECD average. On the other

Table 6.4   Unemployment: stylized facts for the Nordic, the Continental and the Anglo-Saxon model

	Nordic	*Continental*	*Anglo-Saxon*	*OECD*
Average 1955–69	2.0 (0.9)	1.6 (0.8)	2.8 (1.9)	3 (0.2)
Average 1970–79	2.7 (1.9)	2.8 (1.6)	4.3 (2.5)	4.5 (0.8)
Average 1980–89	4.7 (2.8)	7 (2.6)	7.6 (2.5)	7 (0.9)
Average 1990–2002	7.5 (3.8)	7 (2.9)	7.5 (1.9)	7.1 (0.6)

Notes:
The averages are not weighed. Figures between brackets are the dispersion as measured by the standard deviation.

Sources: The calculations are based on OECD, Main Economic Indicators; OECD Labour Force Statistics and Layard et al.(1991).

hand, Table 6.4 clearly shows increasing unemployment in the Nordic countries coupled with increasing dispersion. Unemployment in the continental European countries has also become far more dispersed over time. Both groups have far higher dispersion than countries with the Anglo-Saxon model; and far higher than the OECD average as a whole. Finally, it must be noted that total unemployment figures hide the structure of unemployment, and in particular, the differences between long-term and short-term unemployment. In this respect, continental Europe performs worst: the share of long-term unemployed in total unemployment is highest for continental Europe (Delsen and van Veen, 1992; Nickell, 1997; OECD, 2004).[7]

6.4   THE BENEFITS OF LABOUR MARKET INSTITUTIONS

It is pertinent to ask why labour markets differ so much. As discussed in a preceding section, one argument is that labour market institutions not only generate costs, but also benefits. Claimed benefits relating to the various types of labour market institutions are the avoidance of unrest in the labour market, reduction of poverty and more equal income redistribution. In the following section, these benefits are discussed in the context of the various types of labour market institutions.

6.4.1   Labour Market Disputes

One of the claimed benefits of the Nordic model and the continental European corporatist model is that coordinated wage bargaining structures and long consultation processes result in consensus policy in which labour disputes are scarce. Table 6.5 reveals whether the various labour market models have a different score on this variable.

Note that the figures for Denmark, Sweden and for France are biased for the period 1993–2002. This is because of an outlier in 1998 for Denmark and an outlier in 1995 for France and for Sweden.[8] Therefore the figure without this outlier is also shown between brackets. Table 6.5 clearly shows that the number of working days lost per 1000 employees has consistently been lowest in the continental European model. On average, the number of days lost is more similar in the Nordic and Anglo-Saxon models than in the continental Europe model.

What is the relevance of this data on the strike activity? In a recent paper, Blanchard and Philippon (2004) argue that when wages are determined by collective bargaining in a right-to-manage framework, the effects on unemployment of shocks depend on the speed of learning (that is, discovering the true state of the economy) by the unions. Blanchard and Philippon argue that this speed depends on the quality of labour relations, which they measure by strike intensity. They argue that this quality is negatively related to unemployment: a high quality of labour relations (low strike activity) suggests a high level of cooperation between unions and employers and lower unemployment after a shock. Consequently, in the case of adverse shocks (demand shocks, productivity shocks and interest rate shocks), unions will quickly realize what is happening and will quickly learn to adjust their perceptions and act accordingly. Blanchard and Philippon's empirical research confirms the hypothesis. It therefore seems worthwhile for future research to elaborate on the importance of the quality of labour relations for labour market performance and in particular on the relationship between labour market institutions and the quality of labour relations.

Table 6.5   Labour market models and labour disputes

	Countries	Working days lost per 1000 employees		
		1984–88	1989–93	1993–2002
Nordic or social	Denmark	250	30	177 (48)
democratic model	Finland	470	170	110
	Norway	150	60	85
	Sweden	100	70	29 (13)
Continental European	Austria	3	10	1
or conservative	France	60	30	98***(62)
corporatist model	Germany	50	20	5
	The Netherlands	10	20	19
Anglo-Saxon model or	Canada	450*	266**	187
liberalist-	United Kingdom	400	70	24
individualistic model	United States	70*	64**	45
	Australia	238*	177**	75
	New Zealand	567*	107**	25

Sources: 1984–93 is taken from Adnett (2002), Table 1.8, p. 29. The figures show averages over the listed period. 1993–2002 is taken from Monger (2004).
  *   The period 1985–88 from Sweeny and Davies (1996), Table 1.
  **   Data from Sweeny and Davies (1996), Table 1.
  *** Covers only the period 1993–97.
  Figures are checked with the Federation of European Employers (FedEE), website (http://www.fedee.com/strikes.html).

Table 6.6   Relative poverty and labour market models

		Relative child poverty (mid-1990s)[a]	Relative poverty rates for the total population 1987–2000[b]	Poverty scores 1990–2000[c]
Nordic or social democratic model	Denmark	5.1 (18)	8.6	8.51
	Finland	4.3 (21)	5.2	7.57
	Norway	3.9 (22)	6.4	5.22
	Sweden	2.6 (23)	6.5	3.18
Continental European or conservative corporatist model	Austria	-	8.5	4.90
	France	7.9 (15)	8	3.65
	Germany	10.7 (12)	6.8	-0.27
	The Netherlands	7.7 (16)	5.9	3.49
Anglo-Saxon model or liberalist-individualistic model	Canada	15.5 (7)	11.7	-3.41
	United Kingdom	19.8 (4)	12.1	-2.78
	United States	22.4 (2)	17.1	-11.41
	Australia	12.6 (8)	12.4	1.14
	New Zealand	-	-	-

Notes:
a   Measures the proportion of children below one half of the overall median of disposable income. The number between brackets shows the ranking out of 23 OECD countries.
b   Relative poverty is the percentage of individuals with a disposable income of less than 50% of the median disposable income.
c   Poverty scores are z-standardized scores and measure the number of standard deviations that a countries' poverty rate differs from the average poverty rate in 19 Western industry countries. A positive figure denotes lower poverty rates.

Sources:
a   see Jäntti and Bradbury (2003), Table 2.
b   The figures are averages over the period 1980–95 and taken from the website of the Luxemburg Income Studies under the LIS Key Figures.
c   These rates are taken from Merkel (2004), p. 41, Table 1.

6.4.2   Labour Market Institutions and Redistribution Goals

Agell (2003) has pointed out that labour market institutions might differ between countries because they incorporate cultural values about equity. Thus any discussion on the appropriateness of labour market institutions links up with notions of efficiency–equity in different countries. In particular, Agell discusses relative poverty and data on the distribution of income (see also Merkel, 2004 on this point). The data generated in the Luxemburg Income Studies provide information concerning poverty, standards of living

Table 6.7   Income distribution and labour market institutions

		P90/P10 Ratio (mid-1990s)[a]	Gini mid-1990s[b]	Gini 70-90 (% change)[c]	Gini (1999)[d]
Nordic or social democratic model	Denmark	3.15	26	22 (-4.9)	25
	Finland	2.68	23	23 (9.1)	29
	Norway	2.83	24	26 (9.4)	
	Sweden	2.61	22	23 (-1.0)	
Continental European or conservative corporatist model	Austria	3.73	28	-	28
	France	3.54	29	29 (-1.7)	30
	Germany	3.18	26	28 (6.4)	27
	The Netherlands	3.15	25	25 (11.8)	27
Anglo-Saxon model or liberalist-individualistic model	Canada	4.13	31	30 (2.3)	
	United Kingdom	4.57	34		32
		5.57	37	34 (10)	
	United States	4.33	31	31 (5.2)	
	Australia	-	-	-	
	New Zealand				

Notes:
a   P90/P10 ratio is defined as the ratio of the income of the person at the 90th percentile to the person at the 10th percentile.
b   The Gini coefficient measures income inequality and lies between 0-100. The lower the Gini coefficient, the more evenly income is distributed. The Gini coefficient in the mid 1990s is based on adjusted disposable income.
c   The Gini coefficient 70-90 is based on equivalent household disposable income per individual and measures income inequality over the period of the mid-1970s to the mid-1990s.
d   Data for 1999 on equivalent total net household income and income inequality is only measured for EU countries.

Sources:
a   The ratio is based on data from the Luxemburg Income Study. Taken from Smeeding (2002), Figure 1.
b   The Gini coefficient is calculated from data from the Luxemburg Income Study, see Smeeding (2002), Figure 1.
c   The data are collected by the OECD and are based on data from national authorities, see Oxley et al (1997), Table 1, p. 62.
d   The Gini 1999 is based on data from the Consortium of Household panels for European socio-economic Research (CHER), see Papatheodorou and Pavlopoulos (2003), Table 1, p. 12.

and income inequality in the various countries considered here (with the exception of New Zealand which does not contribute data to the LIS project).

Here we will relate these measures to the various labour market models. Table 6.6 lists the results for poverty measures.

The picture for the poverty figures is clear, consistent and striking. Relative poverty rates in the US are twice as high as in France or in Denmark. Furthermore, about 22 per cent of children live in relative poverty in the US. This is high in comparison with, for example, Sweden where only about 2.5 per cent of children live in relative poverty. The countries that have implemented the Nordic model or the social democratic model have the lowest poverty rates. On the other hand, high poverty rates are to be found in the countries that use the Anglo-Saxon model. Although there might be no clear causality between the level of poverty and the labour market model, it appears that the Nordic model has a far more attenuating effect on poverty than the Anglo-Saxon model.

Table 6.7 shows income distribution data in a number of OECD countries. Again the picture is clear: income inequality is consistently highest in the Anglo-Saxon countries and lowest in the Nordic countries under the social democratic model.

Despite the use of different data sources and different time periods, Table 6.7 shows a clear picture. If we measure disposable income, income equality is highest in the Nordic countries and lowest in the countries where the Anglo-Saxon model prevails. Despite the increasing trend in income inequality in a number of countries (see Smeeding, 2002 for evidence), the Gini coefficient in the mid-1990s and in 1999 does not differ to a large extent from the Gini coefficient over the period of the mid-1970s to mid-1990s.

Atkinson (2003) discusses these changes in the Gini coefficient and distinguishes between countries where the Gini follows the shape of a U without a serif and a U with a serif. In the case of the U without a serif, income inequality has continued to increase while in the other case the rise in income inequality has come to an end. Atkinson shows that based on pre-tax income from the Luxembourg Income Study, the Gini coefficient for a number of OECD countries first decreased, then stayed the same and thereafter increased between 1950 and 2000. Unfortunately, the data do not give a clear answer as to whether the U-shapes are with or without a serif, but it would be worthwhile to investigate this point further.

6.5   ARE DIFFERENCES IN LABOUR MARKET INSTITUTIONS RELATED TO DIFFERENCES IN CULTURAL VALUES IN COUNTRIES?

From the analyses so far, we can conclude that groups of countries differ in their labour market institutions. In addition, these labour market institutions have their own costs and benefits. The costs materialize in relatively slow adjustment to disequilibria in the labour market. The benefits show in the quality of the labour relations and in the degree of income equality which is much higher in social democratic countries than in liberal countries.

Most research that investigates labour market problems focuses on the cost side and stress the idea that labour market institutions in the Nordic and in the continental European countries cause high and persistent unemployment. Hence, it is argued, to solve unemployment, institutions must change in the direction of the Anglo-Saxon model. The evidence that we have shown in the previous sections, however, clearly shows that the benefits of the various systems differ as well. So the correct shape of labour market institutions depends on a country's trade-off between costs and benefits of labour market institutions (see also de Neubourg and Castonguay in this volume).

Is there any evidence that countries value equity? To examine this proposition, the work of Geert Hofstede is relevant. Hofstede (1991) has extensively researched cultural differences between countries using a number of variables to measure cultural differences. One such variable is the extent to which societies are more collectivist or based on a prevalence of the interest of the individual. Hofstede states:

Individualism pertains to societies in which the ties between individuals are loose: everyone is expected to look after himself or herself and his or her immediate family. Collectivism as its opposite pertains to societies in which people from birth onwards are integrated into strong, cohesive ingroups, which throughout people's lifetime continue to protect them in exchange for unquestioning loyalty. (p. 51)

Hofstede has tried to assess empirically the level of individualism in a society by interviewing a large number of IBM employees in a number of different countries. The results of this research together with a number of relevant differences between collectivist and individualist societies are listed in Table 6.8.

The differences between a collectivist and an individualist society are clear: in a collectivist society collective interests prevail over individual interests. Hence in some societies, equality of income distribution, reduction of poverty and a sufficient level of social security are valued at a higher level than in other societies. If this is correct, then labour market institutions can very well differ between the European countries. As the right-hand side of Table 6.8 shows, the countries under investigation have different individualistic indices. The Anglo-Saxon countries occupy the first places in the ranking, as an expression of their individualist character. The continental European countries follow, while the Nordic countries seem to be more collectivist.

Table 6.8　Individualism index values for selected countries[3].

Selected key differences between collectivist and individualist societies		Individualism index[a]		
Collectivist	Individualist			
Collectivist interests prevail over individual interests	Individual interests prevail over collectivist interests	Nordic or social democratic model	Denmark Finland Norway Sweden	74 (9) 63 (17) 69 (13) 71 (10/11)
Dominant role of the state in the economic system	Restrained role of the state in the economic system	Continental European or conservative corporatist model	Austria France Germany the Netherlands	55 (18) 71 (10/11) 67 (15) 80 (4/5)
Economy based on collective interests	Economy based on individual interests	Anglo-Saxon model or liberalist-individualistic model	Canada United Kingdom United States Australia New Zealand	80 (4/5) 89 (3) 91 (1) 90 (2) 79 (6)
Harmony and consensus in society are ultimate goals	Self-actualization by every individual is an ultimate goal			

Notes:

a　The index ranges from close to 0 for the most collectivist country to close to 100 for the most individualistic one. The score rank (out of 50 countries and three regions) is listed between brackets.

Source: Hofstede (1991). The differences between collectivist and individual interests are taken from Table 3.3 (p. 67) and the index from Table 3.1 (p. 53).

6.6　POLICY IMPLICATIONS

We started the analysis by surveying research results concerning the role of labour market institutions on labour market performance. One major, albeit carefully drawn, conclusion of research in this area has been that European labour markets should be shaped more like the US labour market because the performance of the US labour market has been much better in the past. The chapter has argued, however, that the results of the institutions on the labour market cannot be discussed via unemployment only. It has been argued and shown that the difference in labour market institutions not only influences (un)employment, but also influences poverty, income distribution and labour relations.

In this context, Freeman (1995) has made an interesting contribution to the discussion. He claims that labour market institutions must be seen as part of the larger economic system in which they operate. And economic systems differ in their tightness of the linkage between economic agents: 'in a welfare state economic agents are more tightly linked than in decentralized economies' (Freeman, 1995, p. 17). This links up with the propositions of Hofstede: the collective interest is more important in welfare states than in decentralized economies. The interesting point that Freeman makes is that such a system approach implies that one cannot change only one element without changing the system itself. A recent example can be found in Dutch labour relations. In 2003, given the slowdown of economic growth in the Netherlands, unions and employers' organizations agreed, in the true Dutch spirit, to moderate wage developments: the agreement was to have zero wage changes in the collective agreements. However, the Dutch government is determined to reform the operation of a number of institutional features of the labour market, such as entrance to disability schemes and so-called pre-pension systems. The unions (and for some issues employers' organizations as well) have expressed their disagreement with the reforms and this led to unrest on the Dutch labour market in autumn 2004. The reaction of the unions was that if the reforms were implemented, the agreement for wage moderation would be cancelled. Thus for the unions, wage moderation fits in a specific type of welfare state and one cannot simply change a few parts. Thus changes that aim at labour market reforms might result in higher wage claims. As a side-effect, some commentators and economists have argued that this labour market conflict showed the failure of central agreements and of the Dutch *polder* model. However, in the spirit of the Dutch culture, all parties were convinced that labour conflicts do not solve any problem and were convinced that unions, employers and the government had to solve these problems at the negotiation table. This has happened and the problems were smoothly and quickly solved. Basically this was an example of an argument that was put forward in van Veen (1997). There it was argued that if unions value a decent level of social security benefits, they will be willing to pay for this. However, if the level decreases, unions will want compensation. Consequently, the relationship between changes in social security contributions and changes in the wage rate need not be positive.[9] This is the disciplinary effect that can be offered by centralization of wage bargaining. Similar arguments can be put forward in cases where governments want to reduce employment protection. If employment protection is reduced, employees face a higher risk of being dismissed. Employees might therefore ask for a higher risk premium and consequently a higher wage.

What are the policy implications of the preceding discussion? First, as has been argued extensively (Freeman, 1995; Boeri, 2002; Blanchard, 2004) labour market reforms are costly. They do happen, but in various directions and mostly at the margin (see Boeri, 2002 on this issue and the database of the Fondazione Rodolfo Debenedetti)[10]. So the potential implications of these reforms should be carefully thought through. Second, in any reforms, the spirit of original design of the labour market institutions must be respected. To quote Boeri (2002): 'The various Social Europe(s) ... may simply reflect heterogeneous preferences of EU-citizens' (p. 8) and 'reforms ought to be respectful of the initial conditions and by imposing the same pattern of adjustment to the different European social policy models, there is a high risk of jeopardising altogether reform efforts' (p. 9). Third, and this follows from Freeman, labour market reforms can only be a success if they are taken at once (and not in small parts) with a clear view about the future of labour market relations and the welfare system. A number of separate changes in labour market institutions will probably lead to worse outcomes.

6.7   CONCLUSIONS

This chapter has discussed the costs and the benefits of labour market institutions. The costs of high levels of employment protection and high levels of social security benefits are rigidities on the labour market, mainly high and persistent unemployment (we have left the question whether this is an increase in the NAIRU out of the discussion). We have shown, however, that different types of labour market institutions coincide with differences in labour disputes, in poverty rates and in equality of income distribution. It was shown that different types of labour market institutions coincide with whether societies are more collectivist or individualist oriented and therefore differences in labour market institutions may be related to differences in preferences in a society. If this is correct, changing parts of labour market institutions is likely to provoke resistance because labour market institutions are part of the broader settings of the welfare state.

NOTES

1. This chapter was presented as a paper at the second CofFEE-Europe workshop in November 2004 in Maastricht. I thank the participants of this workshop for their valuable comments.
2. Note that we state 'the analysis of country-specific variables' because insofar as country dummies are incorporated in various studies, the change in the fit is discussed. Generally the fit improves but the discussion lacks further analysis.
3. See also the chapter by Baccaro and Rei in this volume which examines the relationship between unemployment and labour market institutions.
4. Note that the Mediterranean countries are rapidly evolving from their traditional models to more continental European types of labour market models. This process accelerated in particular in the late 1990s. However, for the period under consideration, the differences in institutions are still too large to allocate these countries to one of the models.
5. See Bruno and Sachs (1985) and Cörvers and van Veen (1995) for an overview of various classifications. Although for the majority of countries the classification is clear, for some countries the classification varies. Australia is one such example and mixes corporatist characteristics (centralized wage bargaining) with characteristics of the liberalist model (low benefit replacement rates). However, since Australia is hardly classified as a corporatist country we have allocated Australia in the liberalist model. On the other hand, the Dutch and, to some extent, the Austrian labour market seem to be on the edge of the social democratic and the corporatist model.
6. Quite some research is based on this Nickell database, although it covers the period 1989–94. One may wonder whether these figures are still relevant, in particular for Europe. Although the closer cooperation in the European Union has brought about some harmonization, there still is the difference between the Nordic model and the corporatist model. The result of the cooperation seems the disappearance of the Mediterranean model.
7. The most recent figures (for 2003) show that the incidence of long-term unemployment (12 months and over) as a percentage of total unemployment for the Anglo-Saxon countries is 13.7, for the Nordic countries it is 17.2 and for the corporatist countries the figure equals 34.5. Note that this is by no means an atypical picture; see *OECD Employment Outlook* (2004), Statistical Annex, Table G.
8. We define an outlier in the period 1993–2002 as a value that is more than three times as large as the maximum value of the series without the outlier. In addition, there can only be one outlier, thus if two values are very high, neither is considered an outlier.
9. The findings of Batyra and Sneessens in this volume suggest otherwise. One reason for this difference might be that public goods are not incorporated in the utility functions in Batyra and Sneessens.
10. The Fondazione Rodolfo DEBENEDETTI offers a documentation centre on social policy reforms and EU labour markets. The material collected at the Fondazione is available to researchers interested in these issues. See http://www.frdb.org.

REFERENCES

Adnett, N. (1996), *European Labour Markets, Analysis and Policy*, New York: Longman.
Agell, J. (2003), 'Efficiency and Equality in the labour market', *CESifo Forum*, **4** (2), 33–42.
Atkinson, A. (2003), 'Income inequality in OECD countries: data and explanations', *CESifo Economic Studies*, **49** (4), 479–513.
Baker, D., A. Glyn, D. Howell and J. Schmitt (2002), 'Labour market institutions and unemployment: A critical analysis of the cross-country evidence', *Working paper*

P 2002–17, Center for Economic Policy Analysis, New School University, New York.

Blanchard, O. (2004), The economic future of europe, *NBER Working Paper* No. 10310.

Blanchard, O. and J. Wolfers (1999), 'The role of shocks and institutions in the rise of European unemployment: the aggregate evidence', *NBER Working Paper* No. 7282.

Blanchard, O. and T. Philippon (2004), 'The quality of labor relations and unemployment', *NBER Working Paper* No. 10590.

Boeri, T., (2002), *Social Policy: One for All?*, unpublished paper prepared for a CEPII conference on Policy Competition and the Welfare State, The Hague, 29–30 November.

Bruno, M. and J. Sachs (1985), *The Economics of Worldwide Stagflation*, Cambridge, MA: Harvard University Press.

Calmfors, L. and J. Driffill (1988), 'Centralization of wage bargaining', *Economic Policy*, 3, 13–61.

Cörvers, F. and T. van Veen (1995), On the measurement of corporatism, *Labour*, 9 (3), 423–442.

Delsen, L. and T. van Veen (1992), 'The Swedish Model: relevant for other European countries?', *British Journal of Industrial Relations*, 30 (1), 83–105.

Freeman, R. (1995), 'The large welfare state as a system', *American Economic Review*, 85, (2) (May), 16–21.

Hofstede, G. (1991), *Cultures and Organizations*, London: McGraw Hill.

Jäntti, M. and B. Bradbury (2003), 'Child poverty across industrialized countries', *Journal of Population and Social Security/The Japanese Journal of Population*, 1 (supplement), 385–410.

Keynes, J.M. (1939), *The General Theory of Employment, Interest and Money*, London: Macmillan.

Krueger, A. (2000), 'From Bismarck to Maastricht: the march to European Union and the labor compact', *Labour Economics*, 7, 117–134.

Layard, R., S. Nickell and R. Jackman (1991), *Unemployment, Macroeconomic Performance and the Labour Market*, Oxford: Oxford University Press.

Merkel, W. (2004), 'Welke landen zijn sociaal rechtvaardig?' (What countries are socially just?), *Socialisme en Democratie*, 10 (11), 34–44.

Monger, J. (2004), 'International Comparisons of labour disputes in 2002', *Labour Market Trends* (published by the UK Governmental Statistical Service), (April), 145–152.

Nickell, S. (1997), 'Unemployment and labor market rigidities', *Journal of Economic Perspectives*, 11 (3), 55–74.

North, D. (1990), *Institutions, Institutional Change and Economic Performance*, Cambridge, UK: Cambridge University Press.

OECD, *Main Economic Indicators*, various volumes, Paris: OECD.

OECD, *Labour Force Statistics*, various volumes, Paris: OECD.

OECD (2004), *OECD Employment Outlook*, Paris: OECD.

Oxley, H., J-M Burniaux, T. Dang and M. d'Ercole, (1997), 'Income distribution and poverty in 13 OECD Countries', *OECD Economic Studies, 29*, 55–94.

Papatheodorou, C. and D. Pavlopoulos (2003), 'Accounting for inequality in the EU: income disparities between and within member states and overall income inequality', *Document 9*, CHER, Consortium of Household Panels for European Socio-Economic Research.

Smeeding, T. (2002), 'Globalization, inequality and the rich countries of the G–20: evidence from the Luxemburg Income Study', *Luxemburg Income Study Working Paper 320.*

Sweeny, K. and J. Davies (1996), 'International comparisons of labour disputes in 1994', *Labour Market Trends* (published by the UK Governmental Statistical Service), **April**, 153–159.

Veen, T. van (1997), *Studies in Wage Bargaining*, PhD thesis, University of Maastricht.

7. Institutions and Unemployment in OECD Countries: A Panel Data Analysis

Lucio Baccaro and Diego Rei[1]

7.1 INTRODUCTION

In this chapter, we estimate the impact of a country's institutional setting on its rate of unemployment by means of panel regressions covering 18 OECD countries in the period 1960–98. We are by no means the first to undertake a similar task (See Elmeskov et al., 1998; Nickell et al., 2001; Nunziata, 2005, 2002; IMF, 2003), but our results, like those of Baker et al. (2002, 2004), are at odds with those of a large portion of the literature and suggest that the prevailing deregulatory view, according to which unemployment is caused by institutional rigidities and should be addressed through systematic deregulation (see Siebert, 1997), is less robust than it is often made out to be.

Our specification follows closely on the one in IMF (2003) – the paper with perhaps the strongest evidence supporting the deregulatory view. Both our data and models present, however, what we consider plausible changes, which are illustrated below. We focus our analysis on data averaged over five years. There are several features of the estimated models that suggest this as a suitable path to take, in particular the sluggishness of most institutional measures and the statistical properties of models.

Our preferred model is a reduced model in first differences, with only one macroeconomic control (the interest rate), the six institutional variables for which reasonably complete measurement series are available (employment protection, unionization rate, benefit replacement rate, tax wedge, central bank independence and wage coordination), and no interactions. Such a simple and parsimonious model gives labour market institutions more than a fair opportunity to explain changes in unemployment rates. The results, however, show that most institutional variables are insignificant or negatively signed, except the unionization rate, whose positive impact on unemployment seems robustly significantly different from zero, and which has a modest effect according to our point estimates. Overall, we find little support for the deregulatory view. Restrictive macroeconomic policies and institutions (like central bank independence) supporting them appear to play a more important role in explaining variation in unemployment.

7.2 DATA AND MODELS

We conduct our analysis on the dataset provided to us by Baker et al. (2005).[2] This contains a series of macroeconomic and institutional measures for 18 OECD countries between 1960 and 1998.[3] This database is, in turn, very similar to the one used by IMF (2003), except for small changes in the data (in particular concerning the years 1996–1998, and/or specific countries).[4] Both these datasets are extensions of the original Nickell and Nunziata (2001) database of labour market institutions.[5] Information on the various measures can be found in the Annex.

Our basic model is the following:

$$u_{i,t} = \beta_0 + \sum_j \gamma_j x_{j,it} + \sum_n \eta_n z_{n,it} + \sum_p \sigma_p h_{p,it} + \delta_i + \alpha_t + \varepsilon_{i,t} \qquad (7.1)$$

where u_{it} is the unemployment rate in country i at time t, the xs are j institutional variables, the zs are n macroeconomic controls, the hs are p interactions, the δ_is are (N-1) country-specific fixed effects, the α_ts are (T-1) year dummies, and $\varepsilon_{i,t}$ is the stochastic residual.

We also estimate a model with random effects, where the intercept β_{0i} is assumed (somehow incorrectly, as we argue below) to be a random variable $\beta_{0i} = \beta_0 + \upsilon_i$, with a mean value β_0 and a country-specific term υ_i, where υ_i is a random variable with zero mean and σ_υ^2 variance. The random effects model's residual is thus $\omega_{i,t} = \varepsilon_{i,t} + \upsilon_i$.

For reasons explained in section 7.3 below, the fixed effects model is also estimated in first differences, where first differencing wipes out the country fixed effects. The vector of institutional variables is the following:

$$\sum_j \gamma_j x_{j,it} = \gamma_1 EP_{i,t} + \gamma_2 UD_{i,t} + \gamma_3 BRR_{i,t} + \gamma_4 TW_{i,t} + \gamma_5 CBI_{i,t} + \gamma_6 BC_{i,t} \qquad (7.2)$$

with *EP* the employment protection index, *BRR* the benefit replacement rate, *UD* union density, *TW* the tax wedge, *CBI* a central bank independence index and *BC* an index of wage bargaining coordination.[6] The vector of macroeconomic variables includes:

$$\sum_n \eta_n z_{n,it} = \eta_1 RIR_{i,t} + \eta_2 PROD_{i,t-1} + \eta_3 DCPI_{i,t} + \eta_4 TOTS_{i,t} \qquad (7.3)$$

where *RIR* is the real interest rate, *PROD* is the (lagged) change in labour productivity,[7] *DCPI* is the change in the consumer price index, and *TOTS* is the terms of trade shock measure. Finally, the vector of interactions includes:

$$\sum_{p}\sigma_{p}h_{p,it} = \sigma_1 EP_{i,t} * BC_{i,t} + \sigma_2 UD_{i,t} * BC_{i,t} + \sigma_3 BRR_{i,t} * BC_{i,t} +$$
$$\sigma_4 TW_{i,t} * BC_{i,t} + \sigma_5 CBI_{i,t} * BC_{i,t}$$

(7.4)

and $\sigma_6 BD * BC_{i,t}$ or σ_7 *Benefit Generosity*$_{i,t} * BC_{i,t}$ where indicated. Every interactive term is expressed as deviation from the sample average ψ. This allows us to interpret the coefficient of each institutional variable as the coefficient of the hypothetical country characterized by the average level of a given institutional measure (see Nunziata, 2002, p. 8).

Our specification follows closely on IMF (2003), which, in turn, draws heavily on Nickell et al. (2001) (see IMF, 2003, p. 146). The IMF stands out among others (Elmeskov et al., 1998; Nickell et al., 2001; Nunziata, 2005, 2002) because it includes both indicators of labour market institutions as well as a central bank independence index, and hence aims at investigating the effects of both labour market and monetary institutions. Compared with other models, our specifications present a number of changes.

First, we choose to estimate our models with data averaged over five years rather than with annual data (see Daveri and Tabellini, 2000; Nickell, 1997; Baker et al., 2002; Belot and van Ours, 2001, for a similar choice). The advantages of five-year averages are multiple. Five-year aggregates are certainly more appropriate than annual data for an indicator like the employment protection index, which is based on interpolation from a few observations (see Baker et al., 2004, p. 6). In general terms, since the institutional variables vary little over time, an analysis with averaged data should produce better results. Indeed, in the presence of fixed or sluggish variables like most of our institutional variables, the researcher should be careful not to confuse observations with cases. As noted by Wilson and Butler (2004), in a fixed effects context, what really matters is not the number of data points but whether there is dynamic variation in the data or not: 'When significant variation exists across time – in both the dependent and independent variables – each year constitutes a legitimate observation. However, if little variation occurs across time, then ... treating each year of data as a unique observation' is not justified (Wilson and Butler, 2004, p. 18; see also Kittel, 1999, p. 245 for similar views). The obvious drawback of this approach is a lower number of observations over time for each country, which also implies lower statistical power. Also, if some of the effects are purely short term, we may not be able to pick them up by averaging the data. In a related paper (Baccaro and Rei, 2005), we also estimate a number of models using annual data, with results that are largely similar to those obtained with five-year averages.

Second, we use a different, and arguably better, measure of wage bargaining coordination, elaborated by Lane Kenworthy. This measure 'does not attempt to capture the degree of actual wage coordination in each country', which tends to give rise to impressionistic and possibly endogenous assessments (in the sense that the assessment of the degree of wage coordination in a particular country may be influenced by how well or badly the country in question performs), but rather is based on 'a set of expectations about which institutional features of wage setting arrangements *are likely to generate* more or less coordination' (Kenworthy, 2003, p. 5).[8] Two features of the bargaining system are likely to generate coordination: the degree of centralization of bargaining and the degree of employer coordination. The countries are scored year by year from one to five based on a range of secondary sources, covering the 1960–98 period. However, because Spain and Portugal had an atypical bargaining process, if at all, for a large part of this period, these two countries are not coded and are therefore excluded from our sample.

Third, our set of interactions is different from the IMF (2003) and others (Belot and van Ours, 2000, 2001; Nickell et al., 2001) because, unlike other specifications, which contain a rather eclectic set of interactions, we focus on the interaction between the degree of wage coordination in the economy and the various institutional variables. This modelling choice is in line with a basic tenet of the 'variety of capitalism' literature (see Hall and Soskice, 2001), that institutions function differently in different types of economic systems, and that the key factor distinguishing between different types of capitalism is the degree of coordination in economic transactions – of which wage bargaining coordination is of paramount importance.

If the deregulatory view of unemployment were true, the coefficients of our institutional variables, with the exception of the coordination variable, would be positively signed and statistically different from zero. This is because, in an imperfect market scenario, in which wages are determined as the outcome of bargaining between firms and workers, the labour market institutions either directly increase the bargaining power of unions (for example the unionization rate or employment protection), or reduce the willingness and capacity of the unemployed to bid down the wages of the employed (unemployment benefit replacement and duration), and, in so doing, indirectly increase the bargaining power of workers (see Nickell et al. 2001). The tax wedge variable should also be positively associated with unemployment because, if the tax wedge is not entirely paid for by workers, it should negatively affect labour demand and, through this channel, unemployment. Since our tax wedge variable includes employer-paid taxes (for a full description see the Annex), this relationship should hold. We expect the sign of the interaction terms between institutions and the level of bargaining coordination to be negative because a more coordinated bargaining system should help economic actors internalize the systemic consequences of their action.

7.3 RESULTS

In columns 1 and 2 in Table 7.1, we estimate our full fixed effects model, with all macroeconomic predictors and interaction terms. Our models present serial correlation of the residuals and panel heteroscedasticity, as is usual with this data structure. We deal with these problems by using two alternative methods: one is OLS with the Newey-West robust standard errors, the other is Feasible (panel) weighted least squares (FWLS) modelling for (unit level) heteroscedasticity and serial correlation of the residuals with corrections for heteroscedasticity and serial correlation (with a common rho-Prais Winsten transformation).[9] In both cases, we seek to eliminate the likely cross-sectional correlation of the errors via the insertion of time dummies.[10] Among the macroeconomic variables, only the real interest rate is significant and signed according to prediction (that is, positive). The other macroeconomic predictors are surprisingly positive rather than negative. All are, however, insignificant. This insignificance is not unexpected with five-year averages. In fact, variables like changes in consumer price indexes, in terms of trade, and in productivity are likely only to affect short-term adjustment processes of the unemployment rate to its long-term equilibrium and it is not unusual that they are not significantly different from zero when longer time frames are considered. According to mainstream macroeconomic theory, for example, if there is a trade-off between unemployment and inflation, this is, at best, limited to the short run and should disappear in the medium to long term.

Among the institutional variables, employment protection is positive and insignificant. This variable is measured through a time-invariant index for Australia, Canada, Japan, New Zealand, Switzerland and the US. These are for the most part countries with low protection and higher than average unemployment (except Japan, for which the opposite holds). The fact that they do not participate in the determination of the employment protection coefficient in models with country fixed effects may explain the positive sign. Union density is (as in models with yearly data, see Baccaro and Rei, 2005), both positive and significant. Benefit replacement rate is, contrary to predictions, negative but insignificant (except at the 10 per cent level in

Table 7.1   Five-year data. Full models in levels. Static (intercept, country and time dummies omitted).

Dependent variable	OLS robust with country and time dummies	FWLS corrected for hetero-skedasticity and serial correlation (common Rho)	OLS Robust	FWLS corrected for heteroskedasticity and autocorrelation	OLS Robust	FWLS corrected for hetero-skedasticity and serial correlation (common Rho)
Real interest rate	0.315 (3.40)**	0.282 (3.71)**	0.262 (3.19)**	0.216 (2.98)**	0.251 (3.41)**	0.24 (4.00)**
Change in inflation	0.065 (0.37)	0.028 (0.2)	-0.013 (0.08)	-0.071 (0.52)	-	-
Terms of trade shocks	0.092 (0.27)	0.038 (0.16)	0.063 (0.18)	-0.158 (0.61)	-	-
Lag. product. change	0.202 (1.17)	0.136 (1.19)	0.194 (1.14)	0.111 (0.97)	-	-
EP	1.259 (1.04)	0.652 (0.72)	0.925 (0.76)	0.51 (0.61)	1.493 (1.5)	0.977 (1.46)
UD	0.09 (1.76)•	0.067 (2.20)*	0.083 (2.01)*	0.077 (2.75)**	0.103 (3.28)**	0.101 (4.11)**
BRR	-0.011 (0.62)	-0.013 (0.88)	-0.019 (1.11)	-0.02 (1.47)	-0.019 (1.19)	-0.021 (1.64)•
TW	-0.092 (1.45)	-0.103 (2.23)*	-0.064 (1.01)	-0.069 (1.45)	-0.044 (0.89)	-0.051 (1.3)

135

Continued

CBI	3.80 (1.73)•	4.69 (2.92)**	4.05 (2.27)*	4.14 (2.81)**	4.28 (2.45)*	4.10 (2.83)**
BC	0.195 (0.78)	0.085 (0.41)	0.12 (0.53)	-0.109 (0.63)	-0.001 (0.01)	-0.162 (1.07)
BC*UD	0.001 (0.03)	-0.008 (0.63)	-	-	-	-
BC*TW	0.005 (0.19)	-0.008 (0.43)	-	-	-	-
BC*EP	0.451 (0.82)	0.658 (1.74)•	-	-	-	-
BC*BRR	-0.016 (1.37)	-0.014 (1.49)	-	-	-	-
BC*CBI	-0.843 (0.8)	-0.667 (0.71)	-	-	-	-
Observations	121	121	121	121	134	134
Wald test country dummies[a]	$F_{(17, 81)} = 9.50$	$\chi_{(17)} = 151.29$	$F_{(17, 86)} = 9.14$	$\chi_{(17)} = 148.1$	$F_{(17, 102)} = 10.13$	$\chi_{(17)} = 135.51$
Wald test on time dummies[a]	$F_{(7, 81)} = 6.32$	$\chi_{(7)} = 85.44$	$F_{(7, 86)} = 6.97$	$\chi_{(7)} = 80.14$	$F_{(7, 102)} = 6.81$	$\chi_{(7)} = 81.14$
Wald test on interaction coefficients[b]	$F_{(5, 81)} = 0.72$ [0.61]	$\chi_{(1)} = 7.25$ [0.20]	$(3, 81) = 0.50$ [0.67]	$\chi_{(3)} = 1.55$ [0.67]	-	-

Continued

Dependent variable	OLS robust with country and time dummies	FWLS corrected for hetero-skedasticity and serial correlation (common Rho)	OLS Robust	FWLS corrected for heteroskedasticity and autocorrelation (common Rho)	OLS Robust	FWLS corrected for hetero-skedasticity and serial correlation (common Rho)
Estimated Rho	0.3	0.26	0.32	0.25	0.32	0.44
LM autocor-relation test[b]	-	$\chi_{(1)} = 10.95$ [0.009]	$\chi_{(1)} = 7.39$ [0.006]	$\chi_{(1)} = 12$ [0.0005]	$\chi_{(1)} = 13.86$ [0.0001]	$\chi_{(1)} = 18.47$ [0.0001]
Wald hetero-skedasticity test[b]		$\chi_{(18)} = 26.2$ [0.09]	$\chi_{(18)} = 122.6$ [0.79]	$\chi_{(18)} = 27.1$ [0.07]	$\chi_{(18)} = 212$ [0.00]	$\chi_{(18)} = 25.3$ [0.11]
Adj R Square	0.79	-	0.79	-	0.81	-

Notes:
a. All p-values for the tests in these rows are approximately equal to zero.
b. p-values reported in indented parentheses.
All values in normal parentheses give absolute values of z statistics.
• significant at 10%, * significant at 5%, ** significant at 1%.

column 6 in Table 7.1). The tax wedge is also negative, again contrary to predictions, but it is only significant in one of the six models, that is, at the 5 per cent level in column 2   in Table 7.1. This somewhat surprising result could be an indication that taxation is entirely paid for by actual wages, that is, it is the workers who shoulder the burden of the taxes through a reduction of the market clearing wage, and, for this reason, unemployment does not increase. Because it reduces take-home pay, taxation may even increase labour supply for given wage levels, which may explain the negative sign. Central bank independence is positive and significant in all models shown in Table 7.1.

Wage coordination is positive but insignificant in columns 1 and 2, and mostly negative and insignificant in the others. It bears noting, however, that wage coordination is negative and highly significant when country dummies are not controlled for (see Baccaro and Rei, 2005, Table 8). The central bank independence variable behaves in the opposite way. This coefficient is much greater, and significant, when country fixed effects are controlled for (see Baccaro and Rei, 2005, Table 8). None of the interactions terms are significantly different from zero, with the exception of the interaction between coordination and employment protection, which is positive and significant at the 10 per cent level with FWLS (but whose sign appears to jump depending on specification: see Table 8 in Baccaro and Rei, 2005). Comparing these results with those of models with yearly data, presented in Baccaro and Rei (2005, Tables 3 to 6), which show a greater number of significant interaction coefficients (negatively signed), one is led to conclude that the degree of wage coordination moderates the effects of institutions only in the short term, that is, with yearly data, and not when data are averaged over longer time frames. Overall, FWLS seems to provide more optimistic estimates of the standard errors, and hence lead to higher significance levels than OLS. This can be interpreted either as a confirmation of the Beck and Katz (1995, 1996) critique of FWLS, or as a consequence of FWLS's greater efficiency.[11] We also estimated a dynamic model with fixed effects, that is, with a lagged dependent variable among the regressors (see Baccaro and Rei, 2005, Table 9). With T = 8, this is more than likely to suffer from Nickell–Kiviet bias (Nickell, 1981; Kiviet, 1995). The coefficient of the lagged dependent variable is very high, 0.94, notwithstanding the downward bias, and highly significant. We interpret this result as a warning that we may have a problem of non-stationarity and as a reminder that the model in levels is possibly underspecified, as shown by the high significance coefficient of the lagged dependent variable.

The remaining columns 5 and 6 in Table 7.1 exclude, for the sake of greater efficiency, first the interaction variables and then the macroeconomic variables that do not appear significant according to a joint significance test, that is, all except the real interest rate.

Few variables appear robust throughout all specifications in Table 7.1: the real interest rate, union density and the central bank independence index. The magnitude of all coefficients is quite similar across models, even though the effects of some institutional variables like employment protection, union density and central bank independence seem to become greater in the more parsimonious models with only the real interest rate. It is interesting to note that even with parsimonious models – that is with only one macroeconomic control, the institutional variables, and no interactions – no systematic support is found in the data for the deregulatory view. Benefit replacement and tax wedge are negative. Employment protection is positive but insignificant. Only union density is in line with theoretical predictions. Its magnitude is around 0.1. The coefficients of the real interest rate and central bank independence variables, both positive and highly significant, seem to point in the direction of restrictive macroeconomic policies as determinants of unemployment.

Table 7.2 moves from levels to first differences. The reasons behind this choice are the following: first, the results of integration tests show that five-year data are non-stationary and the models we are estimating do not appear to be co-integrated (see Appendix 2 to Baccaro and Rei, 2005).[12] The data in five-year averages are integrated of order one, which justifies first-differencing. Second, differencing the data eliminates serial correlation of the error (we reject the null at the 5 per cent level in all cases). A t-test on the lagged dependent variable (not reported here) shows that this should not be included in a model in first differences, unlike a model in levels. Therefore, a model in first differences seems better behaved statistically than a static model in levels. We present two sets of estimates: one is FWLS with correction for heteroscedasticity, the other is OLS with the White-robust standard errors. The coefficients have to be interpreted as the effect of average changes in independent variables over five-year spans on changes in unemployment in the same period, controlling for other determinants. This interpretation does not seem at odds with the basic policy question underlying this and other studies; namely understanding how unemployment would change over five years if institutions were to change over the same period.

One would expect similar coefficient estimates from models in differences and in levels. This is indeed the case with most variables, but there are a few exceptions, as revealed by comparing the results reported in Tables 7.1 and 7.2. Not surprisingly, variables based on indicators, which change little over time, and especially employment protection and wage coordination, are the ones for which coefficient estimates vary the most. For example, employment

Table 7.2   Five-year data. Full and reduced models in first differences (intercept and time dummies omitted).

Dependent variable	FWLS	OLS with White robust standard errors	FWLS	OLS with White robust standard errors
Real interest rate	0.224 (2.42)	0.219 (2.20)*	0.265 (4.49)**	0.273 (3.73)**
Change in inflation	-0.077 (0.32)	-0.16 (0.64)	-	-
Terms of trade shocks	0.161 (0.77)	0.031 (0.12)	-	-
Lag. product. change	-0.152 (1.31)	-0.101 (0.75)	-	-
EP	-1.715 (1.78)•	-1.747 (1.99)*	-1.083 (1.35)	-1.121 (1.58)
UD	0.095 (2.44)**	0.11 (2.12)*	0.102 (2.99)**	0.108 (2.53)*
BRR	-0.013 (0.67)	-0.004 (0.19)	-0.007 (0.44)	-0.005 (0.23)
TW	-0.065 (1.31)	-0.063 (1.21)	-0.064 (1.42)	-0.071 (1.70)•
CBI	4.301 (2.14)*	4.34 (2.09)*	4.121 (2.29)*	4.364 (1.99)*
BC	-0.079 (0.37)	-0.061 (0.23)	-0.239 (1.80)•	-0.162 (1.05)
BC*UD	-0.018 (1.36)	-0.004 (0.28)	-	-
BC*TW	-0.011 (0.59)	-0.019 (0.97)	-	-
BC*EP	0.507 (1.38)	0.604 (1.34)	-	-
BC*BRR	-0.001 (0.13)	-0.002 (0.16)	-	-
BC*CBI	-0.892 (0.84)	-0.691 (0.68)	-	-

Continued

Dependent variable	FWLS	OLS with White robust standard errors	FWLS	OLS with White robust standard errors
Observations	103	103	116	116
Adj R-square	-	0.26	-	0.26
LM autocor-relation test[a]	$\chi_{(1)} = 2.62$ [0.11]	$\chi_{(1)} = 1.9$ [0.15]	$\chi_{(1)} = 0.33$ [0.56]	$\chi_{(1)} = 0.39$ [0.52]
Wald test on macroeco. variables (RIR)[a]	$\chi_{(3)} = 2.6$ [0.45]	$F(3, 87) = 0.55$ [0.65]	-	-
Wald test on interactions[a]	$\chi_{(3)} = 4.67$ [0.46]	$F(5, 82) = 0.45$ [0.48]	-	-
Wald test on time dummies[a]	$\chi_{(5)} = 15.57$ [0.008]	$F(5, 82) = 1.07$ [0.38]	$\chi_{(7)} = 14.79$ [0.039]	$\chi_{(7)} = 7.6$ [0.37]

Notes:
a. p-values reported in indented parentheses.
All values in normal parentheses give absolute values of z statistics.
• significant at 10%, * significant at 5%, ** significant at 1%.

protection is positive (albeit insignificant) when the models are estimated in levels, and negative (at times even significant) when the same models are estimated in differences. As argued above, this index is time-invariant for Australia, Canada, Japan, New Zealand, Switzerland and the US. These are countries with low protection (high in the case of Japan) and high (low in the case of Japan) unemployment. They do not participate in the determination of the coefficient when the models are in levels and there are country dummies. This tilts the estimate towards a positive association. Similarly, wage coordination is positive (albeit insignificant) in three models in levels, while it is always negative in differences. The countries in which the wage coordination index is time-unvarying and which do not affect the coordination coefficient in levels (with country dummies) are Austria, Germany, Japan and Switzerland, all characterized by high coordination and low unemployment on average across the time period. This, again, biases the estimate in levels towards a positive sign. Interestingly enough, the other index, that of central bank independence, has similar coefficients and standard errors in both levels and differences.

Other coefficients do not vary much. The real interest rate variable is positive and significant in both levels and differences models, and its magnitude similar. The other macroeconomic variables are not significant, either in levels or in differences. Union density is positive and significant, and its magnitude is around 0.1. The benefit replacement rate is negative (and significant in one of the specifications in levels: column 6 of Table 7.1). The tax wedge is negative and significant in one specification in levels and one specification in differences. Interactions are not significantly different from zero (with one exception, that between coordination and employment protection, which is positive and significant at the 10 per cent level in column 2 of Table 7.1). The Wald test reveals that their removal does not significantly reduce the fit. The coordination coefficient increases its absolute magnitude when interactions are omitted and is negative and significant at the 10 per cent level with FWLS estimation.

Table 7.3 presents specifications that include the benefit duration variable. Two different measures of benefit duration are used: the one appearing in the Nickell et al. (2001) database (columns 1, 3, 5 and 7), and the one kindly provided by Baker et al. (2003), respectively (columns 2, 4, 6 and 8). The latter comprises more complete series for countries over time. Both of these measures are not without problems, in our opinion, because they measure benefit duration as a weighted average of benefit replacement rates for the years following the first one (and thus do not capture lengths shorter then the year). However, in this analysis we chose to employ them. In columns 1, 2, 5, and 6, the benefit replacement rate variable and the benefit duration variable are entered separately; in columns 3, 4, 7 and 8 the two are combined (by multiplication) in a single variable, which we call 'benefit generosity.' Columns 1 to 4 are estimated by FWLS modelling for (unit level) heteroscedasticity only; columns 5 to 8, by OLS with White robust standard errors.

None of the two benefit-related variables is significant when entered individually. Benefit replacement rate is negative as in the previous tables, while the sign of benefit duration depends on the measure used: it is positive with the Nickell et al. (2001)'s measure in columns 1 and 5, and negative with the Baker et al. (2003)'s measure in columns 2 and 6. Benefit generosity is instead positive, significant (at the 10 per cent level) only with the first measure of benefit duration, and with FWLS, not with the second measure, or OLS. The other coefficients do not change much, with one exception: the wage coordination measure, which is negative across models, becomes

Table 7.3 Five-year data. Alternative estimates with the insertion of the benefit duration and benefit generosity variables. Data in first differences (intercept and time dummies omitted).

Dependent var.	FWLS	FWLS alternative BD	FWLS BG	FWLS alternative BG	OLS ROBUST	OLS ROBUST alternative BD	OLS ROBUST BG	OLS ROBUST alternative BG
Real interest rate	0.275 (4.66)**	0.277 (4.70)**	0.267 (4.60)**	0.264 (4.42)**	0.285 (3.80)**	0.28 (3.69)**	0.281 (3.77)**	0.28 (3.75)**
EP	-1.387 (1.65)•	-1.101 (1.37)	-1.235 (1.48)	-0.917 (1.13)	-1.331 (1.77)•	-1.12 (1.53)	-1.282 (1.90)•	-1.09 (1.67)•
UD	0.101 (2.74)**	0.087 (2.49)*	0.101 (2.84)**	0.088 (2.52)*	0.125 (2.69)**	0.101 (2.30)*	0.126 (2.71)**	0.101 (2.34)*
BRR	-0.003 (0.18)	-0.009 (0.52)	-	-	-0.004 (0.21)	-0.006 (0.29)	-	-
BD	0.225 (0.13)	-1.433 (1.33)	-	-	0.093 (0.05)	-0.439 (0.38)	-	-
Benefit generosity	-	-	0.041 (1.64)•	0.03 (1.18)	-	-	0.026 (1.02)	0.022 (0.85)
TW	-0.048 (0.98)	-0.063 (1.4)	-0.066 (1.47)	-0.082 (1.88)•	-0.059 (1.24)	-0.069 (1.65)•	-0.072 (1.65)•	-0.081 (2.08)*
CBI	4.45 (2.44)*	4.093 (2.29)*	4.58 (2.56)*	4.413 (2.50)*	4.456 (2.04)*	4.346 (2.01)*	4.579 (2.05)*	4.615 (2.14)*

143

Continued

Dependent var.	FWLS	FWLS alternative BD	FWLS BG	FWLS alternative BG	OLS ROBUST	OLS ROBUST alternative BD	OLS ROBUST BG	OLS ROBUST alternative BG
BC	-0.271 (2.05)*	-0.267 (2.01)*	-0.259 (2.00)*	-0.244 (1.84)•	-0.2 (1.26)	-0.166 (1.07)	-0.186 (1.17)	-0.154 (0.97)
Observations	110	114	110	114	110	114	110	114
Adj. R square	-	-	0.26	0.26	0.27	0.27	-	-

Notes:
All values in normal parentheses give absolute values of z statistics.
• significant at 10%, * significant at 5%, ** significant at 1%.

significant with FWLS (but not with OLS). Tax wedge has a negative sign and is often significant.[13]

Table 7.4 compares fixed effects and random effects specifications of the model in levels. Random effects are used by Elmeskov et al. (1998). Columns 1 and 3 in the table are the same as in Table 7.1. Columns 2 and 4 report the corresponding random effect estimates. In the present context we prefer fixed effects. It is, however, interesting to compare the results of the two at this point.

There are both theoretical and methodological reasons behind the choice for a fixed effects specification. In a fixed effect model, we introduce a country-specific intercept δi, which is intended to capture country-specific and time-invariant unobservable determinants of unemployment, and can also serve as a country-specific fix for possible misspecification.[14] The use of fixed effects is legitimate if the goal is to draw 'inferences that are going to be confined to the effects *in* the model' (Hsiao, 1986, p. 43). In the random effects model, it is assumed that the intercept is a random variable that is a function of a mean value (the constant) plus a random error. It is also assumed that the groups (in this case, countries) are random draws from a population, about whose parameters inferences are being made. The baseline hypothesis for consistent estimates from a random effects model is the absence of correlation between the unit-specific effects (which are considered part of the error term) and the other covariates.

The model appears better specified with fixed effects, as shown by the R-squared statistics in Table 7.4. Indeed, country dummies seem to capture a large share of the variation in the unemployment rate. We also tested for fixed vs. random effects specification through a Hausman test. If the null hypothesis cannot be rejected, then it is safe to use random effects since we can assume no correlation between the covariates and the error term. When the full models with all macroeconomic predictors were compared, the null hypothesis was rejected. However, we could not reject the null hypothesis at the 5 per cent but only at the 10 per cent level, when the more parsimonious models were considered (columns 1 and 2). The random effect specification appears thus borderline acceptable compared with the fixed effects one, based on the Hausman test. However, non-randomness of the sample and better specification still make one prefer the fixed effects model to the random effects one.

One of the reasons why the random effects specification is worth considering is that, dispensing with country dummies, it allows all countries to contribute to the determination of the coefficient estimates, including for those variables like employment protection, central bank independence and wage coordination, which are based on time-unvarying (for some countries) or sluggish indices. Random effects makes use of the between-country variation as well as the within-country one, and takes into account that the

Table 7.4   Five-year data. OLS model with fixed and random effects estimation.

Dependent variable	Static model with fixed effects[a]	Static model with random effects[a]	Model with macroeco. variables and fixed effects	Model with macroeco. variables and random effects
Real interest rate	0,251 (3.41)**	0,234 (2.68)**	0,262 (3.19)**	0,255 (2.36)*
Change in inflation	-	-	-0,013 (0.08)	0,073 (0.3)
Terms of trade shocks	-	-	0,063 (0.18)	0,008 (0.02)
Lag. product. change	-	-	0,194 (1.14)	0,215 (1.34)
EP	1,493 (1.5)	0,447 (0.71)	0,925 (0.76)	-0,18 (0.23)
UD	0,103 (3.28)**	0,053 (2.67)**	0,083 (2.01)*	0,034 (1.49)
BRR	-0,019 (1.19)	-0,019 (1.36)	-0,019 (1.11)	-0,017 (1.17)
TW	-0,044 (0.89)	-0,021 (0.62)	-0,064 (1.01)	-0,007 (0.17)
CBI	4,284 (2.45)*	2,818 (1.79)•	4,053 (2.27)*	2,086 (1.24)
BC	-0,001 (0.01)	-0,496 (2.53)*	0,12 (0.53)	-0,379 (1.76)•
Observations	134	134	121	121
Adj. R-squared	0,75	0,5	0,74	0,51
Hausman test [b]	$\chi_{(14)} = 22.74$ [0.065]		$\chi_{(17)} = 211.45$ [0.0000]	

Notes:
a. With time dummies.
b. Ho: Difference in coefficients is not systematic. p-values reported in indented parentheses.
All values in normal parentheses give absolute values of z statistics.
• significant at 10%, * significant at 5%, ** significant at 1%.

data are clustered in cross-sections (differently from a pooled OLS regression).

Some of the changes between the two specifications are remarkable. The employment protection variable is generally positive and insignificant in both fixed and random effects reduced-model specifications (in levels). However, the magnitude is much lower in the random than in the fixed effects model. Employment protection is even negative in column 4, which uses a random effect specification. Similarly, the central bank independence coefficient has greater magnitude and lower standard error with fixed than with random effects. The greatest change concerns the coordination variable, which is negative and significant when random effects are considered (consistent with most literature; see, for example, Aidt and Tzannatos, 2002) but not when country dummies are inserted. Also, the magnitude of the union density coefficient is cut by about half when one shifts from fixed to random effects models.

7.4 OVERVIEW OF FINDINGS

In this chapter, we estimated various kinds of models, notably fixed effects in levels, random effects in levels, as well as models in first differences, in order to examine the proposition that a positive variation of labour market institutions in the OECD is positively associated with the unemployment rate. We used several kinds of estimation techniques: FWLS and OLS (normally with some form of robust standard errors). In this section, we provide a summary of results.

First difference models are preferable because the five-year series are non-stationary and do not seem to be cointegrated. Also, five-year models in first differences do not seem to require a lagged dependent variable, unlike the models in levels. Another reason is that with first differences the ratio between parameters and observations is much lower, because first differencing wipes out the fixed effects; therefore, coefficient estimates are probably more precise.[15]

The real interest rate is always a positive and significant predictor of unemployment. Its long-term coefficient is around 0.25, both in levels and in differences. The latter value implies that for every 4 per cent increase in the real interest rate, there is a corresponding 1 per cent increase in unemployment. Real interest rates affect demand, especially for consumer durables, investment goods and exports. Our findings suggest that these depressing effects are not just limited to the short run, but also impact upon medium-to-long term unemployment and are, in this respect, a confirmation of Ball's argument (Ball, 1999, p. 189) that 'determinants of aggregate demand have ... effects on long-run as well as short-run movements in unemployment'.

Other macroeconomic variables seem to have a more fleeting impact. Inserted only as precautionary controls, given the relatively large time span of our averaged data, all of these variables confirmed that if they have any effect on unemployment then this is limited to the short period (see Baccaro and Rei, 2005, for a confirmation of this finding). This may imply that if real wage resistance mediates the effect of these variables, this effect is short term and disappears when longer time frames are considered.

Among the institutional variables, employment protection is hardly ever significantly different from zero. This is in line with theoretical arguments, according to which the impact of employment protection on unemployment stocks is indeterminate as employment protection reduces employment and unemployment flows simultaneously and these effects tend to cancel each other out (see, for example, Blanchard and Wolfers, 1999, p. 8; Nickell, 1997, p. 66). It is also to be noted that the employment protection index is based on a limited number of observations, which are interpolated. The employment protection estimates vary considerably between levels and differences. The coefficient is generally positive, but insignificant, in levels, and generally negative, and even significant, in differences. We attribute at least part of this shift to the influence of fixed effects when the measure, as in the case of some countries, is time-invariant. We conclude that this variable does not seem to have a robust impact on aggregate unemployment.

Contrasting with theoretical predictions, the benefit replacement rate variable is almost always negative and almost always insignificant. It may be that if benefit replacement is a form of insurance (see Agell, 1999, 2000), the cost of such insurance is borne by workers through lower real wages. It could also be that the positive impact of benefit replacement on unemployment (for example, by increasing the reservation wage) is counterbalanced by a negative effect linked with a better match between jobs and worker skills when benefit replacement rates are higher.

The benefit duration variable we employ does not seem to have strong effects on unemployment. First, its sign depends on the measure used: it is positive with the Nickell et al. (2001) one and negative with the Baker et al. (2003) one. Second, the benefit generosity measure we constructed by multiplication with the benefit replacement rate is positive, but it is significant only with the first measure of benefit duration, and with FWLS, not with the second measure, or OLS. We conclude from these results that if there is an impact of the benefit system it is a combination of a long duration and high replacement rate that matters.

The tax wedge estimates are also somewhat surprising, in that they are negative with annual data and five-year data, and sometimes significant. If the impact of the tax wedge depends on what portion of it is not paid for by workers through lower real wages and contributes, therefore, to increase the real cost of labour per worker, then one has to conclude that, on average, the whole tax wedge is paid for by workers, controlling for other variables in the model. The negative effect on unemployment may depend on the fact that lower take-home pay shifts the labour supply curve rightward, that is, for given wage levels, workers increase their labour supply.

Union density is the one institutional variable that appears to have a robust positive impact on unemployment, independent of specification or estimation method used. This effect may be due to unionization increasing wages above the market clearing level. According to our models, however, this increase seems of limited magnitude. The union density coefficient is normally 0.1. This implies that a 10 per cent increase in union density is, on average, associated with a 1 per cent increase in overall unemployment, controlling for other determinants.[16] There is no evidence with five-year data (unlike yearly data, see Baccaro and Rei, 2005, Tables 2, 3 and 4) that the positive effect of union density declines with growing coordination, that is, that a more encompassing bargaining system partially internalizes the externalities caused by wage pressure.

The central bank independence coefficient large and always significant, which suggests that an increase in central bank independence leads to greater unemployment, controlling for other determinants of unemployment and especially for the degree of wage coordination. Our point estimates with five-year data – greater than four – suggest that the transition from a totally independent to a totally politically dependent monetary authority is associated with a decrease in unemployment by more than 4 percentage points.[17] Interestingly enough, the effect of central bank independence is net of the effect of real interest rates in our model, since the latter are controlled for. The two measures, central bank independence and real interest rates, are weakly correlated with one another (the correlation coefficient is around 0.14). We interpret the results as follows: the central bank independence index captures the more or less restrictive monetary policy stance of the country in the particular year. Its coefficient reflects the effect on unemployment of restrictive monetary policies through some form of Ball-type mechanism, such that restrictive monetary policies lead to a temporary increase in unemployment, which then becomes permanent probably, as argued by Ball (1999), because some form of hysteresis intervenes. The coefficient of the real interest rate variable captures instead those effects of the real interest rate on unemployment that do not depend on the particular stance of the central bank, but on other factors (for example perceived country risk or others).

The wage coordination variable is insignificant and negatively signed in most specifications. The effect of coordination is however stronger when we resort to random effects models. If fixed effects are accounted for, either directly, or indirectly by taking first differences, then this variable does not seem to have a significant impact on unemployment. If, however, fixed effects are not included in the model (for example, in random effects models), the coefficient of the coordination variable is negative and significant. It is possible that with better-specified models we could be able to dispose of country dummies (which are nothing more than labels) and be able to appreciate the cross-sectional effect of the wage coordination variable. For the time being, however, a model without fixed effects seems more than likely to suffer from omitted variable bias.

Among the interaction variables, none of them seems to have a significant impact. If on one hand this contradicts the results obtained with yearly data (see for example Hall and Franzese, 1998, or Baccaro and Rei, 2005), this is probably explained by the fact that wage coordination alters the impact of institutions only in the short term.

7.5   CONCLUDING REMARKS

In this chapter, we examined what kind of support data on OECD countries provide for the deregulatory view of unemployment, according to which variations in unemployment are explained by variations in labour market and other institutions.

Our preferred model is a fixed effects model in first differences with data averaged over five-year periods. We arrived at it by testing down from our initial specification. It is a highly parsimonious model, in which only the interest rate appears as macroeconomic control alongside the institutional variables, and there are no interaction terms. This model (just like the others we estimate in this chapter) provides very little support for the view that one could reduce unemployment simply by getting rid of institutional rigidities. We find that an increase in interest rates raises unemployment and that countries that augment the level of independence of their central bank end up augmenting the unemployment rate as well. Changes in employment protection, benefit replacement rates and tax wedge do not seem to have a significant impact on unemployment. The one institutional variable we find to be positively associated with changes in unemployment is the union density variable. Other interesting results from our analysis concern the bargaining coordination variable, which turns out to be mostly an insignificant predictor when fixed effects are controlled for, in contrast with most literature that attributes to it a negative impact on unemployment.

What transpires from these findings is that unemployment is mostly increased by policies and institutions that lead to restrictive macroeconomic policies. Obviously, there could be more fine-grained effects of institutions that are not captured by our models. For example, labour market institutions may affect different demographic groups in different ways, so that even though there is no average effect on unemployment, there are distinct effects on group-specific employment and unemployment rates, for example for women and the youth (see Bertola et al., 2003). Similarly, as argued by Blanchard and Wolfers (1999), institutions may impact upon unemployment not so much directly as by magnifying the effects of adverse macroeconomic shocks. However, as far as pooling available time-series data on institutions for OECD countries allows one to tell (Freeman, 2005), we can exclude that systematic deregulation of labour markets would solve the unemployment problem.

ANNEX

The Data

We use the time-series cross-section (TSCS) dataset made available to us by Baker et al. (2004). This is based on the IMF (2003) dataset with some modifications. The IMF dataset, in turn, updates the Nickell and Nunziata (2001) (henceforth NN) dataset. The latter is mostly based on information gathered by the OECD. The modifications introduced by Baker et al. concern specific countries and/or the years 1996–98, and are drawn from other OECD databases (for details, see Baker et al., 2004). The bargaining coordination (BC) index we use is a new measure elaborated and made available to us by Lane Kenworthy.

The countries included in the sample are Australia, Austria, Belgium, Canada, Denmark, Finland, France, Germany, Ireland, Italy, Japan, Netherlands, New Zealand, Norway, Sweden, Switzerland, the United Kingdom and the United States. The years covered are 1960–98.

Macroeconomic variables

Unemployment Rate (UNR), from IMF (2003). All data are from historical OECD databases for standardized unemployment rate

Real Interest Rates. This is the NN series updated for 1995–99 by the IMF based on OECD Economic Outlook series for long-term interest rates and consumer price deflators. The measure is defined as nominal returns on long-term government bond minus the actual inflation rate over the following year.

Change in Inflation Rate, from IMF (2003). Yearly changes in Consumer Prices Indexes, based on OECD databases. The formula for country i is $CPI_t\text{-}CPI_{t\text{-}1}$

Labour Productivity Growth (lagged), from IMF (2003). The series is based on OECD data. Productivity growth for country i is defined as: $100*((Prod_t\text{-}Prod_{t\text{-}1})/Prod_{t\text{-}1})$.

Terms of Trade Shocks. The measure is defined as first log-difference of the terms of trade multiplied by trade openness. The trade openness of the country is defined as the ratio between imports plus exports to GDP (at constant prices). Raw data on export prices, import prices and trade openness are from OECD databases.

Institutional variables

Employment Protection Legislation (EP), from NN. This variable presents some peculiarities that undermine its strength as an indicator (see Baker et al., 2003, p. 6). The NN measure draws on Blanchard and Wolfers (1999). It is based on two data points for the late 1990s and late 1980s. From these, Blanchard and Wolfers created two other data points interpolating the previous measure for the early 1990s and another one for the early 1980s, simply taking the late 1980s figures which were assumed to be constant. For the years 1960–79, the data come from another source (Lazear, 1990). The measure is a 0–2 index where 2 is the highest level of employment legislation protection.

Union Density (UD). This is the NN series updated for 1995–99 by Baker et al. (2003) based on Ebbinghaus and Visser (2000) as well as other sources. Data are expressed in percentage points.

Benefit replacement rate (BRR). This is the NN measure as modified by Baker et al. (2003), namely 'benefit entitlement before tax as a percentage of previous earnings before tax. Data are averages over replacement rates at two earnings levels (average and two-thirds of average earnings) and three family types (single, with dependent spouse, with spouse at work). They refer to the first year of unemployment' (Nickell et al., 2001, p. 46). Baker et al. introduce minor modifications for three Scandinavian countries in the 1970s and update the series to 1998. The data are in percentage points.

Tax Wedge (TW). Baker et al. (2003, p. 27) update the NN series 'based on changes in the sum of individual (income) tax, social security contributions (employer and employee), payroll taxes, VAT, sales taxes, excise taxes and customs duties, all over GDP ([...] from OECD data).' Data are in percentage points.

Central Bank Independence index (CBI). This is a 0–1 continuous CBI index. The IMF borrowed the series from Rob Franzese (see Hall and Franzese,

1998) and updated it based on information on more recent reforms in Daunfeldt and de Luna (2002).

Index of Coordination in wage setting (BC). The variable is taken from Kenworthy (2003). It is available at: http://www.emory.edu/SOC/lkenworthy/WageCoorScores.xls. The index ranges from 1 to 5 where 1 is the minimum coordination. We introduced minor changes for Ireland between 1988 and 1992 and Italy in the 1990s based on our previous work (Baccaro and Simoni, 2004; Baccaro, 2002).

NOTES

1. Many thanks to participants in the 2nd CofFEE-Europe Workshop, as well as Peter Auer, Rob Franzese, Andrew Glyn, Bernhard Kittel, Naren Prasad and Marco Vivarelli for comments on a previous version of this chapter. The views expressed in this chapter are the authors' only and do not necessarily coincide with those of the International Institute for Labour Studies or the ILO.
2. Many thanks to John Schmitt and his colleagues for making the dataset available to us.
3. The countries we consider in this analysis are Australia, Austria, Belgium, Canada, Denmark, Finland, France, Germany, Ireland, Italy, Japan, the Netherlands, New Zealand, Norway, Sweden, Switzerland, the United Kingdom and the United States.
4. We would also like to thank Xavier Debrun for making the IMF (2003) dataset available to us.
5. This is publicly available at: http://cep.lse.ac.uk/pubs/number.asp?number=502.
6. Some specifications also include $\gamma_7 BD_{i,t}$ for the duration of unemployment benefits, or $\gamma_8 Benefit\ Generosity_{i,t}$ for a variable that multiplies BRR and BD.
7. As in IMF (2003), we lag the productivity variable due to possible endogeneity with unemployment.
8. Many thanks to Lane Kenworthy for permission to use his index. This is available at: http://www.u.arizona.edu/~lkenwor/WageCoorScores.xls
9. Panel-specific rhos would be problematic given the small number of observations over time.
10. The panel corrected standard errors (PCSEs) proposed by Beck and Katz (1995, 1996), which we use in models with annual data in Baccaro and Rei (2005), are not appropriate in this case because this estimator is recommended for panels where T > N. In particular, Beck (2001, p. 274) recommends against using PCSEs when T < 10 since they depend on asymptotic assumptions about T.
11. Beck and Katz (1995) argue, based on simulations, that FWLS estimates of standard errors and significance levels are overly optimistic in short panels and lead to rejection of the null hypothesis that regression coefficients are equal to zero in the population more often than warranted. The Beck and Katz's (1995) critique is directed at the FWLS correction for spatial correlation of the errors in particular. However, it also takes issue with FWLS's correction for panel heteroscedasticity (see Beck and Katz, 1996). 'This is because the weights used in the procedure are simply how well the observations for a unit fit the original OLS regression plane. The second round of FWLS simply downweights the observations for a country if that country does not fit the OLS regression plane well' (Beck, 2001, p. 277)
12. We suspect, however, that the latter result may be due to low statistical power of the test.
13. We also estimated a full model, with the whole set of macro controls, and of interactions, adding the benefit duration and benefit generosity measures. The results are not reported. However, they do not vary much. The interactions are mostly insignificant with three exceptions: the interaction between coordination and benefit duration is negative and significant at the 10 per cent level with FWLS; the interaction between coordination and

benefit generosity is negative and significant at the 10 per cent level with FWLS; the interaction between coordination and employment protection is positive and significant at the 10 per cent level with FWLS when benefit generosity and its interaction are inserted.

14. There could be other variables, not included in the model, which could influence the unemployment rate. Degree of competition in the goods and services markets, degree of labour mobility, demography and so on are all examples of additional control variables that could have been inserted in our models. Lack of data, or of complete time series for some countries, prevented us from estimating a more comprehensive model. We aimed for a specification that was as close as possible to the one used by IMF (2003) and others.

15. With reduced models, there are approximately four observations for each parameter to be estimated when the model is in levels, and eight observations per parameter in first differences. However, the first difference estimator may come at a price. On one hand, we risk exacerbating the problem of measurement error, which may be less severe in the levels equation (see Arellano, 2003, p. 50). On the other hand, since 'the information about the Betas in the regression in first differences will depend on the ratio of the variances $v \Delta$ and $x \Delta$ (where v is the error term and x is an explanatory variable) ... if Var $x \Delta$ is small, regressions in changes may contain very little information about the parameters of interests' (Arellano, 2003, p. 10).

16. The effect could, however, vary across demographic groups and be higher for workers with more elastic supply curves, like women and youth, and lower for workers with less elastic supply curves, like prime-age males (see Bertola et al., 2003).

17. With random effects, the coefficient is somewhat lower.

REFERENCES

Agell, J. (1999), 'On the benefits from rigid labour markets: norms, market failures, and social insurance', *Economic Journal*, **127** (453), F143–F164.

Agell, J. (2000), 'On the determinants of labour market institutions: rent-sharing vs. social insurance', *Working Paper Series* 2000–16, Uppsala University, Department of Economics.

Aidt, T. and Z. Tsannatos (2002), *Unions and Collective Bargaining: Economic Effects in a Global Environment*, Washington, DC: World Bank.

Arellano, M. (2003), *Panel Data Econometrics*, Oxford: Oxford University Press.

Baccaro, L. (2002), 'The construction of "democratic" corporatism in Italy', *Politics and Society*, **30** (2) 327–57.

Baccaro, L. and D. Rei (2005), 'Institutional determinants of unemployment in OECD countries: A time series cross-section analysis (1960–1998)', *Discussion Paper* DP/160/2005, International Institute for Labour Studies, Geneva: ILO.

Baccaro, L. and M. Simoni (2004) 'The Irish social partnership and the "Celtic Tiger" phenomenon', *Discussion Paper* DP/154/2004, International Institute for Labour Studies, Geneva: ILO.

Ball, L. (1999), 'Aggregate demand and long-run unemployment', *Brookings Papers on Economic Activity*, **2**, 189–251.

Baltagi, B. (2001), *Econometric Analysis of Panel Data*, New York: Wiley.

Baker, D., A. Glyn, D. Howell and J. Schmitt (2002), 'Labour market institutions and unemployment: A critical analysis of the cross-country evidence', *Working paper P 2002–17*, Center for Economic Policy Analysis, New School University, New York.

Baker, D., A. Glyn, D. Howell and J. Schmitt (2004), 'Unemployment and labour market institutions: The failure of the empirical case for deregulation', *CEPA Working Paper* 2004–4.

Beck, N. (2001), 'Time-series-cross-section cata: what have we learned in the past few years?' *Annual Review of Political Science*, **4**, 271–293.

Beck, N. and J. Katz (1995), 'What to do (and not to do) with time series cross section data', *American Political Science Review*, **89** (3), 634–647.

Beck, N. and J. Katz (1996), 'Nuisance vs. substance: specifying and estimating time-series-cross-section models', *Political Analysis*, **6**, 1–36.

Belot, M. and J. van Ours (2000), 'Does the recent success of some OECD countries in lowering their unemployment rates lie in the clever design of their labor market reforms?' *IZA Discussion Paper*, 147.

Belot, M. and J.C. van Ours (2001), 'Unemployment and Labor Market Institutions: An Empirical Analysis,' *Journal of the Japanese and International Economies*, **15** (4), 403–418.

Bertola, G., F.D. Blau and L.M. Kahn (2003), 'Labour market institutions and demographic employment patterns', *NBER Working Papers*, No. 9043.

Blanchard, J.O. and J. Wolfers (1999), 'The role of shocks and institutions in the rise of European unemployment: The aggregate evidence', *NBER Working Papers*, No. W7282.

Daveri, F. and G. Tabellini (2000), 'Unemployment, growth and taxation in industrial countries', *Economic Policy*, **30**, 47–104.

Daunfeldt, S.O. and X. de Luna (2002), 'Central bank independence and price stability: evidence from 23 OECD countries.' *Umeå Economic Studies*, **589**, Umeå University.

Ebbinghaus, B and J. Visser (2000), *Trade Unions in Western Europe*, London: Macmillan.

Elmeskov, J., J.P. Martin and S. Scarpetta (1998), 'Key lessons for labour market reforms: evidence from OECD countries' experiences', *Swedish Economic Policy Review*, **5** (2), 205–52.

Freeman R. (2005). 'Labour Market Institutions Without Blinders: The Debate over Flexibility and Labour Market Performance', *NBER Working Papers*, 11286.

Hall, P.A. and R.J. Franzese, Jr. (1998), 'Mixed signals: CBI, coordinated wage-bargaining, and European Monetary Union', *International Organization*, **52** Summer, 505-523.

Hall, P.A. and D. Soskice (2001), *Varieties of Capitalism: The Institutional Foundations of Comparative Advantage*, Oxford: Oxford University Press.

Hsiao, C. (1986) *Analysis of Panel Data*, (1st ed.), Cambridge, UK: Cambridge University Press.

IMF (2003), 'Unemployment and Labor Market Institutions: Why Reforms Pay Off?' in IMF, (2003) *World Economic Outlook: Growth and Institutions*, Chapter 4, pp. 129–150, Washington, DC: IMF.

Kenworthy, L. (2003), 'Quantitative indicators of corporatism', *International Journal of Sociology*, **33** (3), 10–44.

Kittel, B. (1999), 'Sense and sensitivity in pooled analysis of political data', *European Journal of Political Research*, **35**, 225–253.

Kiviet, J.F. (1995), 'On Bias, inconsistency and efficiency of various estimators in dynamic panel data models', *Journal of Econometrics*, **68**, 53–68.

Lazear, E.P. (1990), 'Job security provisions and employment', *Quarterly Journal of Economics*, **105**, 699–726.

Nickell, S.J. (1981), 'Biases in dynamic models with fixed effects', *Econometrica*, **49**, 1417–1426.

Nickell, S.J. (1997), 'Unemployment and labour market rigidities: Europe versus North America', *Journal of Economic Perspectives*, **11** (3), 55–74.

Nickell, S.J. and L. Nunziata (2001), *Labour Market Institutions Database*, unpublished, London School of Economics, available at http://cep.lse.ac.uk/pubs/abstract.asp?ID=502

Nickell, S.J., L. Nunziata, W. Ochel and G. Quintini (2001), 'The Beveridge Curve, Unemployment and Wages in the OECD from the 1960s to the 1990s', in P. Aghion, R. Frydman, J. Stiglitz and M. Woodford (eds.), *Knowledge, Information and Expectations in Modern Macroeconomics: in Honor of Edmund S. Phelps*, Princeton University Press, 2002.

Nunziata, L. (2005), 'Institutions and wage determination: a multi-Country approach', *Oxford Bulletin of Economics and Statistics*, **67** (4), 435–466.

Nunziata, L. (2002), 'Unemployment, labour market institutions and shocks', *Nuffield College Working Papers in Economics*, W16.

Siebert, H. (1997), 'Labour market rigidities: at the root of unemployment in Europe', *Journal of Economic Perspectives*, **11** (3), 37–54.

Wilson, S.E. and Butler, D.M. (2004) *A Lot More to Do: The promise and peril of panel data in political science*, unpublished paper, available at http://www.stanford.edu/class/polisci353/2004spring/reading/wilson_butler.pdf.

8. The Institutional Determinants of Labour Market Performance: Comparing the Anglo-Saxon Model and a European-Style Alternative

Henri de Groot, Richard Nahuis and Paul Tang[1]

8.1 INTRODUCTION

Variation in work intensity is an important source of variation in per capita income levels. For the richest countries, it is a more important source than differences in labour productivity: whereas Americans are on average richer than Europeans, workers in the United States and in the richest European countries are by and large equally productive. Instead, the difference in the number of hours worked is mainly responsible for the huge difference in GDP per capita (see for example de Groot et al., 2004).

A cursory look at the data provides a first impression of labour market performance in Europe compared with the United States. Table 8.1 ranks OECD countries according to the total number of hours worked per inhabitant. In addition, the table contains information on the average number of hours worked per worker, the number of employed workers per capita (that is, the employment rate)[2] and the standardized unemployment rate. Clearly, the United States is on top in terms of hours worked per inhabitant. This mainly reflects long working days compared to the other countries, most notably the European countries. Indeed, when countries are ranked according to hours worked per worker, the United States also comes out on top. The picture is less clear-cut when the number of employed workers per capita is considered. The Scandinavian countries (but also the Netherlands and Portugal), the other Anglo-Saxon countries (Australia, Canada, New Zealand and the United Kingdom), Japan and Switzerland score about equally well (or even better) than the United States. Also the picture is not clear-cut when the number of unemployed workers is considered. For most European countries,

Labour Markets and Labour Market Policies

Table 8.1   Hours worked (per worker and per inhabitant), employment and unemployment in the OECD in 2000 (US = 1)

	Hours per inhabitant	Hours per worker[a]	Employment rate[a]	Unemployment rate[b]
US	1.00	1.00	1.00	1.00
Japan	0.99	0.96	1.04	1.18
Switzerland	0.93	0.85	1.10	0.65
Portugal	0.93	0.94	0.99	1.03
Australia	0.92	0.96	0.96	1.58
Canada	0.92	0.95	0.97	1.70
New Zealand	0.89	0.93	0.95	1.50
Denmark	0.84	0.82	1.03	1.10
Sweden	0.83	0.86	0.97	1.48
United Kingdom	0.83	0.88	0.95	1.33
Ireland	0.81	0.90	0.89	1.05
Finland	0.80	0.87	0.92	2.43
Austria	0.76	0.81	0.94	0.93
Italy	0.75	0.87	0.87	2.63
Norway	0.75	0.73	1.02	0.88
Germany	0.74	0.82	0.90	1.98
The Netherlands	0.72	0.72	1.00	0.70
Spain	0.71	0.97	0.74	2.83
France	0.66	0.82	0.80	2.33
Belgium	0.65	0.83	0.79	1.73

Notes:
a.   Based on own computations using GGDC: Total Economy Database 2004 (University of Groningen and the Conference Board).
b.   Based on information on the standardised unemployment rate from the OECD (2001), Nickell and Nunziata (2001) and Golden et al. (2002).

Sources: We refer to the Annex for an extensive description of the data sources.

the unemployment rate exceeds that of the United States, although important exceptions exist: Austria, the Netherlands, Norway and Switzerland. The many exceptions make it difficult to assert as a rule that the European welfare states tend to discourage employment and to result in open and hidden unemployment.

The contrast between Europe and the United States has led to a call for reforms in Europe. Barriers to competition in goods, capital and labour markets, 'the result of too many and too great a diversity in regulations across countries', are thought to reduce the incentive to work (Baily and Kierkegaard, 2004). The European Council has backed this call for reform. In Lisbon it has drawn up an agenda for reform which the Council expected will make the European economy in 2010 the most competitive in the world. It has reaffirmed this agenda on later occasions. Nobel Prize winner Gary Becker (2002, p. 24) sees a watershed in European economic policies: 'Until recent years, most continental European politicians and intellectuals dismissed what they derisively called the British and American "Anglo-Saxon" model of competition and price flexibility. Yet a quiet but enormous change may be taking place in European attitudes toward competition in labour and other markets.' This change in attitude is, however, also cause for concern in Europe. The same institutions that are considered inefficient and rigid, also reduce income inequality. A shift towards an Anglo-Saxon model does not necessarily imply that European countries would adopt this model in full. Rather, they may adopt elements from the Anglo-Saxon model, while at the same time aiming for a European-style alternative, in which not only efficiency but also equity is valued. Of course, such an alternative would almost certainly involve difficult trade-offs between efficiency and equity.

This chapter aims to describe the variation in the labour market performance of OECD countries and to analyse the role of institutional factors in explaining this variation. We consider the effect of institutional factors on employment, measured in persons and in hours, as well as on income distribution.

Much research on labour market institutions and economic performance is already available. Most of this literature, however, tends to analyse the measures of labour market performance more or less in isolation, focusing on unemployment, participation or hours worked separately. The most prominent example of this literature – which also provides a good account of previous contributions – is Nickell and Layard (1999).[3] While our analysis is closely related to theirs, we make a further contribution to this literature by analysing more dimensions of labour market performance in a unified framework.

A second strand of literature takes up the question of what institutional settings best serve the goal of optimizing social-economic performance. An interesting example of this literature is Boeri (2002).[4] He considers the social-economic performance of four different 'social policy models', that he associates with groups of countries, that is, the Nordic, the Anglo–Saxon, continental Europe and the Mediterranean countries. Performance is evaluated on the basis of income inequality, protection against labour market risk and rewards to labour market participation. Based on cross-country comparisons supplemented with micro-econometric evidence, Boeri concludes that both the Nordic countries as well as the Anglo-Saxon countries score well on all indicators and can compete with the US. Our analysis supplements this approach by considering a wide range of institutional characteristics and their effect on efficiency as well as equity, using systematic econometric analysis exploiting both cross-sectional as well as time-series variation. Despite the attractiveness of cross-country analysis, the limitations of such approaches have to be acknowledged. These are concisely summarized in Freeman (1998).[5]

We proceed in the following manner. In section 8.2, we compare several dimensions of labour market performance across time and countries. Section 8.3 discusses trade-offs among various indicators for social-economic performance and characterizes variation in the institutional context of the countries that we consider in our analysis. A systematic econometric analysis of the determinants of variation in labour market performance is subsequently presented. Concluding remarks are offered in section 8.4.

8.2   LABOUR MARKET PERFORMANCE IN THE UNITED STATES AND EUROPE

Work intensity in the United States (hours worked per inhabitant) is the highest of OECD countries. It exceeds that of European countries by almost 25 per cent. A first factor that can explain this is that workers in the United States have long working days. The title of a book by Juliet Schor – *The Overworked American* – is telling in this respect. A second possibility is that the United States is successful in mobilizing its working-age population to participate in the labour market. If this goes hand in hand with succesful matching of these people with jobs (and hence with low unemployment), effective use is made of the available people. A final explanation may be that the age structure of the US population is such that many people are of working age (being neither too young nor too old to participate in the labour market). The rapid ageing of the population that several European countries are experiencing may be relevant in this respect.

8.2.1   A Decomposition of Hours Worked per Inhabitant

To examine these possible explanations, for all countries in our sample we decompose the difference in the number of hours worked per inhabitant with the US into its four constituent factors, that is, hours per worker, the employment rate (that is, one minus the unemployment rate), the number of workers and active job seekers as a fraction of the working-age population (that is between 15 and 65), and the working-age population as a fraction of the total population.[6] Figure 8.1 shows for four European countries with different developments – the Netherlands, France, Ireland and Finland – to what extent these four factors have contributed historically to the relative difference in the number of hours worked per inhabitant with the US.[7]

France is an example of a country facing a continuously increasing gap in terms of hours per inhabitant with the US. This gap has doubled over the last 20 years, driven by a combination of a shrinking labour force and a gradual decline in the number of hours worked per worker (relative to the US). In the early 1980s, the Netherlands was characterized by a huge gap with the US of about 40 per cent. It has since managed to reduce this gap slightly. The key factor here is the increase in the labour force, which has partly been offset by a gradual decline in the number of hours worked per worker. Finland has experienced the most dramatic decline in hours per inhabitant. Starting in 1980 with a lead over the US of approximately 5 percentage points, it is now more than 20 percentage points behind. This development is driven by the combination of a huge increase in unemployment, a shrinking labour force and a decline in hours per worker. Finally, Ireland has gone through a period of decline, followed by a period of catching up with the US. The initial decline was the result of reduced hours per worker, a shrinking labour force and increased unemployment. Since the late 1980s, the trends of increasing unemployment and a shrinking labour force have been reversed, resulting in an increase of hours worked per inhabitant (despite a declining trend of hours worked per worker).

Table 8.2 decomposes for a broader sample of countries (mainly in Europe), the gap in hours worked with the United States for the year 2000. The countries are ranked from high to low according to the relative number of hours worked per inhabitant.[8] For most countries, the gap is largely explained by a relatively low number of hours worked per worker. In addition, for countries such as Spain, France, Belgium and Ireland, the low number of hours worked is also, to a large extent, the result of a small labour force as a proportion of the working-age population. Unemployment adds to the problem most notably for countries such as France, Italy and Spain. Variation in the pattern of ageing (or greening) of the population explains only a small part of the variation in hours per capita.

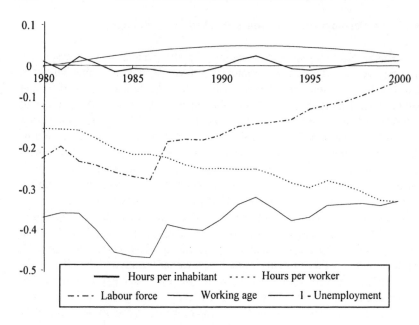

Figure 8.1a   The hours gap: The Netherlands

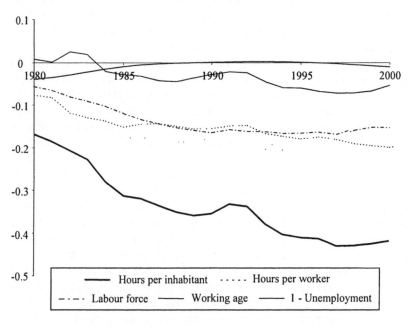

Figure 8.1b   The hours gap: France

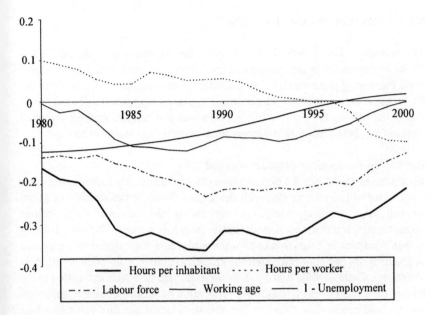

Figure 8.1c   The hours gap: Ireland

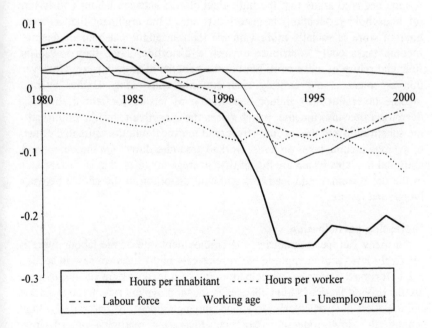

Figure 8.1d   The hours gap: Finland

8.2.2   How to Close the Hours Gap?

The European Union would like to close the income gap with the United States as expressed in the Lisbon targets. Increasing work intensity is – apart from increasing productivity – an important means to this end. How can the EU achieve this ambition? The discussion above suggests two broad ways, that is, increasing the number of hours worked and increasing the number of workers (by either increasing participation or reducing unemployment).

Increasing the number of hours worked
As aforementioned, for the richest members of the European Union, the main contributor to the income gap with the United States is the number of hours worked (per worker). However, increasing this number has serious shortcomings and does not unequivocally improve welfare. One shortcoming is that increases in hours worked might partly be compensated by decreases in productivity per hour (although the empirical evidence for such an effect is not strong; Cette, 2004). A second, more important disadvantage is that more labour time means less leisure time. The value of leisure does not appear in income and production statistics, but this does not make this value any less real. Similarly, official statistics ignore the value of household production.

One needs to argue that the individual choice between labour and leisure (or household production) is distorted to make the argument that an extra hour of work is socially more valuable than an additional hour of leisure.[9] Income taxes could contribute to such a distortion, since they lower the financial return of extra work but not the benefits of extra leisure. However, this argument is not entirely clear-cut, nor convincing. Higher average income taxes not only induce substitution of leisure for labour, but also decrease (after-tax) income, which raises the incentive to work. Empirically the substitution and the income effect tend to cancel out; the estimated effects of average income taxes on hours worked are rather low.[10] On the other hand, marginal tax rates which are higher than average tax rates, that is, progression in the tax system, could lead to significant distortion in the choice between labour and leisure.[11]

Increasing participation
In many European countries, the employment rate of the labour force is relatively low (and unemployment is relatively high).[12] As we saw in section 8.2.1, for most countries, participation and to a lesser extent unemployment are the driving factors behind changes in the employment rate. Labour market participation is particularly low and unemployment is particularly high among the low-productive workers. Increasing participation of low-productive workers in the labour market would be expected to reduce the

Table 8.2 The hours gap with the US explained: a decomposition, 2000

Percentage difference in	Hours per capita	Hours per worker	Workers[a]	Labour force[b]	Working age population[c]
Japan	-0.6	4.4	-0.7	1.3	3.2
Switzerland	-7.5	-16.8	1.4	5.7	2.1
Portugal	-7.8	-6.7	-0.1	-3.7	2.7
Australia	-8.3	-4.4	-2.4	-3.4	1.9
Canada	-8.4	-4.9	-3.0	-3.9	3.4
New Zealand	-12.0	-6.8	-2.1	-2.2	-0.9
Denmark	-17.1	-19.8	-0.4	2.1	1.1
Sweden	-18.1	-14.7	-2.0	1.1	-2.5
United Kingdom	-18.4	-12.8	-1.4	-3.3	-0.9
Ireland	-21.3	-10.0	-0.2	-12.7	1.6
Finland	-22.4	-13.8	-6.1	-4.0	1.5
Austria	-27.7	-21.3	0.3	-9.5	2.7
Italy	-28.1	-14.0	-7.0	-9.5	2.4
Germany	-30.5	-20.4	-4.1	-8.9	3.0
The Netherlands	-33.1	-33.3	1.2	-3.8	2.7
Spain	-33.6	-3.0	-7.9	-26.0	3.3
France	-41.8	-19.9	-5.7	-15.2	-1.1
Belgium	-42.5	-19.0	-3.1	-20.0	-0.4

Notes:
[a] As fraction of labour force.
[b] As fraction of working-age population.
[c] As share of population.

Source: We refer to the annex for an extensive description of the data sources.

overall average productivity per hour due to a composition effect. Furthermore, more easily than with the choice between labour and leisure, it can be argued that open and hidden unemployment creates an important distortion. Moreover, unemployment is often involuntary. And even if drawing an unemployment benefit or other type of social benefit is voluntary, the social security arrangements do distort the individual choice. An example may help to clarify this. The participation of workers older than 55 is strikingly low in many countries. The reason lies primarily in the design of schemes for early retirement, which may give little incentive to continue working. People who retire early hardly experience an income loss, while the close link between the last earned wage and old-age benefits makes elderly workers reluctant to accept lower wages when getting older – even though they are not as productive as they used to be. The social security system then provides firms and workers with a way of escaping the conflict of interests.

8.3   AN EMPIRICAL APPROACH

Institutional factors are commonly recognized as key determinants of labour market performance (Nickell and Layard, 1999). These factors include, for example, the duration of unemployment benefits, active labour market policies and employment protection. In order to identify the effects of labour market institutions on performance, we undertake a multivariate analysis. Central in the analysis are regressions in which the hours worked per worker, the participation rate, the unemployment rate and a measure for income inequality are related to various institutional characteristics of national labour markets. Our data set covers 18 OECD countries[13] and averages for seven five-year periods from 1960 to 1995 which yields (at most) 126 observations.

8.3.1   Characterizing the Countries in the Sample

Before turning to the regression results, we first examine our data set. We do so by characterizing the various dimensions of labour market performance for clusters of countries. In defining the clusters, we follow Esping-Anderson (1999) who breaks down the group of rich countries into three groups according to the social models that the countries have adopted: corporatist, social democratic and liberal. Broadly speaking, the first category comprises continental Europe, the second Scandinavian countries and the third Anglo–Saxon countries.[14]

Figure 8.2 shows for each of the groups, four efficiency indicators for labour market performance: participation, employment (defined as 1 minus the unemployment rate), income equality (defined as 100 minus the income inequality measure provided by Galbraith and Kum, 2002), and hours worked per worker.[15] On the axes is the measure of economic performance of the respective group of countries divided by the average measure of performance of all countries. A score of 100 thus means that the group of countries scores equal to the average of all countries. Figure 8.2 shows that the Anglo-Saxon model does not outperform the others on all counts: the participation rate is on average the highest in the social-democratic countries, the differences in the employment rate are small, and income inequality is high.

Figure 8.3 shows several characteristics of labour market institutions for the same three groups of countries. It is immediately clear that in the liberal countries the government intervenes less in the labour market than in the other (groups of) countries. For example, the level and duration of unemployment benefits are on average lower in the liberal countries than elsewhere. Figure 8.3 also illustrates an interesting difference among the European countries. The social-democratic countries have on average the highest benefit level (and the highest tax wedge). They have a higher benefit level than the corporatist countries and combine this with higher expenditures on active labour market policies, with shorter benefit duration and less employment protection. This suggests that social security in the social-democratic countries is more geared towards reintegration into the labour market than in the corporatist countries, possibly explaining the difference in the participation rate between the two groups of countries. We now turn to the regression analysis to see whether it confirms these notions derived from a partial consideration of the data.

8.3.2   A Systematic Econometric Approach

One complication typically encountered when undertaking regression analyses is that labour market characteristics tend to be mutually correlated. Thus the effect of a single factor may be hard to isolate, since it will affect not only the performance of the labour market directly, but also the other institutional factors. For example, a country with a strong trade union movement is likely to have a high replacement rate and a progressive tax system.

We proceed therefore in the following manner. In the first step we include in the equation only variables for which the mutual correlation is relatively low. In doing so, we avoid potential problems of multi-collinearity. Table 8.3 reports the correlation among the explanatory variables for the average of the period 1989–94. The correlation coefficients are below 0.5 for four variables: benefit level or replacement rate, benefit duration, a measure for employment protection and a measure for active labour market policies.[16] In the second step the tax wedge between the labour costs for employers and the net wage for employees is introduced into the regression equation. This variable is *a priori* thought to have an important impact on the number of hours worked. By

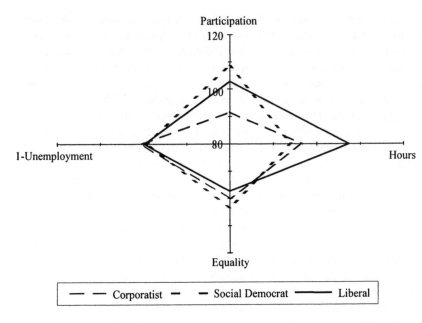

Figure 8.2   Performance in Esping-Anderson groups (average 1989–94)

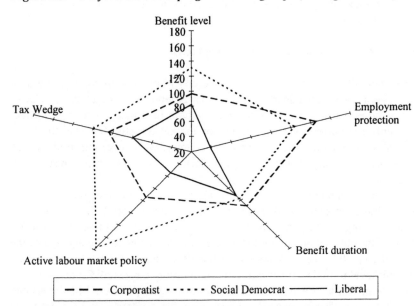

Figure 8.3   Labour market characteristics in Esping-Anderson groups (average 1989–94)

introducing the tax wedge separately, its interaction with other labour market characteristics becomes clear. The third and final step is to add measures for the unions' role in the labour market, that is, the degree of centralization in wage bargaining (called coordination) and the extent to which workers are covered by collective agreements (called coverage).

Of course, the potential problem with multi-collinearity calls for a careful interpretation of the results in the second and third step. The fact that the qualitative results (that is, the signs of the relationship) are not seriously affected by the inclusion of such variables gives confidence in the results obtained.

Table 8.3   Correlations between policy instruments, average of 1989–94

	Benefit level	Benefit duration	Employ- ment protection	Active LM policies	Union coordin- ation	Union coverage	Tax wedge
Benefit level	1.00	-0.25	0.32	0.41	0.15	0.25	0.36
Benefit duration		1.00	0.03	-0.26	0.27	0.42	-0.07
Employment protection			1.00	0.47	0.55	0.52	0.55
Active LM policies				1.00	0.33	0.36	0.51
Union coordination					1.00	0.36	0.06
Union coverage				.		1.00	0.06
Tax wedge							1.00

Source: We refer to the Annex for an extensive description of the data sources.

8.3.3   The Regression Results

Table 8.4 reports the estimation results.[17] Below, we will first discuss the results of the first step, in columns I, IV, VII and X. Later we shift attention to the other columns. We discuss the results presented in Table 8.4 horizontally, that is, we discuss the effect of each policy instrument on various indicators of social-economic performance separately.

Table 8.4 Labour market policy and performance (1960–95)

Dependent variable, logarithm

	Participation rate			Standardized unemployment rate			Hours per worker			Income inequality		
	I	II	III	IV	V	VI	VII	VIII	IX	X	XI	XII
Replacement rate	0.012 (0.21)	0.016 (0.27)	-0.007 (-0.12)	1.281* (1.95)	0.722 (1.15)	0.864 (1.38)	-0.274*** (-5.26)	-0.215*** (-4.09)	-0.226*** (-4.30)	-0.080*** (-3.66)	-0.032 (-1.63)	-0.028 (-1.33)
Benefit duration	-0.060** (-2.08)	-0.032 (0.96)	0.006 (0.13)	0.456 (1.27)	0.818** (1.99)	0.878 (1.65)	-0.011 (-0.48)	-0.014 (-0.48)	-0.032 (-0.88)	-0.051*** (-3.10)	-0.109*** (-6.43)	-0.125*** (-5.61)
Employment protection	-0.042** (-2.59)	-0.040** (2.41)	-0.042** (-2.18)	-0.120 (-0.65)	-0.303** (-2.05)	-0.183 (-0.99)	-0.074*** (-4.01)	-0.034* (-1.80)	-0.047** (-2.53)	-0.006 (-0.65)	0.018** (2.17)	0.017* (1.71)
Active labour market policy	0.003*** (4.81)	0.003*** (4.71)	0.004*** (4.55)	-0.012* (-1.96)	-0.016*** (-2.66)	-0.010 (-1.57)	0.001 (1.53)	0.002** (2.68)	0.002* (1.97)	-0.003*** (-13.75)	-0.003*** (-10.61)	-0.003*** (-7.94)
Tax wedge	- -	-0.021 (0.19)	0.125 (0.78)	- -	2.518*** (2.66)	1.796 (1.28)	- -	-0.408*** (-4.07)	-0.381*** (-3.57)	- -	-0.287*** (-6.55)	-0.316*** (-5.21)
Coordination	- -	- -	0.007 (0.41)	- -	- -	-0.216* (-1.76)	- -	- -	0.015 (1.28)	- -	- -	0.002 (0.28)

Continued

	Participation rate			Standardized unemployment rate			Hours per worker			Income inequality		
	I	II	III	IV	V	VI	VII	VIII	IX	X	XI	XII
Union coverage	-	-	-0.036* (-1.81)	-	-	0.085 (0.51)	-	-	0.005 (0.27)	-	-	0.008 (1.20)
Time trend	0.000 (0.15)	0.000 (-0.17)	-0.001 (-0.68)	0.055*** (7.18)	0.045*** (5.40)	0.046*** (4.67)	-0.004* (-1.70)	-0.003 (-1.63)	-0.003* (-1.71)	0.003*** (5.46)	0.004*** (7.19)	0.004*** (7.06)
Constant	4.209*** (154.52)	4.206*** (85.01)	4.209*** (77.03)	-4.715*** (-9.92)	-5.447*** (-8.40)	-5.148*** (-8.00)	7.712*** (127.79)	7.833*** (138.14)	7.813*** (129.72)	3.496*** (204.39)	3.599*** (185.59)	3.597*** (155.77)
R^2	0.203	0.204	0.228	0.370	0.381	0.391	0.545	0.697	0.707	0.511	0.675	0.679
Number of observations	126	118	118	126	118	118	50	47	47	95	89	89
F-statistic	6.113	4.753	4.021	14.071	11.368	8.750	10.533	15.328	11.473	18.607	28.393	21.196

Notes:
t-statistics are reported in brackets below the parameter estimates.
All equations have been estimated without country-specific fixed effects.
* statistical significance at 10% level.
** statistical significance at 5% level.
*** statistical significance at 1% level.

171

A higher replacement rate corresponds with less inequality (column X) but with more unemployment (column IV). Furthermore, a higher rate is associated with less hours worked. This may indicate that a higher replacement rate gives rise to a more equal income distribution resulting in a smaller reward for working longer hours. Clearly, for this policy instrument, a trade-off between equity and efficiency seems to result. The effect on the participation rate is positive although small and far from statistically significant.[18] One explanation is that the replacement rate has two opposing effects. A higher rate leads to less labour demand and, thus, to more unemployment. It also encourages labour supply. A better insurance against unemployment risk, a higher replacement rate, provides a higher incentive to enter the labour market. The net effect of the replacement rate on participation is hence ambiguous.

The duration of unemployment benefit has a similar impact on unemployment and inequality as the level. Specifically, duration is positively related to unemployment and negatively related to inequality. In addition, it has a negative effect on participation, but not a significant effect on hours worked. In short, as was the case with benefit level, for benefit duration a clear trade-off also arises.

Employment protection also has a negative (and statistically significant) effect on participation and on hours worked. Since it tends to reduce inequality, a trade-off seems to arise. However, the effect on inequality is small and statistically insignificant. Interestingly, employment protection does not have a significant impact on unemployment. The main effect of employment protection is to reduce labour market flows, from employment to unemployment and vice versa. This probably means it would have more of an impact on the duration of unemployment rather than the rate of unemployment.[19]

The results for active labour market policies particularly stand out. Whereas the other three policy instruments give rise to a trade-off, spending on active labour market policies (per unemployed) does not. This type of spending boosts the rate of participation (column I), lowers the rate of unemployment (column IV), increases hours worked (column VII) – albeit not statistically significant – and reduces income inequality (column X). These results show that some forms of active labour market policy are effective, helping those with a relatively bad position in the labour market and a relatively low income.[20] Of course, the results show only the benefits of these policies, but not their financial costs. Moreover, it remains unclear which forms of active labour market policy are effective.

The results of the second step in which the tax wedge is added seem to fit the rule that creating jobs comes at the expense of more pronounced inequality. The tax wedge mitigates income differences, reduces hours worked and increases unemployment. The effect on participation is insignificant. Including this variable in the second step does not alter the result that active labour market polices have allowed countries to achieve better combinations of equity and efficiency: the effect of including the tax wedge on the coefficient for active labour market policies is small, both in terms of size as well as in terms of significance. The coefficient for spending on unemployed workers is hardly affected. Including the tax wedge reduces the effect of the replacement rate on unemployment and inequality – and these two variables are no longer significant. This may not seem surprising, given the fact that a higher replacement rate implies more expenditure (on unemployment benefits) and a higher tax burden. However, including the tax wedge magnifies the effect of benefit duration on unemployment as well as on inequality. Moreover, the effect of employment protection on income inequality even gets an unexpected sign.

The results of the third step are, one might say, reassuring. Even though the two union variables are strongly correlated with the other measures for labour market institutions, including them does not change the regression results much. Most affected is the coefficient for employment protection.

For policy-making, the results are interesting. As we illustrated in the introduction, several European countries face relatively low employment rates and high unemployment rates as compared to the US. This has given rise to several policy initiatives reforming the labour market and social security programmes, aimed at increasing participation and alleviating the unemployment problem (for example, Baily and Kirkegaard, 2004) However, achieving that usually gives rise to a dilemma. As a rule, a trade-off between employment and inequality emerges. Reducing benefit duration, for example, has the effect of raising participation, but also brings about more income inequality. Not surprisingly, this and similar measures often meet fierce social and political resistance and fuel the fear that Europe will end up with an American-style society in which everyone works because they have no other form of income support, and in which social-economic distinctions are sharp.

An exception to the rule is active labour market policy, which comprises amongst other things assistance with job search and schooling of (unemployed) workers. This type of instrument is effective in raising participation as well as reducing inequality. It has allowed countries like Denmark and Sweden to combine relatively generous social security systems (when measured by the replacement rate) and limited inactivity among the labour force. The regression analysis provides no conclusive evidence, but does suggest that European countries can improve employment while maintaining income equality by investing in active labour market policies. Not every form of active labour market policy is effective, though. The available evidence is scant, but already makes this apparent as seen for example, in Koning and Vollaard (2000), and Martin (2000). Their study is similar to this one in its set-up, covering the same time span and countries. It essentially extends the analysis in this chapter by investigating the impact of more detailed types of active labour market policies on labour market performance. The categories of expenses on active labour market policies that are distinguished are labour market training, youth measures, subsidized employment, employment measures for the disabled and employment services and administration. Systematic evaluations are still, however, needed. The OECD (2001) concludes from the few evaluations available that some inexpensive policies, like job-search assistance, are among the most cost-effective for a substantial number of unemployed. De Groot et al. (2004) come to a similar conclusion on the basis of a regression analysis.

Finally, the income gap between the richest European countries and the United States stems mainly from a difference in hours worked. If reducing the gap is the aim, the regressions do not provide reassuring results. Hours worked in Europe are on average relatively low since the tax wedge is relatively high, and income inequality is relatively low (as result of a high replacement rate). In other words, the reward for working longer hours is rather low in Europe. Changing this is one way to close the income gap with the United States, but at the expense of more income inequality, both before and after taxation.

8.4   CONCLUSION

US citizens are on average far richer than Europeans. Production per capita is on average more than 30 per cent higher in the United States than in the European Union. This does not result from a general gap in technology. It also does not result from a general difference in participation in the labour market. In fact, some European economies are better at providing jobs than the American economy. Instead, the income difference arises from a difference in hours worked. Whereas Americans work on average 1865 hours per year, Europeans work only around 1600 hours. There is a concomitant difference in income per capita but not necessary in welfare, since the income statistics ignore the value of leisure and household production.

Behind the averages are important differences within Europe. In continental Europe (that is, Belgium, France, Italy and Germany) participation is far lower than on the other side of the Atlantic. The explanation which is most often offered is the extensive social security system in continental Europe. Implementing lower and less generous social security coverage would help to make Europe more 'competitive' and would help to raise the rate of participation. The fear is that this would come at the expense of larger, American-style income differences.

The panel-data analysis for OECD countries undertaken in this chapter shows why different countries achieve different combinations of social-economic performance. Income redistribution (through a social security system) does not necessarily lead to lower participation and higher unemployment as long as countries supplement it with active labour market policies. These results are robust in a statistical sense. For hours worked, however, a trade-off is more difficult to escape. The tax wedge has an important negative effect on hours worked. Since it directly affects the choice between work and leisure, this is hardly surprising. At the same time, reducing the tax wedge probably requires reducing public expenditure and will lead to larger after-tax income differences.

ANNEX

Data Sources

This Annex describes the sources and content of the data used in this study.

Hours per inhabitant, employment rate and hours per worker
These data are taken from GGDC Total Economy Database 2003 (GGDC, 2004). The database contains series for real GDP, population, employment, annual working hours, GDP per capita, GDP per person employed and GDP per hour. It covers 74 countries from 1950 onwards.

Details on the data sources used for Table 8.4
- Participation: taken from Nickell and Nunziata (2001). Defined as total civilian employment normalized on the working age population (15–64) (from CEP OECD data, updated by authors).
- Hours worked per worker: Own computations based on data taken from GGDC Total Economy Database 2003 and 2004 (University of Groningen and the Conference Board; data are available at www.eco.rug.nl/ggdc).
- Inequality: Estimated Household Income Inequality taken from Galbraith and Kum (2003). We refer to Nahuis and de Groot (2003) for a more extensive discussion on available inequality measures. An alternative though less attractive variable available for long time spans is the Theil inequality measure provided by the University of Texas Inequality Project (UTIP). This measure is based on pay inequality in the manufacturing sector.

- Standardized unemployment rate: taken from Belot (2003).
- Replacement rate: taken from Nickell and Nunziata (2001). They use Benefit Replacement Rates data provided by OECD with one observation every two years for each country in the sample. The data refer to first year of unemployment benefits, averaged over family types of recipients, since in many countries benefits are distributed according to family composition. The benefits are a percentage of average earnings before tax.
- Employment protection: taken from Nickell and Nunziata (2001). They use information from Blanchard and Wolfers (2000) who use an employment protection time varying variable from 1960 to 1995, each observation taken every five years. Range is {0,2} increasing with strictness of employment protection.
- Benefit duration: An index. See Nickell and Nunziata (2001) for details.
- Active-labour-market policy: taken from Nickell (1997).
- Coordination: Belot (2003).
- Union coverage: taken from Belot (2003).
- Tax measures: Data on average and marginal taxes are taken from the OECD. Our measure for tax progression is derived from the average and marginal tax data.
- Tax wedge: Our measure for the tax wedge is taken from Nickell and Nunziata (2001) and is equal to the sum of the employment tax rate, the direct tax rate and the indirect tax rate (see Nickell and Nunizata for details).

NOTES

1. Henri de Groot and Paul Tang would like to dedicate this chapter to the memory of Richard Nahuis who so sadly and unexpectedly passed away during the proof-reading stage of this chapter.
    The authors would like to thank the participants at the CofFEE-Europe workshop and Michèle Belot, Henk Don, Sjef Ederveen, Casper van Ewijk, Theo van de Klundert, Pierre Koning and Ruud de Mooij for discussions and comments.
2. We define the employment rate here as the share of employed in the total population. A more commonly used indicator for economic performance in this respect is the participation rate that is defined as the share of the labour force in the population aged between 15 and 65. Evidently, the employment rate is related to participation, but note that the latter also includes the unemployed in the numerator and excludes persons aged below 15 and above 65 from the denominator.
3. Other examples include Daveri and Tabellini (2000) and Scarpetta (1996).
4. See also Andersen (2004) for a more in-depth analysis of the Scandinavian welfare model.
5. Although Freeman acknowledges the usefulness of cross-sectional analyses as a complement to within-country studies that exploit changes in institutions over time and comparisons of groups of workers that are covered by different institutions, he points out two important problems with cross-country analyses. Most importantly, he points out the possibility that countries differ in many institutional dimensions, implying that differences

in outcomes can be explained in different ways. Furthermore, he points to the possibility that institutions that work in one country may not work in another because of other differences in institutions that mutually interact. Acknowledging these difficulties, we argue that macroeconomic cross-country studies extended with time series analysis are a useful complement to more microeconomic-oriented studies.

6   More specifically, we use the definition $H/P = (H/W)*(W/F)*(F/P_A)*(P_A/P)$, where H is the total number of hours worked, P is the population, W is the number of people with a job, F is the size of the workforce (people with a job plus the unemployed), and P_A is the number of people aged between 15 and 65. Taking logs and differences with the United States, we arrive at relative differences between a country and the United States. Note that the empirical basis for this decomposition is slightly different from the information that was presented in Table 8.1. There we showed hours per inhabitant (H/P), hours per worker (H/W), workers per inhabitant (W/P), and the unemployment rate $(1 - W/F)$.

7.   Similar figures for all other countries are available in the Annex to this chapter, which is available at www.henridegroot.net/downloads.asp (under 'notes and appendices').

8.   Note that the numbers in Table 8.1 and Table 8.2 are strongly related. In Table 8.1, we showed hours per inhabitant of a country relative to that of the US, whereas in Table 8.2 we decompose the difference between the log of the number of hours worked per inhabitant of a country and that of the US into its components (see note 6 for the definition of the number of hours worked per inhabitant resulting in our decomposition).

9.   Of course, in many jobs workers have no choice over the number of hours worked. Hours worked are often institutionally constrained. Workers for whom the constraint is binding might also face a different valuation at the margin.

10.   Kimball and Shapiro (2003, p. 1) write that 'One of the best-documented regularities in economics is that – when they affect all members of a household proportionately – large, permanent differences in the real wage induce at most modest differences in the quantity of labor supplied by a household ... The standard explanation is that the substitution and income effects of a permanently higher real wage are of approximately the same size'.

11.   However, lowering tax progression is not without risks. Decreasing progressivity makes it more difficult to redistribute income but could also have important side-effects on macroeconomic productivity, especially in Europe. For example, progressive taxes help to moderate wage demands (of trade unions) and in this way help to reduce unemployment.

12.   In our dataset, for 14 OECD countries the simple coefficient of correlation between the average participation rate and the average standardized unemployment rate in the period 1989–94 is -0.83.

13.   These countries are Australia, Austria, Belgium, Canada, Denmark, Finland, France, Germany, Ireland, Italy, Japan, the Netherlands, New Zealand, Norway, Sweden, Switzerland, the United Kingdom and the United States.

14.   More specifically, the corporatist countries are Austria, Belgium, France, Germany, Italy, the Netherlands and Japan; the social-democratic countries are Denmark, Sweden, Finland and Norway; and the liberal countries are Ireland, the United Kingdom, the United States, Switzerland, Australia, Canada and New Zealand.

15.   The data sources are given in the annex.

16.   Even for these variables, the mutual correlation is not negligible.

17.   Our data for active labour market policies are taken from Nickell (1997). Their availability is restricted to the periods 1984–89 and 1989–94. In order optimally to exploit the information in our dataset for the other variables and to avoid serious biases in the estimates for active labour market policies, we have filled the non-available data for active labour market policies in our dataset with expenditures on active labour market policies in the closest period for which data are available. We have analysed the robustness of our results by (1) performing the analysis without filling the series for active labour market policies (and accepting the loss of observations that results); (2) using data on active labour market policies from the OECD that cover a longer time span; and (3) using lags of active labour market policies to account for the possible problem of endogeneity. These sensitivity tests are reported in de Groot et al. (2004). The data on benefit duration are taken from Nickell and Nunziata and contain several zeros. We find these slightly

suspicious. The results in Table 8.4 are based on information on benefit duration in which the zeros have been replaced by the value for benefit duration in the closest year for which information is available. As with active labour market policies, we have done sensitivity analyses to establish the robustness of the results for this change to the original data supplied by Nickell and Nunziata.
18. Nickell (1997) comes up with a similar result.
19. Indeed, Nickell (1997) finds that employment protection has a positive effect on long-term unemployment and a negative effect on short-term unemployment.
20. We performed some additional robustness checks (see de Groot et al., 2004). The results in general, and particularly the impact of active labour market policies, are robust to changes in data sources, i.e. the countries that are included, the time period that is considered, the estimation technique used, etc.

REFERENCES

Andersen, T.M. (2004), 'Challenges to the Scandinavian welfare model', *European Journal of Political Economy*, **20**, 743–754.
Baily, M.N. and J.F. Kirkegaard (2004), *Transforming the European Economy*, Institute for International Economics, Washington, DC.
Becker, G.S. (2002), 'Is Europe starting to play by US rules?', *Business Week*, April 22.
Belot, M. (2003), *Labor Market Institutions in OECD Countries: Origins and Consequences*, PhD thesis, Center for Economic Research, Tilburg University, Tilburg, The Netherlands.
Blanchard, O. and J. Wolfers (2000), 'The role of shocks and institutions in the rise of European unemployment: The aggregate evidence', *Economic Journal*, **110** (462), C1–33.
Boeri, T. (2002), *Making Social Europe(s) Compete*, unpublished paper prepared for a conference at Harvard University on Transatlantic Perspectives on US–EU Economic Relations: Convergence, Conflict and Co-operation, 11–12 April.
Cette, G. (2004), 'Is hourly labour productivity structurally higher in some major European countries than it is in the United States?' *International Productivity Monitor*, **10** (spring), 59–68.
Daveri, F. and G. Tabellini (2000), 'Unemployment, growth and taxation in industrial countries', *Economic Policy: A European Forum*, **15**, 47–88.
Esping-Andersen, G. (1999), *Social Foundations of Post-industrial Economics*, Oxford: Oxford University Press.
Freeman, R. (1998), 'War of the models: which labour market institutions for the 21st Century?', *Labour Economics*, **5** (1), 1–24.
Galbraith, J.K. and H. Kum (2002), 'Inequality and Economic Growth: Data Comparisons and Econometric Tests', *Inequality Project Working Paper No. 21*, University of Texas.
Galbraith, J.K. and H. Kum (2003), 'Estimating the inequality of household income: filling gaps and fixing problems in Deininger & Squire', *Inequality Project Working Paper No. 22*, University of Texas.
GGDC Groningen Growth and Development Centre (2004), *Total Economy Database (2004)*, available at http://www.eco.rug.nl/ggdc, University of Groningen, Groningen, The Netherlands.

Golden, M., P. Lange and M. Wallerstein (2002) 'Union centralisation among advanced industrialised societies: An empirical study', dataset available at http://www.shelley.polisci.ucla.edu/data.

Groot, H.L.F. de, R. Nahuis and P. Tang (2004), 'Is the American model Miss World? Choosing between the Anglo-Saxon Model and a European Style Alternative', *CPB Discussion Paper no. 40*, Netherlands Bureau for Economic Policy Analysis (CPB), The Hague, The Netherlands: CPB.

Kimball, M.S. and M.D. Shapiro (2003), *Labor Supply: Are the Income and Substitution Effects Both Large or Both Small?*, Unpublished paper, University of Michigan.

Koning, P. and B. Vollaard (2000), 'Arbeidsbemiddeling en -reïntegratie van werklozen: welke rol heeft de overheid te spelen?', *CPB Document no. 118*, Netherlands Bureau for Economic Policy Analysis (CPB), The Hague, The Netherlands: CPB.

Martin, J. (2000), 'What works among active labour market policies: rvidence from OECD vountries' experiences', in OECD, *Policies Towards Full Employment*, Paris: OECD.

Nahuis, R. and H.L.F. de Groot (2003), 'Rising skill premia: you ain't seen nothing yet?', *CPB Discussion Paper no. 20*, Netherlands Bureau for Economic Policy Analysis (CPB), The Hague, The Netherlands: CPB.

Nickell, S. (1997), 'Unemployment and labor market rigidities', *Journal of Economic Perspectives*, **11**, 55–74.

Nickell, S. and R. Layard (1999), 'Labour market institutions and economic performance', in O. Aschenfelter and D. Card, *Handbook of Labor Economics*, Amsterdam: Elsevier Science.

Nickell, S. and L. Nunziata (2001), Labour Market Institutions Database, (Version 2.00, 1960–95).

OECD (2001), *Employment Outlook 2001*, OECD, Paris.

Scarpetta, S. (1996), 'Assessing the role of labour market policies and institutional settings on unemployment: a cross-country study', *OECD Economic Studies*, **26** (2), 43–98.

9. Enhancing Productivity: Social Protection as Investment Policy

Chris de Neubourg and Julie Castonguay

9.1 INTRODUCTION

Under the Lisbon Agenda, the EU member states agreed to make major efforts to become the most competitive economic area in the world. Often, either explicitly or implicitly, EU social policy practices are presented as obstacles towards this policy objective. This chapter argues that on the contrary that:

- the trade-off between equity and efficiency only exists under very specific assumptions;
- social policy can increase productivity and efficiency by reducing transaction costs and poverty;
- there is no reason to believe that we could not make further progress in making social policy more (cost-) efficient and effective;
- a simplified social policy framework, recognizing both incentives and implementation costs as relevant design parameters, can contribute to improving effectiveness and efficiency.

9.2 EQUITY AND EFFICIENCY: OPTIMAL SOCIAL PROTECTION

Traditionally it is assumed that there is a direct trade-off between equity and efficiency; making an economy more equitable can be done only at the expense of less efficient production and thus less overall wealth. This is reflected in the shape of the 'social policy production possibility frontier' ABC in Figure 9.1. However, economic growth theory and empirical research on the relationship between growth and equity seem to point to a more complicated analysis. From an international comparative and long-term historical perspective, there are good reasons to believe that, at least for certain stages of economic development, (a certain degree of) equity and economic growth are preconditions for each other rather than competing economic forces. Rethinking the shape of the social policy production possibility frontier (SPPPF) in Figure 9.1, we should at least assume that for (very) low values of equity and efficiency, the relationship is positive and upward sloping and goes through the origin since it is hard to imagine that an economy could produce wealth without redistribution if all the wealth were kept. For this reason, the curve OBC would appear to be a reasonable representation. This relationship is, however, asymmetric in the sense that in an economy with wealth perfectly equitably distributed (by whatever mechanism), production and thus efficiency is still possible (hence C in the OBC-SPPPF).

   If it is argued in policy discussions that social policy decreases efficiency and thus the competitiveness of an economy, then in fact it is argued that:

1. the economy produces social policy on the social policy production possibility frontier; and
2. the economy produces social policy on a point at the right of B (for example D in Figure 9.1).

   This empirical assessment is difficult to prove (or disprove) but it is highly unlikely. There is no reason why the current situation of the European economies could not be characterized by either any point left of B on the frontier (for example D') or any point below OBC (for example E). In both cases, improvements in social policy and equity could be made without damaging efficiency or could even stimulate efficiency. While it is impossible to illustrate empirically that D' or E are close to current reality, it is equally impossible to sustain the argument that we produce social policy on a point on the SPPPF at the right of D: the latter is much more restrictive in its assumptions on the possibilities.

   Moreover, in a dynamic environment allowing technical progress, we can also shift the SPPPF outwards by improving the design of, instruments used in and/or implementation of social policy. The SPPPF would then take the shape of OB'C' and we would shift towards an optimistic version of the world allowing more efficiency and more equity at the same time, features that would continue in the future.

   This chapter develops the arguments along these lines. It illustrates how more equity may lead to more efficiency by reducing transaction costs and poverty. It demonstrates that social policy is important in reducing poverty, and that poverty reduction is not just a by-product of more economic growth. Poverty reduction is also shown to be a driving force behind the increase in both equity and efficiency. The chapter argues that cutting expenditure on

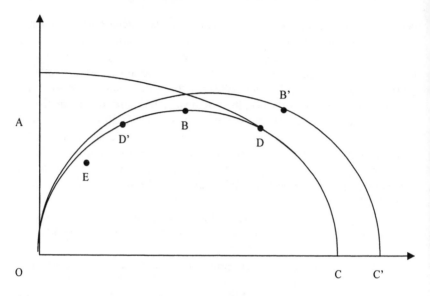

Figure 9.1   Social Policy Production Possibility Frontier

social policy does not necessarily lead to lower costs. A way to improve the actual technology of social policy design in an attempt to shift the SPPPF outwards is also explored in the chapter.

9.3   MORE EFFICIENCY THROUGH MORE EQUITY

9.3.1   Social Protection Increases Productivity because it Reduces Poverty

On the household level, poverty leads to lower investment in and accumulation of human and social capital as well as risk-averse behaviour leading to suboptimal choices of the risk management portfolio (Holzmann and Jorgensen, 2002). If social policy can reduce poverty, it hence will stimulate productive investment and contribute to more efficiency.

The question that must be considered first, however, is whether there are serious differences in poverty levels between countries. The following analysis refers mainly to differences between continental Europe on the one hand and the USA and the UK on the other.

Since 2001, all members of the European Union have agreed to provide the European statistical agency, Eurostat, with a set of social indicators called the Laeken Common Indicators of Social Inclusion. In view of the fact that poverty has multiple dimensions, the Laeken Common Indicators include various poverty lines as well as different types of poverty measurement in order to depict poverty in a manner that is most informative of the situation in each country. In Table 9.1, some of these poverty rates are presented for the nine European countries under study as well as the United States. The most striking feature that can be seen from this table is the large gap between the poverty rate in Europe and the poverty rate in the United States, whereby the poverty rate in the latter is almost three times as large as the poverty rate in Belgium, Germany, the Netherlands and Sweden. The rate in the United Kingdom is between that of the Northern European countries and the Southern

Table 9.1   Laeken Common Indicators of Social Inclusion, 2001

	Risk-of-Poverty[a]				Persistent risk-of-poverty[b]		Relative risk-of-poverty gap[c]
	40%	50%	60%	70%	60%	50%	
Belgium	2	6	13	21	7	3	15
France	4	9	15	23	9	3	19
Germany	3	6	11	19	6	3	19
Italy	8	13	19	27	13	7	28
Netherlands	4	6	11	19	5	2	20
Portugal	6	13	20	28	15	8	22
Spain	7	13	19	27	10	6	24
Sweden	2	5	9	17	-	-	17
United Kingdom	5	11	17	26	10	5	23
United States[d]		17.5					

Notes:
a   In percentage of median income.
b   The share of persons with an income below the risk-of-poverty threshold (percentage of median income) in the current year and at least two of the preceding three years.
c   The difference between the median income of persons below the at-risk-of-poverty threshold, expressed as a percentage of the at-the-risk-of-poverty threshold.
d   Figure from the United States from an OECD study by Oxley et al. (1999), refers to the year 1995. Oxley et al. used a methodology similar to that used by Eurostat, which is a measure of poverty that is relative to the 50% median income of the population.

Source: Eurostat (2004).

Southern European countries shown in this table. This rank order holds no matter which poverty rate is used for comparison.

Further to this, using survey data on large samples of the Luxembourg Income Study group, Ritakallio (2002) comes to similar conclusions concerning the country rankings, although different poverty levels are found. In this study the United Kingdom ranks in a position between the countries of northern continental Europe and the United States. According to these estimates, poverty (measured as having a disposable income of less than 50 per cent of the median income) was 17.5 per cent in the United States in 1995 while the rate in continental European countries was around 7.5 per cent with Sweden as low as 3.2 per cent. The poverty rate in the United Kingdom was 12.4 per cent.

Smeeding and Rainwater (2004) compare living standards across nations based on real income comparisons using Purchasing Power Parities (PPPs). A comparison of the purchasing power of persons in various deciles across 13 countries in the OECD area was made (see Table 9.2). Their analysis indicates that while the average American has a higher living standard than the average resident in the other countries considered[1] (columns 1 and 2 in Table 9.2), this does not hold for the entire spectrum of the income distribution. Despite the higher aggregate and average standard of living in the United States, people in the lower deciles of the income distribution are far worse off in that country than poorer persons or households in all other countries if compared to the median income of their own country (column 3, Table 9.2). Even if compared with the median US income, the poor in the other countries are better off with the exception of the poorer people in the United Kingdom (column 4, Table 9.2). The income distribution in the United States is the most unequal distribution of adjusted household income. This is not simply due to the fact that richer households have a much higher disposable income, but also to the fact that poorer Americans have a seriously lower disposable income than people in lower-income strata in the other countries. While the average French or Dutch citizen has a real income of approximately 80 per cent of that of an average American, the low-income (10th decile) French or Dutch person has an income that is 110 per cent of the income of the low-income American (for details see Smeeding and Rainwater, 2004).

According to the study by Ritakallio (2002) and as shown in Table 9.3, (after taxes-/after benefits-) poverty rates increased by 2.5 per cent in the United States in the period 1981–95 while in the same period comparable poverty rates in France and Sweden and Norway did not change. Poverty (Germany, the Netherlands) increased by approximately the same percentage as in the United States while the increase in the United Kingdom was larger

Table 9.2   Income of average person and average person in the tenth decile
             (D10): international comparison 1999

	Average person relative to US person (PPP)	Average overall GDP per capita relative to US	Average D10 as % of median income country (PPP)	Average D10 as % of median income United States (PPP)
Belgium	87	73	59	47
Denmark	811	80	54	43
France	79	65	54	43
Germany	79	70	54	44
Netherlands	80	77	56	43
Sweden	68	68	60	40
United Kingdom	69	68	46	33
United States	100	100	38	39

Note:
Difference between columns three and four due to difference in the equivalence scale used; for details see source.

Source: compiled from Smeeding and Rainwater (2002).rates in some other countries

(5 per cent). Note that the poverty rates in Canada and Finland actually declined over the same period.

Assessing the dynamics of poverty and considering indicators on how long people stay in poverty is also necessary for comparative purposes. If people are temporarily poor, the behavioural consequences noted at the beginning of this section may be much milder. Table 9.4 illustrates this issue. Considering disposable incomes after taxes and transfers, it can be seen that in the continental European countries, between 1 and 2 per cent of the population was poor over a five-year period. This is a considerably smaller percentage of the population than in the United Kingdom and the United States where, respectively, 6.1 and 4.6 per cent of the population was poor throughout the period. The same difference can be observed when considering the percentage of the population who were poor at least once during the five-year period as well as the exits from poverty during the same period (columns 4 and 5 in Table 9.4). More than a quarter of the population in the United States and more than one-third of the population in the United Kingdom experienced

Table 9.3   Poverty rates (% of population < 50% of median): rounded changes 1981–95

	Absolute change in poverty rates after transfers	Absolute change in poverty rates before income transfers
Canada	-1	6
Finland	-3	11
France	0	8
Germany	3	6
Netherlands	3	2
Norway	0	6
Sweden	0	9
United Kingdom	5	13
United States	2.5	5

Source: compiled from Ritakallio (2002), pp. 13, 14, 16.

experienced poverty during the early 1990s. In the continental European countries, the equivalent percentage was around 12 per cent in the Netherlands and Sweden and 20 per cent in Germany. Consistent with this, many more people experienced an exit from poverty in that period in Germany, the Netherlands and Sweden (overall around 40 per cent of the poor) compared with the United Kingdom and the United States, where only around 30 per cent of persons were able to do so.

Summarizing, it can be said that in terms of both levels and duration of poverty the United States and the United Kingdom show a worse performance than the continental European countries (to a lesser or greater extent depending on the figures chosen). In the United States and the United Kingdom more people experience poverty and stay longer in poverty than in the continental European countries. The standard of living of the poor in the former countries is also worse than in the latter group of countries.

Poverty does not affect all groups in a society evenly. Moreover for some groups, particularly children, longer spells of poverty have much deeper consequences than for others. This is especially important in this context

Table 9.4   Dynamic poverty rates

	Year	Poor throughout the period – % of population	Poor at least once over the period – % of population	Exits from poverty* as % of poor
Post-taxes and transfers				
Canada	1990–95	1.8	28.1	41.8
Germany	1991–96	1.8	19.9	37.0
Netherlands	1991–96	0.8	12.1	43.7
Sweden	1991–96	1.1	11.9	36.3
United Kingdom	1991–96	6.1	38.4	29.1
United States	1989–93	4.6	26.0	28.6
Pre-taxes and transfers				
Canada	1990–95	14.3	42.0	17.1
Germany	1991–96	14.4	38.0	13.8
Netherlands	1991–96	13.5	32.2	12.3
Sweden	1991–96	19.0	45.4	11.6
United Kingdom	1991–96	23.1	54.4	12.3
United States	1989–93	8.3	31.5	20.4

Note:
* The number of poor in period t who exit poverty in t+1, averaged over the period.

Source: Oxley et al.(2000a).

because of the crucial role that human capital investments play for economic growth and competitiveness.

Table 9.5 shows estimates of the number of children living in households with earnings of less than 50 per cent of the median income. Again the same type of differences can be observed: in 1995 in Sweden and Belgium less than 5 per cent of children lived in poor households. In France, the Netherlands and Germany this figure was around 10 per cent or less, while in

Table 9.5   Percentage share of children living in households with less income than 50% of median income

Country	Year	Child poverty rate
Belgium	1995	4.1
Canada	1995	14.2
France	1994	7.1
Germany	1994	10.6
Italy	1993	18.8
Netherlands	1995	9.1
Sweden	1995	2.7
United Kingdom	1995	18.6
United States	1995	23.2

Source: Förster (2000)

Italy, the United Kingdom and the United States approximately one in five children, or more, lived in poor households. This has serious consequences, not only for the circumstances in which the children grow up but especially for the related incentives and opportunities for investment in human capital (and thus for economic productivity and the future income positions of the children involved), particularly in countries like the United States where access to good-quality education is expensive. Poor children in the United States, and particularly in the United Kingdom, have considerably less purchasing power (and thus are worse off) than their peers in poor households in continental Europe. This is illustrated by the figures in the column of Table 9.6 headed 'Real incomes'. The figures express the purchasing power of low-income children (1st decile of the income distribution) in all countries as a percentage of disposable income for the same group of children in the United States (putting the United States at 100). Consistent with the previous figures, children of low-income families are best off in Sweden, the Netherlands, Belgium, Germany and France and worst off in the United Kingdom. In the former group of countries they have a considerably higher purchasing power than in the United States, while low-

Table 9.6   *Real standards of living for children: disposable income for children in lowest decile (D1) expressed as index with the United States = 100 and decile ratio D10/D1 (mid-1990s)*

	Real incomes	Decile ratio (D10/D1)
Belgium (1996)	126	2.89
France (1994)	126	3.11
Germany (1994)	114	3.03
Netherlands (1994)	120	2.62
Sweden (1995)	137	2.02
United Kingdom (1995)	89	4.10
United States (1997)	100	5.11

Note:
Figures are calculated on 1997 US PPP adjusted dollars per equivalent person, weighted for the number of children in each unit size.

Source: Smeeding and Rainwater (2002), Figures 3 and 6.

income families with children in the United Kingdom have considerably less purchasing power in terms of income than their US peers.

Looking at the differences from an equal opportunity point of view, Smeeding and Rainwater (2002) calculated the real income gap between children from the lowest decile and the children from the highest decile (again expressed in PPPs). This information is presented under the column 'Decile ratio (D10/D1)' of Table 9.6. The decile ratio (D10/D1) is more than 5 for the United States and more than 4 for the United Kingdom, indicating that families with children from the highest income group (D10) can spend as much as five times more in the US and four times more in the UK than families with children from the lowest income group (D1). In the continental European countries this ratio is between 2 and 3, with Sweden showing the smallest difference (2.02). In dollar terms, the income gap between the average child in the highest income group compared with the average child in the lowest income group is about US$40 000 per year for the United States and US$14 000 a year for Sweden (for details see Smeeding and Rainwater, 2004).

On the basis of the previous analyses it can be concluded that there are large and systematic differences between continental Europe on the one hand and the Anglo-Saxon countries (the United Kingdom and the United States) on the other, with the United Kingdom often taking a middle position between the first and the second group and with the Southern European countries performing less well than the other continental European countries. The question is whether these systematic differences in distributional performance can be explained by differences in the social protection systems in place in these countries or whether they can be explained by other factors. Alesina and Glaeser (2004) explore the economic interpretations for explaining the differences illustrated above. Their explanations are based on:

1. the Romer–Meltzer–Richard model – that redistributive policies are the logical consequence of more people being poor relative to the average;
2. the theory of the prospect of upward mobility – which is that people who expect future increases in income will be opposed to higher taxes and that economies with better prospects for future upward mobility will tend to oppose higher taxes; and
3. differences in the efficiency of tax collection.

They find, however, that none of these explanations stand up to empirical scrutiny.

They point to the major influence of more elaborate social protection systems and use political economy to explain why continental European countries have built different and more encompassing social protection systems than the Anglo-Saxon countries. Assessing the exact role of Social Protection systems for explaining the differences in distributional performance between Europe and the United States is not an easy task, but all empirical information points to the fact that social protection systems do have a considerable influence.

The pre-tax and transfer figures for the dynamics of poverty are presented in Table 9.4. These data show that the rate of long-term poor in the population before transfers and taxes is lower in the United States than in any European country. The United Kingdom and surprisingly Sweden have the highest rates of poverty. The same broad ranking of countries applies for the occasionally poor (at least once in the five-year period). Looking from this perspective, the United Kingdom social protection system delivers good results as does the Swedish system. Comparing the upper and lower parts of Table 9.4, it is not difficult to conclude that direct taxes and social transfers contribute substantially to the alleviation of poverty in all countries, although in the United States less markedly so than in others.

The role of the social protection system can also be judged from international differences in the poverty risk between households with an earning parent and households without one. In Europe the differences are much smaller, indicating that the social protection system steps in to 'correct' the differences between the two groups of households. The differences between such households in the United States are larger (see Oxley, Dang, Förster and Pellizari, 2000).

A number of studies have estimated the impact of taxes, transfers and other income components on inequality and poverty. The most comprehensive results are found in an OECD study by Oxley et al., (1999) where changes in the Gini coefficients are decomposed by income component for 13 countries. The results indicate that, in all the countries, taxes and transfers played a significant role in containing the growing inequality due to growing differences in market earnings. Similar results were found by Ritakallio (2002). Table 9.7 shows the contribution of various elements of disposable income to inequality. It can be seen that taxes and transfers played a major role. The fact that transfers seemingly have a smaller influence is a result of the methodology (see Oxley et al., 1999, for an explanation of the Shorrocks decomposition that was used) and the fact that taxes affect the entire income distribution while transfers primarily affect the bottom part.

Table 9.7   Contribution of income components to the level of inequality: Shorrocks decomposition; percent and changes in percentage points

| | % contribution to total inequality of disposable income | | | | |
	Earnings	Capital and self-employment	Transfers	Taxes	Total transfers and taxes
Belgium, 1995	67.5	88.7	-0.5	-55.7	-56.2
Germany, 1994	115.9	29.9	0.6	-46.4	-45.8
Italy, 1993	41.4	95.4	4.3	-41.1	-36.8
Netherlands, 1994	131.1	45.4	-12.5	-63.9	-76.4
Sweden, 1995	138.3	26.5	4.7	-69.5	-64.8

Source: Oxley et al., (1999).

Another OECD study (Förster, 2000) indicated that in many OECD countries the main contributor to widening income inequality has been the widening distribution of gross earnings. Gross earnings and even more so, income from capital and self-employment, have become more important in explaining differences in the growth path of disposable incomes. The share of market income in the three bottom deciles in many OECD countries is small (generally less than 12 per cent), while the share of market income going to higher incomes is large (between 47 and 77 per cent depending on the item). In all countries the share of earnings going to the lower seven deciles of the distribution declined between 1980 and 1995 (except for Ireland where the share of market income in the deciles 4 to 7 increased). Among market incomes, the dispersion of capital and self-employment related earnings have a faster growth path than of other earnings (mainly labour). The increased dispersion of labour market income was particularly evident in Australia, Denmark, France, the Netherlands, Sweden and the United States. Dispersion of capital income and income from self-employment has increased particularly in Canada, Finland, Germany, Italy, Sweden and the United Kingdom. The study further supports the thesis of an 'employment polarisation' (Gregg and Wadsworth, 1996) indicating that an important aspect of increased inequality is due to the relative income positions of 'fully employed' households, where all adult members are employed, and 'workless' households, where no adult member is employed. This phenomenon was found to be important in nine of 11 European OECD countries.

The effect of employment concentration among a specific group of households (as opposed to employment dispersed among all households) on increased income inequality is not easily assessed. In the OECD study by Förster (2000) increased income inequality mainly due to the fact that there were relatively more 'workless' households holds only for France and Greece; in most other countries income inequality increased because of increasing inequality within the group of 'fully employed households' as well as within the group of 'workless households'. Only in the United States and in Germany was the disparity between the two groups the major contributor to the increased inequality.

The fact that inequality increased far more than poverty rates, indicates that the importance of taxes and government transfers has increased over the period from the early 1980s to the mid-1990s. This is exactly what has been found in various studies for the majority of the countries considered here (see for example Förster, 2000; Behrendt, 2000a; Cantillon and van den Bosch, 2000). This indicates a kind of paradox in the sense that in a period where social protection systems have been heavily criticized for overburdening the economy, they have become more and more important in terms of their distributional effects. Market forces have led to an increase in inequality and social protection arrangements have been responsible for counteracting this. There are two notable exceptions here: the Netherlands and the United Kingdom. In both countries the shrinking of the welfare state has contributed more to the increase in income inequality than increasing earning differentials (Caminada and Goudswaard, 2000).[2]

It is also interesting to try to understand who is losing and who is gaining. Relative positions of various groups changed during the 1980s and 1990s and countries may be divided into three groups according to the distributional outcomes (Förster, 2000). In the Nordic countries (and also partially in the United States) redistribution has been from the active age-groups towards both the elderly and children. In the other European countries the young, including children, particularly lost in income shares, while the elderly and the middle age groups gained. In the United Kingdom, the losses were situated at both ends of the income distribution while only those on middle incomes gained.

Cantillon and van den Bosch (2000) simulated overall poverty rates for 2005 and 2010 under two different assumptions: that all incomes rise by 2 per cent and that all incomes with the exception of transfer incomes rise by 2 per cent.[3] The results, shown in Table 9.8, again illustrate the importance of social protection systems in alleviating poverty in OECD economies. When all transfer incomes increase by the same percentage as other incomes, poverty in Europe is reduced to 10.1 per cent in 2005 and to 7.9 per cent in 2010. However, when transfer incomes are frozen on their 1995 level, poverty rates would be 14.6 in 2005 and 13.6 per cent in 2010 (note that the 1995 poverty level is 17.2 per cent and 60 per cent of median income is used as the poverty line in all cases). The biggest effect would be experienced by aged persons, but poverty incidence would also increase considerably for children. This illustrates how even small adjustments in benefits (like not indexing benefits to the growth of other incomes) change the (relative) poverty count. Social protection systems have an important influence on poverty rates.

In summary, the impact of social protection systems is huge. While the continental European countries show internationally the highest income inequality before taxes and benefits, they display smaller inequalities after taxes and benefits. The interventionist and universalistic oriented social protection systems play an important role in this 'correction'. They also produce considerably lower poverty rates than other countries, reducing poverty to less than 7 per cent of the population compared with 17.5 per cent for the United States, with the United Kingdom and the Mediterranean countries taking an intermediate position. This ranking in 'poverty performance' holds whatever type of measurement or count is used and the

*Table 9.8   Simulated poverty rates in the European Union in 2005 and 2010
            using a constant poverty line; 2 per cent income growth of all
            incomes and of all incomes excluding transfer income*

	All incomes grow 2%		All incomes except transfers grow 2%	
	2005	2010	2005	2010
All households	10.1	7.9	14.6	13.6
All individuals	9.4	7.4	12.9	11.9
Children	10.3	8.0	13.3	11.7
Non-aged adults	9.2	7.3	11.5	10.3
Aged persons	10.2	7.7	18.0	18.3

Source: Cantillon and van den Bosch (2000), pp. 15, 16.

changes in poverty rates over the last decades show divergence between these
groups of countries rather than convergence. Social protection systems in
continental Europe are also more effective in the sense that they manage to
reduce the duration of poverty and the incidence of poverty over the life
cycle of individuals and households. The impact of social protection systems
is even more pronounced for children. While more than one out of five
children in the United States lives in poor households, this is only the case for
less than 4 per cent of the children in Belgium and Sweden.

9.3.2 Social Protection Decreases Productivity because it Increases Costs

Undeniably, the public organization of a social protection system changes the
economy; it has to be financed and benefits of any type influence the
economic behaviour of economic agents. Presenting social policies
theoretically as classic cases of market distortions, however, is not very
helpful in context. Empirical evidence, on the other hand, concerning the
combined effects is partial and usually considers single types of instruments
only. It is nevertheless possible to identify a number of factors that are
important when trying to explain why more social protection and more social
policy   expenditures   may   frustrate   competitiveness.   Social   policy
expenditures increase labour costs, crowd out other allocations on the capital
market, may lead to overconsumption (especially in health) and lead to moral

hazard providing disincentives to perform (especially through employment protection) and disincentives to active labour market participation. These propositions are examined below.

9.3.3 Cutting social policy expenditures does not necessarily lead to reduction in costs and hence does not lead directly to enhanced competitiveness

The main argument used by proponents of a reduction in social policies refers to costs, whereby production costs are assumed to increase and thus aggregate wealth is assumed to be lower than either would be without the social protection system. This is, however, only half of the reasoning because while social protection does indeed increase some of the costs, it also decreases other costs, both for individual agents and on an aggregate level. Table 9.9 summarizes the cost pressures of social protection on the economy and on individual agents, distinguishing between financing and benefits. The arrows in the table reflect upward and downward pressures. From the table it

Table 9.9   Main effects of social policy on the economy

		Micro-level (enterprises/individuals)	Macro-level (economy)
Financing	enterprises	↑ taxes and contributions	↑ crowding out on capital market
		↓ benefits subsitutes firm arrangements	↓ cheaper through economy wide risk pooling
	individuals	↑ risk pooling larger base ↑ taxes and contributions ↓ risk pooling	↑ increases labour supply ↓ reduces labour supply
Benefits	enterprises	↑ moral hazard wage pressure	↑ crowding out on labour market ↑ employment costs in stagnant services
		↓ adjustment costs	↓ increase in economic and social stability (aggregate demand)
	individuals	↑ moral hazard	↓ positive attitudes safety net
		↓ mobility cost ↓ human capital investment	↑ social stability (f.e. immigration) ↓ social stability

can be seen that the upward and downward pressures level out. Cost reductions are mainly due to efficiency gained in pooling of resources (and risks) and in reducing transaction costs of investment and transaction costs of economic adjustments.

The question of the ultimate effect is empirical and impossible to answer using available information. It is sufficient to note in the context of this chapter, however, that it is not necessarily true that lower social policy expenditures (less equity) means more efficiency or more economic growth.

The main underlying argument rests on the observation that social protection is not only producing equity, but that it also covers risks encountered by the economic agents (de Neubourg and Weigand, 2000). Prevention of hazardous situations, mitigation of effects of damaging events and facilitating the ability to cope with 'bad luck', are all functions of a well-working social protection system. That also implies that in the absence of a social protection system, the costs related to these risks do not disappear and still have to be paid for in the economy. In the absence of a publicly organized system, the costs of these risks are shifted towards what we have called elsewhere the other corners of the 'Welfare Pentagon' (de Neubourg, 2002). This means that costs incurred by the social protection system in many cases are still present in the economy. This is illustrated in Tables 9.10 and 9.11.

Table 9.10   Gross and net public and private expenditure on social protection, including health care, as a percentage of GDP, 1993

	Public gross	Public net	Private	Total (public net + private)
Belgium	27.3	n.a.	1.9	n.a.
Denmark	31.0	26.8	1.7	28.4
Germany	28.3	26.6	4.4	31.0
Netherlands	30.2	25.1	5.0	30.1
Sweden	38.0	34.1	2.9	37.0
United Kingdom	23.4	23.2	4.7	27.9
United States	15.6	15.5	11.9	27.4

Source: Berghman et al. (1998).

Table 9.11   Expenditures on social protection in Sweden and the United States as a percentage of GDP and as a percentage of household expenditures, 1990

	Sweden	USA
	As a percentage of GDP	
Public social expenditures	33.1	14.6
Tax expenditures	0.0	1.3
Private education	0.1	2.5
Private health	1.1	8.2
Private pensions	1.8	3.0
Total	35.5	28.3
	As a percentage of private household expenditures	
Health education and pensions	2.7	18.8
Day care	1.7	10.4
Total	4.4	29.2
Taxes	36.8	10.4
Total private + taxes	41.2	39.6

Notes:
a   Tax expenditures for the USA exclude those for pensions
b   Private health data for Sweden are for 1992; US data include 'other social welfare'. Private pensions for Sweden are estimated from employer pension benefits in the OECD national accounts. Swedish tax data are from Sveriges Statistika Aarsbok, 1994 (table T 226). US private pensions and health expenditures data are from Social Security Bulletin, Annual Statistical Supplement, 1992 (table 3A4).

Source: Esping-Andersen (1999), Table 9.1, p. 177.

The last column of Table 9.10 shows a remarkable uniformity in the total net expenditures for social protection among the countries examined here. While the public–private mix differs, especially between the United States and Europe, the overall expenditures are of a similar order of magnitude.

Table 9.11 shows public and private expenditures on social protection and compares Sweden (representing the countries with high levels of public spending on social protection) with the United States (at the lower end of public spending for social protection). As a percentage of GDP, total expenditures for education, child care, health and pensions for the USA are somewhat lower than in Sweden; as a percentage of household incomes, however, US households spend more on these items than Swedish households taking into consideration both private expenditures and taxes. This illustrates the fact that reducing expenditure on social protection does not necessarily lead to lower costs for households, nor indeed for the aggregate economy.

One issue that must be considered is whether public provision is less efficient and less effective than private provision, meaning that social policy may therefore be relatively costly and that less public social protection would therefore be desirable. There are no hard figures comparing the effectiveness of publicly and privately provided goods, but Table 9.4 estimates the share of administration costs in total social expenditures for some European countries and for the EU as a whole. It can safely be concluded that administration costs in most countries are very low and compare favourably with the administration costs of, for example, private pension funds or some types of private insurance (see Mitchell, 1998). The effectiveness of public social policy in terms of effective redistribution and targeting towards the poorest sections of the social spectrum is well documented in other publications (see de Neubourg, 2005a, 2005b). From these studies it is clear that the most developed welfare states, for example in Scandinavian Europe and the Benelux, are highly effective in allocating benefits to the poorest part of the population.

9.3.4 More Efficiency through more Equity

The first section of this chapter argued that there are no reasons suggesting that efficiency and equity are invariably inversely related. Moreover, there are good arguments to defend the proposition that efficiency gains could be made by more rather than less social protection. The second section explored why more social protection may indeed lead to more efficiency. The arguments are related to reductions in poverty and the related growth in human investment and reductions in transaction costs. It was illustrated that economies differ in poverty levels and that social protection plays a major role in explaining these differences. While the cost effects of social policy must be considered, the private costs of risk management in the absence of a public social protection system must equally be taken into account. It was illustrated that in terms of efficiency public systems perform at least as well as private systems.

If social protection can contribute to more efficiency, more productivity, more wealth and increased competitiveness, then it is worth exploring ways to improve the design and the implementation of social protection. It is worth, in the terminology of the first section, seeking opportunities to shift the social protection possibility frontier outwards by improving the production technology. In the following section, a proposal is formulated for part of the social protection system to be provided to the active age-groups.

9.4 A GENERALISED INCOME LOSS INSURANCE WITH NOTIONAL INDIVIDUAL ACCOUNTS

The labour force participation rate and the employment–population ratio are major concerns for EU member states attempting to reach the Lisbon policy objectives. Both are believed to be too low to sustain long-term growth and to keep a sufficiently broad tax-base into the future. Social policy in mature welfare states in Europe is blamed for at least part of the low employment–population ratios. It has been argued that generous early retirement schemes are an important factor lowering the number of workers over 55 years of age. On the other hand, generous unemployment benefit schemes and social assistance schemes are often said to act as disincentives for the unemployed and the non-employed to accept jobs. Despite reforms in many countries including lowering benefits, tightening eligibility rules and reducing benefit duration, the number of unemployed is still very high in many European countries.

The question is whether changes can be made in the existing design of benefits and insurance, so curbing existing trends and stimulating higher activity rates. Social assistance reforms are discussed elsewhere at length (see de Neubourg, 2005) and point in the direction of more financial pressure on the beneficiaries. The more successful practices provide more services to the recipients in terms of childcare facilities, job search assistance, training advice and employment exchange services in order to assist welfare recipients back into the labour market.

It would also be possible the revise entire unemployment benefit, sickness and social assistance schemes towards a simplified system that explicitly links contribution history to benefit entitlement rights without jeopardizing the social elements that form part of these schemes. Such a system is described below and involves the implementation of a unified and compulsory mandated Income Loss Insurance (ILI). The basics are simple.

All participants in the labour market contribute to a mandated publicly managed insurance scheme. They are entitled to receive a benefit whenever they are confronted with a situation that leads to income losses caused by unemployment or sickness for more than a basic period.[4] The level of the benefits is defined as B_1 in Figure 9.2 and is fixed for a period of six months.

After the first six months the benefit level declines gradually to reach zero. The speed of the decline is defined by the length of the contribution period of the insured – the longer the worker has contributed to the insurance, the slower the decline. The exact level (B_1) of the benefit during the first period would be set as a percentage of the last earned wage capped at a predefined level.[5] The benefit is given for a relatively predetermined short period in order to increase financial pressure on the beneficiaries. The period of six months is chosen because empirical evidence shows that after approximately that period, negative duration dependence becomes important.

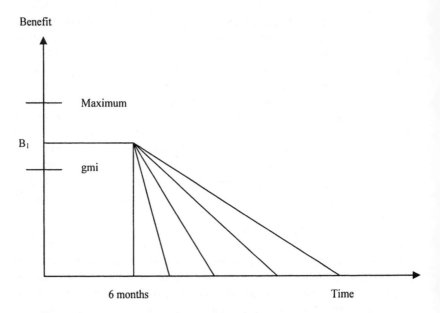

Figure 9.2   Income Loss Insurance with notional defined contributions

The first part of the benefit can be financed out of general revenue; the second part can be financed in a similar way to notional defined contributory pension systems using pay-as-you-go type financing but linking the benefits of the recipients to their actual contribution history, so defining both the level and the duration of the benefit entitlements.[6] The system is simple and can be made very transparent to the workers; just as with pension rights, the social security administration could calculate the level and duration of the benefit to which each contributing worker would be entitled and send them each year a statement specifying their entitlements. It would be expected that the transparency of the regulation combined with an obvious reduction in income after a certain period, would act as positive incentives for the unemployed to search for and accept jobs. It increases the pressure on younger workers (who would have less contribution months) compared to older workers, which seems to be both fair and effective in the sense that younger workers have better chances on the labour market and that eventually further investment in human capital for younger workers would make more sense because of the longer pay-back period. The regulation has both elements of social solidarity and actuarial fairness. Solidarity materializes as a predefined and fixed benefit designed to allow households to adjust a new situation of unemployment and sickness. Actuarial fairness applies to the second (declining) part of the benefit whereby contributors' entitlements are defined in terms of contribution history. The combination of solidarity and actuarial fairness can be expected to provide a solid basis for a stable and infrequently disputed regulation.[7]

The regulation could also be used as alternative to the existing early retirement provisions. Voluntary quits of workers at the end of their careers could be financed out of unused entitlement rights in the second (declining) part of the benefit. As already mentioned (see note 6), this would, however, make the regulation more expensive and more difficult to administer. It might, however, be a viable (and cheaper) option in countries where early retirement schemes are already very expensive. It definitely leaves the decision and its financial consequences more to the beneficiaries and therefore may provide better incentives to higher rates of participation for the older age-groups in the labour market. Another option within a more active labour market policy stance would be to use the first part of the benefit as an employment subsidy (or training subsidy) allowing unemployed workers to offer the unused part of their benefits as a one-off employment subsidy to employers who would employ them within that period. It would not avoid deadweight losses occurring,[8] but would provide a clear incentive both to workers and to employers to avoid long-term unemployment.

9.5 CONCLUDING REMARKS

In this chapter we have argued that social policy can contribute to economic growth and increased competitiveness. We particularly want to stress that improvements in the effectiveness and efficiency of social policy are potentially powerful instruments for reaching the so-called Lisbon policy objectives. The central tenet of the chapter rests on four main arguments. First, there are no theoretical reasons to accept that European economies have reached a position whereby more spending on social policy necessarily reduces economic growth or competitiveness. Second, spending on social policy stimulates economic growth as well as reduces it in the short term; the actual balance is an empirical question that cannot be fully answered with available data sources. Third, social policy contributes to lower poverty and lower inequality and therefore stimulates economic growth in the long term. Fourth, it is possible to redesign part of the social security system in directions that point to a higher employment–population ratio. The essence of that redesign is summarized in Figure 9.3 depicting productivity distributions within a population. Distribution D (the left-hand distribution) is a normal distribution of productivity within a population. Classic social policy, providing a benefit to people outside the production process, basically provides a benefit of level A. The benefit level A acts as a minimum wage since no worker is willing to work for a wage below that level because they can always get the benefit level A. Note that no employer is willing to pay for the services of all the people left of benefit level A, because the productivity of those people would be lower than the minimum wage of level A. In this case a benefit is provided to all the people under the distribution D left of the line AB. This will remain unchanged unless the benefit level line AB is shifted to the left.

It would be desirable to have an activating social policy that is either able to provide the right incentives to beneficiaries and employers to invest in human capital or can provide retraining and jobs that increase the productivity

Productivity

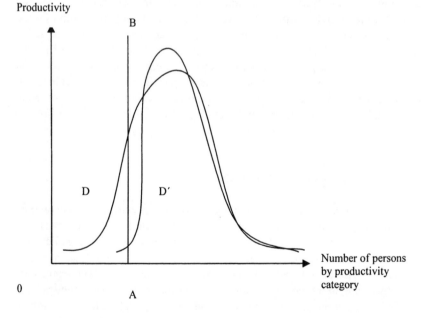

Figure 9.3 Productivity distribution under two types of social policy

productivity of persons left of point A in Figure 9.3. Investment in human capital results in changing the distribution D into the distribution D′ in Figure 9.3. Fewer persons now remain left of the line AB and thus fewer people have to stay out of the labour process. Hence more social policy of the 'right' type will increase overall productivity of an economy and thus its competitiveness.[9]

NOTES

1. The estimates of Smeeding and Rainwater are innovative since they calculate incomes per decile based on measurement of purchasing power. This enables an examination of whether poorer people (here defined as the 10 per cent poorest households in the economy) are better off in terms of what can be purchased with the money available to them. Note, however, that Smeeding and Rainwater use income after taxes and transfers (disposable income) and that there are huge differences, particularly between the USA and continental Europe, in what goods and services are provided by government. This has consequences for what the 'real' purchasing power of all the people in the economy might be. If education and health are basically provided for free (or almost free) as is the case in many countries in continental Europe, than nobody (including the poor) needs to spend private income on these items. This is certainly not the case in the USA where the average resident spends significant amounts on health and education. This implies that the purchasing power adjusted for free health and education of households in continental Europe is underestimated by the figures provided in Table 9.2, or, equivalently, that the income in PPP terms of the US residents is seriously overestimated.
2. Christina Behrendt (2000b) adds another aspect emphasizing that both positive and negative effects are not only to be attributed to levels of spending on social benefits, but that institutional details framing the benefit levels, benefit take-up rates and eligibility rules are also highly relevant. This is also argued by Ritakallio (2002) where the poverty-alleviating impact of social benefits and services is compared. Ritakallio concludes, for example, that systems based on means testing are in general less effective and that this was rather accentuated in the period 1980–95.
3. They also provide estimates under other assumptions of growth rates and for subgroups.
4. Short-term sickness cannot be covered by this insurance since in most cases the worker will not be separated from his or her job. The definition of what is short-term sickness and long-term sickness is important for the implementation of the scheme, but not essential for the purposes of this chapter. Here the insurance is meant to cover the risk of being separated from a job either permanently or quasi-parmanently.
5. The reasons for defining the benefit as a percentage of the last wage (with a maximum) and not as flat rate uniform benefit are: (1) allowing workers to smooth household expenditures and to adjust to the new situation; (2) to point to the (social) insurance character of the benefit; and (3) to smooth macroeconomic shocks when aggregate unemployment is increasing.
6. Note that the system could also be organized as a fully-funded system. Whether that would be desirable in this case is questionable since it would definitely increase the political pressure to pay the saved funds to the workers at the end of their career if they had never been unemployed. This would then turn this provision into an additional pension and would increase the costs considerably. Moreover, it would reduce the socially beneficial idea of solidarity between the employed and the unemployed. Finally, it would increase inequality considerably because workers with interrupted careers, through periods of unemployment or sickness, would be 'punished' again after retirement by facing lower pension benefits.

7. It should be noted that further design issues have to be resolved such as the minimum waiting period for unemployed labour market entrants, the minimum contribution period after a new job has been accepted, the actuarial formula to be applied to define the benefit level and the rate at which it declines when a person has 'used' all his or her rights during a specific benefit period and he or she becomes unemployed or ill again.
8. See Welters (2005), for an interesting discussion of the topic.
9. Similar views on the investment character of some social expenditures are expressed in Esping-Andersen (1999, 2005).

REFERENCES

Alesina, A. and E. Glaeser (2004), *Fighting Poverty in the US and Europe: A World of Difference*, Oxford: Oxford University Press.

Behrendt, C. (2000a), 'Effectiveness of means-tested transfers in Western Europe: evidence from the Luxembourg Income Study', *Journal of European Social Policy* **10** (1), 23–41.

Behrendt, C. (2000b), 'Holes in the safety net? Social security and the alleviation of poverty in a comparative perspective', in R. Sigg and C. Behrendt (eds), *Social Security in the Global Village*, New Brunswick, NJ: Transaction Publisher.

Berghman, J., D. Fouarge and K. Govaerts (1998), *Social Protection as a Productive Factor: Collecting Evidence of Trends and Cases in the EU*, Report at the demand of the EU - DG V, Leuven, Belgium: European Institute of Social Security.

Caminada, K. and K. Goudswaard (2000), 'International Trends in Income Inequality and Social Policy', *International Tax and Public Finance*, **8** (4), 395–415.

Cantillon, B. and K. van den Bosch, (2000), *Back to Basics: The case for an adequate minimum guaranteed income in the active welfare state*, unpublished paper for the International Research Conference on Social Security, Helsinki, Finland, 25–27 September.

Esping-Andersen, G. (1999), *Social Foundations of Postindustrial Economics*, Oxford: Oxford University Press.

Esping-Andersen, G. (2005), 'Indicators and social accounting for the 21st century social policy', in OECD, *Statistics, Knowledge and Policy: Key Indicators to Inform Decision Making*, Paris: OECD.

Eurostat (2004), *European Social Statistics, Social Protection, Expenditure and Receipts 1992–2001*, Luxembourg: European Commission.

Förster, M. (2000), 'Trends and driving factors in income distribution and poverty in the OECD area', *Labour Market and Social Policy Occasional Papers* No. 42, Paris: OECD.

Gregg, P. and J. Wadsworth (1996), 'How effective are state employment agencies? Jobcentre use and jobmatching in Britain', *Oxford Bulletin of Economics and Statistics*, **58** (3), 443–67.

Holzmann, R. and S. Jorgensen (2002), *Social Risk Management: A New Conceptual Framework for Social Protection and Beyond*. Washington, DC: World Bank.

Mitchell, O.S. (1998), 'Administrative costs in public and private retirement systems', in M. Feldstein (ed.), *Privatizing Social Security*, Chicago: University of Chicago Press.

Neubourg, C. de (2002), 'The Welfare Pentagon and the social management of risks', in R. Sigg and C. Behrendt (eds), *Social Security in the Global Village*, New Brunswick, NJ: Transaction Publisher.

Neubourg, C. de (2005), 'Targeted social assistance to the poor and the role of social assistance in Europe', *Maastricht Graduate School of Governance Research Report 2005*, Maastricht, The Netherlands: Maastricht Graduate School of Governance.

Neubourg, C. de, C. Castonguay and K. Roelen (2005), 'Social safety nets and targeted social assistance: lessons from the European experience', forthcoming in *World Bank Social Protection Discussion Papers*, Washington DC: World Bank.

Neubourg, C. de and C. Weigand (2000), 'Social policy as social risk management', *Innovation: The European Journal of Social Sciences*, 13 (4), 401–412.

Oxley, H., J. Burniaux, T. Dang and M. d'Ercole (1999), 'Income distribution and poverty in 13 OECD countries', *OECD Economic Studies*, 29, 55–94.

Oxley, H., T. Dang and P. Antolin (2000), 'Poverty dynamics in six OECD countries', *OECD Economic Studies*, 30, 50–72.

Oxley, H., T. Dang, M. Förster and M. Pellizari (2000), 'Income inequalities and poverty among children and households with children in selected OECD countries: trends and determinants', in K. Vleminckx and T.M. Smeeding (eds) *Child Well-Being, Child Poverty and Child Policy in Modern Nations*, Bristol, UK: Policy Press.

Ritakallio, V.M. (2002), 'Trends of poverty and income inequality in cross-national comparison', *European Journal of Social Security*, 4, 151–177.

Smeeding, T.M. and L. Rainwater (2004), 'Comparing living standards across nations: real incomes at the top, the bottom and the middle', in D.B. Papadimitrou and E.N. Wolff (eds), *What has Happened to the Quality of Life in the Advanced Industrialized Nations?* Cheltenham, UK and Northampton, MA, US: Edward Elgar Publishing.

10. Labour Market Adjustments and Macroeconomic Performance

Anna Batyra and Henri R. Sneessens

10.1 INTRODUCTION

Since the 1970s, unemployment remains the main concern of most EU countries. There are, however, substantial differences between unemployment rates not only across countries but also across regions of the same country. Substantial differences also exist across skill groups. This chapter focuses on the skill dimension and examines the issue in the context of the Belgian economy.

Figure 10.1 illustrates how unemployment rate differences by education level have changed over time in Belgium, from 1977 to 1981, and from 1981 to 1996. These three years are comparable as they all correspond to recession periods. Although the unemployment rate has risen for all education levels, the magnitude of the change is inversely related to the education level: it is negligible for highly educated workers (1.2 percentage points) but considerable for workers with low education levels (13.7 percentage points). Pierrard (2004b) shows that during the late 1970s and early 1980s the difference between low- and high-skilled unemployment rates have risen in a similar fashion in countries like Belgium, France, Germany and the US. However, after 1983, the difference stabilizes in the US while it continues to increase in the other three countries. Belgium, France and Germany are also characterized by stable relative wage incomes (see Pierrard, 2004b, Figures 10.1a and 10.1b).

Biased technological change provides one possible explanation of such asymmetric evolutions. There is ample evidence suggesting that technological progress may have substantially increased the relative demand for skilled workers (see for instance Autor et al., 1998, Berman et al., 1998, Machin and van Reenen 1998). Pierrard and Sneessens (2003b) show that most of the increase in the gap between low- and high-skilled unemployment rates can be explained by relative wage rigidities at a time where biased technological progress increased the net relative labour demand for high-skilled

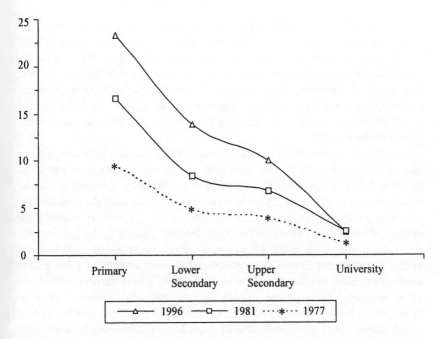

Figure 10.1 *Unemployment rates by education level in 1977, 1981, 1996 in Belgium*

workers. We here built on Pierrard and Sneessens (2003b) to discuss and evaluate the effects of various policy scenarios aiming at decreasing employers' social insurance contributions.

The quantitative evaluations of the effects of permanent reductions in employers' social insurance contributions lead to two common conclusions: (1) the measures targeted at low wages have a much more significant effect on employment compared to non-targeted measures; (2) the effect is stronger the weaker the elasticity of bargained wages to the unemployment rate. The consensus does not extend any further. In particular, we observe differences between the results of macroeconomic and microeconomic studies. The former suggest a more modest impact on employment, as well as a rather significant cost *ex post* per job created (for Belgium see for instance Sneessens and Shadman-Mehta, 2000; Stockman, 2002; Burggraeve and du Caju, 2003; Hendricks et al., 2003; Pierrard, 2004a, 2004b; Bureau federal du Plan, 2005). Microeconomic studies find, on the other hand, very large employment effects, in fact so large that the cost of reductions is more than compensated for by the reduction in the benefits paid to the unemployed and the increase in revenues from labour taxation (see for instance Laroque and

Salanié, 2000; Crépon and Desplatz, 2001 for France); the cost *ex post* of the subsidy is hence negative. This difference between macro and micro studies has occasionally been attributed to possibly large substitution effects between subsidized and non-subsidized jobs, if a job created in a firm leads to a lower activity at a competing firm. In such circumstances, extrapolating micro results at the aggregate level by summing up the number of posts created would be grossly inadequate and largely overestimates the macroeconomic effects of the subsidy.

The results obtained by Pierrard (2004a, 2004b) provide, however, a more convincing explanation of this discrepancy. Pierrard's analysis is based on the simulation of a general equilibrium model incorporating a careful representation of the labour market, taking into account both job creation and job destruction. A number of earlier models of the labour market (for instance Pierrard and Sneessens, 2003a, 2003b) assume an exogenous job destruction rate, as a result of which, a reduction in social contributions affects employment purely through the creation of additional jobs. In the work of Pierrard, the job destruction rate depends on the economic situation of enterprises. Through its impact on the financial position of low-productivity firms, a reduction of social contributions targeted at the lowest wages slows down the destruction of posts on which the workers are paid least. In this setting, a reduction of social contributions affects the level of employment in two ways: by stimulating job creation and reducing job destruction. The simulation of the version of the model incorporating only endogenous job creation predicts employment effects similar to those obtained in the earlier macroeconomic studies; the simulation taking into account both endogenous job creation and job destruction produces a result in line with microeconomic estimations. As in Crépon and Desplatz (2001), Pierrard (2004a, 2004b) suggests that a reduction in social contributions affects employment mainly through its impact on job destruction, which has not been incorporated into traditional macroeconomic evaluations.

Compared with the approach adopted in Pierrard and Sneessens (2003a), the formulation adopted by Pierrard (2004a, 2004b) combines two important elements: the targeting of tax reductions and the endogenous job destruction rate. In section 10.2 we will evaluate the respective importance of these two elements, distinguishing between the effects on employment and welfare of different categories of workers. Moreover, we will pay particular attention to the role of job competition (or the ladder effect), which is important in the following context. Reductions in social contributions targeted at the lowest wages aim to tackle the unemployment problem of the least qualified workers. The underlying analysis is such that high unemployment amongst this category of workers is the result of disequilibrium between the supply of and the demand for this skill type, which arises due to the downward wage rigidity in the region of minimum or reservation wages. A number of studies emphasize, nevertheless, the importance of ladder effect phenomenon induced by a more general weakness of the demand for labour: because of the low probability of contracting a job corresponding with their qualifications, workers accept posts for which they are overqualified, preventing to a certain extent the employment of the least skilled. In section 10.3 we will, therefore, attempt to evaluate the role of job competition and its impact on the effectiveness of the policy of tax reduction targeting. Finally, section 10.4 concludes.

10.2   IMPACT OF POLICY TARGETING

10.2.1   Elements of Theoretical Analysis

Figure 10.2 illustrates two fundamental elements in the analysis of the effects of reductions in social contributions on the employment of workers of a given skill. The downward sloping line represents the effect of a gross wage change on the demand for labour of a certain qualification level. The upward sloping line represents, on the other hand, the effect of an employment change on bargained wages, *ceteris paribus*. At a given gross wage, a reduction of social contributions lowers the wage cost and stimulates labour demand. This is represented in the figure by a shift to the right of the labour demand curve at an unchanged gross wage, employment increases from A to B. For a given size of the tax cut, the employment increase is larger the higher (in absolute value) is the wage elasticity of labour demand. The fall in unemployment and subsequent reactions it causes lead, more or less immediately, to a rise in bargained wages up to the point C. We see that the wage rise reduces the impact of the tax cut on employment. Hence this simple figure shows two reasons in favour of targeting reductions in social contributions to the least skilled workers: the wage elasticity of labour demand for the low skilled is empirically high (the employment increase, which depends on the shape of the labour demand profile, is larger) and the subsequent upward wage pressure is weak (the wage formation profile is flatter).

Nevertheless, this analysis remains both too partial and too simple. It is too partial because it neglects, for example, further effects induced by the tax cut on other factors of production, on saving and investment, on policy financing or job competition. Since a reduction in social contributions involves a redistribution of income, its impact on the welfare of different groups of workers should also be considered, both in the short and the long run. To achieve this, we develop a general equilibrium model incorporating three skill levels in the following section.

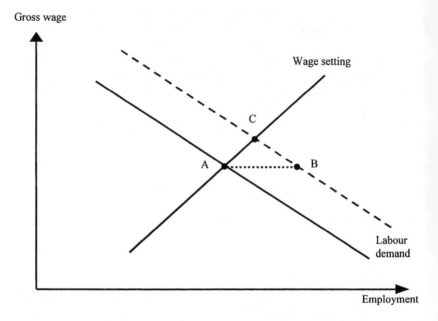

Gross wage

Wage setting

C

A   B

Labour
demand

Employment

*Figure 10.2   Effects of a reduction in social security contributions: partial
analysis*

The analysis is too simple since it rests on an extremely basic
representation of the labour market from which job creation and job
destruction processes are absent. In fact, the transition from unemployment to
employment, and vice versa, is not instantaneous and has been more
accurately presented, as shown in Figure 10.3. The flow into employment (N)
is positively affected by the matching efficiency of jobs to workers (c) and
the conditions in the labour market such as the ratio of jobs to job seekers (θ)
– the outflow rate from unemployment is given by $c.x(\theta)$ as we explain in
equation (10.6) below. On the other hand, a fraction ϕ of jobs is destroyed
each period. Such a destruction occurs whenever the productivity of an
existing job becomes too low to pay the minimum or reservation wage. The
employment effects of a labour tax cut depend on its impact on both the job
creation and job destruction flows. Standard macro analyses emphasize the
job creation channel; Pierrard (2004a, 2004b) emphasizes job destruction.
One of our objectives in this chapter is to assess better the respective
importance of the two mechanisms.

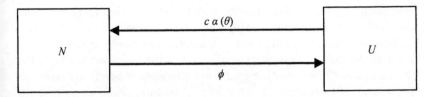

Figure 10.3   Employment in frictional labour markets.

10.2.2   The Model

In this section we construct an intertemporal general equilibrium model. Although rather complex, this formulation is also much more complete. In such a general equilibrium model we can account for the saving and consumption behaviour of households, the interaction of which with the evolution of employment is not negligible. We can also evaluate the effects of the policy on household welfare. The use of an intertemporal dynamic model allows for consideration of the role of expectations and distinguishing between the short and the long run. Such a distinction is important because the effects of the policy might differ in the short and the long run as the result of frictions which exist in the labour market.

Production and factor substitutability

The majority of economic models that analyse the mismatch between the supply of and the demand for skills assume that all firms produce the same good regardless of the technology and the type of workers employed. The total production of the economy is, hence, the sum of firms' individual production. In essence, this setting means that workers with different skills, although having different productivity, are treated as perfect substitutes. Empirical evidence suggests otherwise. We therefore use another approach, adapted from Pierrard and Sneessens (2003a, 2003b), in order to distinguish three qualification levels.

We also distinguish between final and intermediate goods. Final goods are produced using intermediate inputs and capital (representing infrastructure as well as the machines used in the production process). The three intermediate goods we consider here are associated with three different levels of technology and complexity: low-, medium- and high-tech goods and services. We assume that the skill level required in the production of intermediate goods increases with their complexity.

In order to model the technology of the production of final goods, we use a Cobb-Douglas aggregate production function. This implies that the elasticity of substitution between different skill types is equal to one, while the assumption of perfect substitutability would imply that this value is infinite. Manacorda and Petrongolo (1999) find that a Cobb-Douglas function is indeed an appropriate specification to model technological progress biased in favour of the skilled. One direct implication of the described setting is that the intermediate firms producing different intermediate goods are no longer independent of each other. If, for example, the final goods firm decides to employ more of the high-tech input, the marginal productivity of the low-tech inputs will rise, which will in turn stimulate the demand for those inputs. Therefore a rise in high-skilled employment stimulates the demand for low-skilled employment, and vice versa. In the same way, if the final firm invests in capital, this will positively influence the demand for all intermediate inputs and, hence, the employment of all skill groups.

Labour market flows
We consider an economy with a constant population which is comprised of three professional categories, each corresponding to a distinct qualification level (low, medium, high). This partition of the work force is exogenous, determined by the prior investment in human capital (education). There exist three types of jobs, one for each type of intermediate good. These distinct job types vary with respect to the complexity of tasks involved on the job. To start with, we assume a perfectly segmented labour market: the low-skilled workers (respectively skilled and highly skilled) operate exclusively in the low (respectively medium and high) complexity job market.

Labour market flows and relationships between different production sectors are represented in Figure 10.4. The notation is as follows:

$Q_{I,t}$ quantity produced of an intermediate good of type I, where I represents the degree of job complexity, with $I = T, M, B$ (T = top, M = medium, B = bottom,), and t is the time index
y_I worker productivity in each intermediate good sector
$N_{i,t}$ number of jobs in each intermediate good sector
$U_{n,t}$ number of the unemployed of a qualification $n = h, s, l$ (h = high-skilled, s = skilled, l = low-skilled)
ϕ_I job destruction of type I
c_I matching efficiency in type I
$M_{I,t}$ number of matches in each intermediate good sector
$V_{I,t}$ number of vacancies in each intermediate good sector
K_t capital stock in period t
Y_t output produced in period t

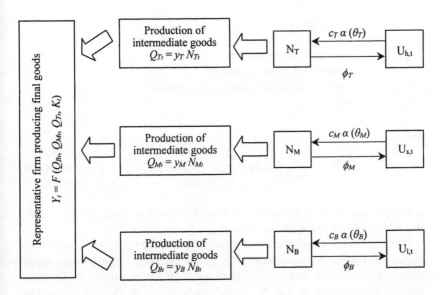

Figure 10.4   Employment and flows in a perfectly segmented labour market

The technology of the final good production is represented by the function:

$$Y_t = F(Q_{B,t}, Q_{M,t}, Q_{T,t}, K_t) \qquad (10.1)$$

The flows in the labour markets are determined by the rates of job destruction and job creation. The duration of an employment spell is the function of all possible developments that can occur and which incite either a firm or a worker to end the contract. We take this into account by assuming that a fraction of existing jobs is destroyed each period. For simplicity, we assume the job destruction rates ϕ_I to be exogenous. The evolution of employment in each intermediate sector is then:

$$N_{I,t+1} = (1-\phi_I) N_{I,t} + M_{I,t} \qquad (10.2)$$

where $M_{I,t}$: number of matches in each intermediate good sector.

Total employment remains constant if the number of jobs destroyed equals the number of jobs created (stationary equilibrium).

Each intermediate firm chooses the number of vacancies to maximize the present value of expected profits:

$$W_{I,t}^F = \rho_{I,t} y_I (1+\tau_I) w_I + E_t [(1-\phi_I) \frac{W_{I,t+1}^F}{1+r_{t+1}} + \phi_I \frac{W_{I,t+1}^V}{1+r_{t+1}}] \qquad (10.3)$$

where the following apply:

$\rho_{I,t}$: market price of an intermediate input;
τ_I : rate of employer social security;
w_{It}: gross wage in each intermediate good sector;
r_t: rate of interest;

and

$$W_{I,t}^V = -a_I + E_t[q_{I,t}\frac{W_{I,t+1}^F}{1+r_{t+1}} + (1-q_{I,t})\frac{W_{I,t+1}^V}{1+r_{t+1}}] \qquad (10.4)$$

is the present value of a vacancy, with a per period recruitment cost a_I and the probability of filling the vacancy is $q_{I,t}$.

The optimal number of vacancies for each firm type is hence a function of current and expected conditions in the goods market and the relevant labour market segment (for example vacancy costs, wage formation or prices of intermediate goods). A job is created when the firm finds a job-seeking worker of the desired qualification level.

In order to account for job matching frictions (coordination problems due to imperfect information), the process of job creation is represented as in Pissarides (2000) by a constant returns to scale matching function in which the number of jobs created is a positive function of the number of vacancies and workers searching for jobs (adjusted by their search intensity which at this stage is equal to one):

$$M_{I,t} = c_I\,M\,(V_{I,t};\ U_{n,t}) \qquad (10.5)$$

The probability of finding a job in the labour market segment I (p, I, t) becomes:

$$p_{I,t} = \frac{M_{I,t}}{U_{n,t}} = c_I\alpha(\theta_{I,t}) \qquad (10.6)$$

In this setting, the probability of finding a job depends on two factors: the matching efficiency in segment I (c_I), and the tightness in that segment (θ_I), which affect positively the probability of a worker contracting a job. The tightness in each segment is measured by the ratio of the number of vacancies $V_{I,t}$ to the number of job seekers $U_{n,t}$.

Saving and investment

Since there are three types of workers, we distinguish between three categories of households. We assume that the least skilled do not save and in each period consume their disposable income from wages and unemployment benefits. This hypothesis seems reasonable since these workers would be paid only a minimum wage. The skilled and highly skilled households, on the other hand, have access to capital markets and choose their profile of saving and consumption to maximize their current and expected future welfare:

$$W_{n,t}^H = U(C_{n,t}) - D(N_{t,t}) + \beta E_t[W_{n,t+1}^H]$$ (10.7)

with respect to the budget constraint:

$$C_{n,t} = \pi_{n,t} + b_{n,t}U_{n,t} + (1-\tau_n)w_{t,t}N_{t,t} + (r_t + \delta)K_{n,t} - I_{n,t} - T_{n,t}$$ (10.8)

where we have:

$C_{n,t}$ consumption of skill group n
$U(.)$ utility of consumption
$D(.)$ disutility of work
B subjective discount factor
$\pi_{n,t}$ share of skill category n in the profits of the intermediate firm
$b_{n,t}$ unemployment benefit received by skill category n
τ_n rate of personal taxation
$K_{n,t}$ capital rented by skill category n
$I_{n,t}$ investment by skill group
$T_{n,t}$ lump sum transfers

In order to model saving and investment behaviour, we have employed a traditional assumption of a representative household for each skill category. This approach assumes that all the workers of each skill would insure mutually within the household against the risk of unemployment. The assumption of perfect insurance is rather strong; it is however indispensable if we wish to avoid the difficulties associated with the heterogeneity of income due to the risk of unemployment in the absence of perfect insurance. The assumption is not damaging since the two categories of workers that save, unlike the least skilled, face a much lower probability of unemployment.

Accumulated savings constitute the stock of capital lent to intermediate firms. The capital market, as well as all goods markets, is perfectly competitive. The equilibrium between supply and demand is ensured by the instantaneous adjustment of prices (the interest rate in the case of capital). Aggregate capital stock is:

$$K_t = \sum_n K_{n,t} \tag{10.9}$$

Wage formation

The presence of imperfect information in the labour market implies that salaries are no longer determined in the equilibrium of supply and demand, but are negotiated between firms and workers. The most common representation of wage negotiations is based on the sharing of an economic surplus. A successful match between a firm and a worker results in a job which adds value and generates an income surplus. This surplus is divided between the firm and the worker; the firm makes a positive profit (the wage paid is smaller than the worker's marginal productivity), while the workers are remunerated above their reservation wage (which in turn depends on their replacement income, the probability that they will find a job elsewhere and the value of their leisure). The key to the partition of the surplus lies in the respective bargaining powers of the firm and the workers. The surplus itself can vary over time in response to variables such as productivity or interest rates. Wages are renegotiated each period. Formally, the result of such negotiations is represented by the maximization with respect to w_l of a Nash product:

$$\left[\frac{W^H_{N_{l,t}}}{U_{C_{l,t}}}\right]^{\eta} [W^F_{l,t} - W^V_{l,t}]^{1-\eta} \tag{10.10}$$

The first and the second term stand for the valuation of the match surplus by the worker and the firm respectively. Parameter η is the bargaining power of the worker. We use this representation of wage bargaining to determine the gross salaries of the skilled and high-skilled workers. We assume, on the other hand, that the least skilled are paid a minimum wage which evolves proportionally to the average wage of other categories of workers. This seems a reasonable assumption since in recent decades, the ratio of the lowest to the highest wages has indeed remained stable in Belgium (OECD, 1996).

Government budget constraint

In order to avoid unnecessarily complicated treatment and notation, we write the government budget constraint as if the government balanced its budget each period[1] and account purely for the elements of the budget associated directly with the labour market. Therefore, in each period, government spending (on government consumption and unemployment benefits) equals revenues (from proportional and lump sum taxation):

$$G_t + [b_{l,t}\, U_{l,t} + b_{s,t}\, U_{s,t} + b_{h,t}\, U_{h,t}] =$$
$$(\tau_l + \tau_B)\, w_{B,t}\, N_{B,t} + (\tau_s + \tau_M)\, w_{M,t}\, N_{M,t} + (\tau_h + \tau_T)\, w_{T,t}\, N_{T,t} + T_t \quad (10.11)$$

where G stands for government consumption and the other terms are as defined earlier. Unemployment benefits $b_{n,t}$ are a fraction (set by legislation) of the gross salaries of workers of type n.

10.2.3   Quantitative Analysis

Our objective is to use the model outlined above to evaluate the quantitative effect of targeted wage cost reductions. The first stage of the exercise involves the calibration of the model, which is to assign to the parameters numerical values compatible with the existing empirical estimations, allowing the model to reproduce the situation observed in the economy at a chosen point in time. Having fixed the parameters, in the second stage we can simulate the model numerically in order to examine the short and long run impacts of changes in the economic environment.

Model calibration
The model is calibrated on quarterly data for the Belgian economy in the mid-1990s. The parameters to be calibrated fall into three categories: (1) standard parameters found in all models of this type (for example, depreciation of capital and intertemporal rate of preference of households); (2) parameters specific to this particular model for which we have direct information; (3) parameters specific to this model but for which we do not have direct information. The values of these latter parameters are fixed so that the model reproduces an economy similar to that of the mid-1990s with respect to a number of endogenous variables (such as unemployment rate, probability of finding a job, probability of filling a vacancy, wage). Below we discuss the most significant elements of calibration.

Standard to RBC models, we set the quarterly depreciation rate of capital at 2.5 per cent and the psychological discount factor at 0.99 which implies a quarterly rate of interest of 1 per cent. The final goods production function is a constant returns to scale Cobb-Douglas form (as in Manacorda and Petrongolo, 1999):

$$Y_t = \varepsilon\, (Q_{B,t})^{\mu}\, (Q_{M,t})^{\nu}\, (Q_{T,t})^{\omega}\, (K_t)^{1-\mu-\nu-\omega} \quad (10.12)$$

The elasticity of final output with respect to capital is a standard value seen in literature (0.33). The coefficients associated with other intermediate inputs are based on the estimation of Sneessens and Shadman-Mehta (2000) in such a way that realistic factor shares can be obtained. In particular, their value of 0.51 for the elasticity of output with respect to the most complex input has been adopted. The elasticity of output with respect to the least complex input (0.05) implies the absolute value of 1.05 of the wage elasticity of demand for the least qualified labour, which seems very reasonable.[2]

The composition of the active labour force (defined broadly to include the workers of pre-retirement age and the older aged unemployed) plays a crucial role. Our objective is to evaluate the impact of a very narrow targeting of reductions in employer social contributions, more narrow than that considered in the work of Sneessens and Shadman-Mehta (2000), Pierrard and Sneessens (2003a, 2003b) or Pierrard (2004a), with exogenous job destruction rates. Those studies distinguish only between two qualification levels, the low and the high skilled. We specify three qualification levels by dividing the low-skilled category into two subgroups: one with low (primary education diploma) and the other with medium (lower secondary education diploma) qualification attainment. These two groups represent respectively 15 per cent and 21 per cent of the active workforce (INS, 1997). Accounting for the unemployed, this partition corresponds well to the percentage of employees paid (sectoral) minimum wages in Belgium: approximately 10 per cent of the salaried population. The high-skilled workers (having completed at least an upper secondary degree) constitute 64 per cent of the work force; their average share in the economy's savings is set at 77 per cent (INS, 1996–97).

Empirical evidence suggests a constant returns to scale Cobb-Douglas matching function:

$$M_{l,t} = c_l \, (V_{l,t})^\lambda \, (U_{n,t})^{(1-\lambda)} \tag{10.13}$$

so that the probability of finding a job in segment l for a worker of the relevant skill n, $c_l \, (\theta_{l,t})^\lambda$, is a positive function of the tightness in that market with constant elasticity λ. Van der Linden and Dor (2001) estimate λ to be 0.4 for Belgium, which we adopt here for each intermediate sector. Since empirical studies provide little information on the values of matching efficiencies c_l, we fix them to reproduce the job-finding probabilities p_n from the mid-1990s, estimated by Cockx and Dejemeppe (2002) to be $p_n = 0.40$, 0.25 and 0.15 for $n = h, s, l$ respectively.

The salaries of the skilled and high-skilled workers are bargained. The bargaining powers for those workers are fixed at 0.6, a value commonly used in models of this type. The least skilled are paid a minimum wage which represents approximately 50 per cent (*ind* = 0.5) of the high-skilled wage (see INS, 1996–97; OECD, 1996) and evolves proportionally to it. This adjustment is subject to time inertia:

$$w_B = ind \left[\alpha_0 \, w_{T,t} + \alpha_1 \, w_{T,t-1} + \alpha_2 \, w_{T,t-2} + \alpha_3 \, w_{T,t-3} + \alpha_4 \, w_{T,t-4} \right] \qquad (10.14)$$

with $\alpha_0 = 0$, $\alpha_1 = \alpha_2 = 0.1$, $\alpha_3 = 0.3$ and $\alpha_4 = 0.5$ as in Pierrard (2004a). Gross replacement ratios (ratios between an average unemployment benefit and gross wages) have been calculated based on wage data from INS (1995–99), benefits data from ONEM (1997) and information on the taxation of benefits from OECD (1997). We fix them at 0.28, 0.36 and 0.57 for the high skilled, skilled and low skilled respectively. We take the rate of employer social contributions as equal to 34 per cent for all intermediate firms ($\tau_T = \tau_M = \tau_B = 0.34$), the value drawn from the model HERMES. The sum of the rates of employee social contributions (13.07 per cent) and personal income taxation (taken from the Social Bulletin of January 1997) gives on average the following rates of personal imposition: $\tau_\lambda = 24$ per cent, $\tau_\sigma = 33$ per cent and $\tau_\eta = 38$ per cent.

Job destruction rates have been chosen to broadly respect the lower bound estimated by van der Linden and Dor (2001) (3.9 per cent per quarter) and to reproduce the unemployment rates in the mid-1990s of 7.9 per cent, 17 per cent and 28 per cent respectively for the low skilled, skilled and high skilled (INS, 1997). In this way we obtain $\phi_I = 3.45$ per cent, 5.15 per cent and 5.8 per cent for $I = T, M, B$ respectively.

According to Delmotte et al. (2001), 52 per cent of vacancies were filled in the course of a quarter in 2000. Their study does not show any systematic differences in the probability subject to vacancy complexity. We therefore calibrate the cost of opening a vacancy in such a way as to obtain a 50 per cent probability of filling a vacancy for all types of jobs. This recruitment cost represents approximately 10 per cent of the total wage cost (Abowd and Kramarz, 2003) and is such that it is more costly to recruit more qualified workers.

Finally, the utility of consumption is assumed logarithmic and the disutility of work is assumed linear:

$$U(C_{nt}) = \ln C_{nt} \qquad (10.15)$$

and

$$D(N_{It}) = d_n N_{It} \qquad (10.16)$$

Table 10.1   Calibration of the model

	Parameters and parameter values					
Labour force shares	α	0.64	γ	0.21		
Matching efficiencies	c_T	0.44	c_M	0.33	c_B	0.24
Matching elasticities	λ	0.4				
Job destruction rates	ϕ_T	0.0345	ϕ_M	0.0515		0.058
Vacancy opening costs	a_T	0.11	a_M	0.09	a_B	0.055
Worker productivities	y_T	1	y_M	0.8	y_B	0.6
Production function	μ	0.51	v	0.11	ω	0.05
Technology	ε	1				
Disutility of work	d_h	0.27	d_s	0.57	d_l	0.75
Saving share	π	0.77				
Worker bargaining power	η	0.6				
Replacement ratios	σ_n	0.28	σ_s	0.36	σ_l	0.57
Minimum wage index	ind	0.5				
Minimum wage inertia	α_0	0	α_1	0.1	α_2	0.1
	α_3	0.3	α_4	0.5		
Personal tax rates	τ_h	0.38	τ_s	0.33	τ_l	0.24
Employer contribution rates	τ	0.343				
Discount factor	β	0.99				
Depreciation	δ	0.025				

with parameters d_n fixed at 0.27, 0.57 and 0.75 for $n = h, s, l$ respectively to close the model and ensure the non-negativity of asset values in the wage bargaining equations. The summary of the calibration is provided in Table 10.1.

Long-run effects of reductions in social security contributions

The values of the endogenous variables obtained in the model calibrated in the manner outlined above will serve as a reference point in the calculation of the effects of different economic policies. The first scenario involves a reduction in employer social security contributions targeted at the lowest wages. The reduction equals x_B and is financed by a lump sum tax $T_{h,t}$ on the high skilled in such a manner that the government budget remains balanced:

$$G_t + [b_{l,t} U_{l,t} + b_{s,t} U_{s,t} + b_{h,t} U_{h,t}] =$$
$$(\tau_l + \tau_B - x_B) w_{B,t} N_{B,t} + (\tau_s + \tau_M) w_{M,t} N_{M,t} + (\tau_h + \tau_T) w_{T,t} N_{T,t} + T_{h,t} \quad (10.17)$$

The value of x_B is such that the *ex ante* cost of the subsidy represents 1 percent of GDP. The long run effects of the policy are summarized in column (a) of Table 10.2. The remaining columns reproduce the results of policies defined in the same way but targeted at different sectors. In all cases, the *ex ante* cost of the reduction remains 1 per cent of GDP. We observe:

1. The number of jobs created lies in the region of 90,000 when the bottom wages are targeted (sector B with the low level of technology); the rise in employment and the level of activity (+1.36 per cent) is sufficiently strong to render the measure self-financing (via the reduction in the total of unemployment benefits paid and the rise in revenues from labour taxation).
2. The effect on employment is more than halved (only 35000 jobs created) when targeting is broader and includes both the low skilled and skilled (sectors $B+M$); such targeting corresponds with that studied by Pierrard and Sneessens (2003a) who obtain some 50000 additional jobs due to the same tax cut; the difference between the two estimations arises essentially as the result of a different effect on wages w_M which in Pierrard and Sneessens (2003a) rise by some 1.2 per cent, compared with 6.4 per cent in our scenario; because they distinguish only two categories of workers, Pierrard and Sneessens (2003a) assume that the salaries of both the low skilled and skilled are indexed on the highest wages, while we assume that w_M is negotiated; they find a positive and non-trivial cost per job created.
3. Policy targeting at relatively high wages (sectors M or T individually) has a weakly positive employment effect (column (c)), or even a negative effect (column (d)); the fundamental reason lies in the reaction of the negotiated gross wages which rise, absorbing the majority of the tax cut; the minimum wage, being indexed on high wages, rises as well and leads to a rather significant destruction of simple jobs.

4. Scenario (d) is especially intuitive: the reduction of social security contributions targeted at the most complex jobs turns out to be counterproductive since it leads to higher expenses associated with the recruitment activity in the sector where such expenses, in the light of labour market tightness in that sector, are not profitable at the margin.
5. It is interesting to note that scenario (a) produces an increase in the welfare of all workers, at least in the long. The rise in the high-skilled welfare is even larger than that observed in scenario (d).

We therefore find, with the respective differences having been considered, broadly the same result as Pierrard (2004a, 2004b): that is, policy targeting at the 10 per cent of workers paid the lowest wages stimulates employment to the extent that the policy measure is self-financing. The effect on employment obtained by Pierrard (2004a, 2004b) is, nevertheless, still three times stronger than that found here in column (a) of Table 10.2. The essential difference in the two formulations lies in the specification of the job destruction process which in Pierrard (2004a, 2004b) depends on the wage cost borne by the bottom-end firms. Consequently, the two channels of job creation and job destruction which a tax cut will impact upon are important: job creation is sufficient to guarantee self-financing; however job destruction seems to be the more powerful one.

Effect of different methods of policy financing
Until now we have assumed that the reductions in social security contributions have been financed by a lump sum tax imposed on the high-skilled household h whose members earn the highest wages. There are, however, alternative methods to finance the reductions and Table 10.3 provides a comparison of various taxation methods: a lump sum tax T, an additional proportional income tax on the high skilled τ_h or an increase in employer social contributions τ_T paid by the most complex firms (sector T). Table 10.3 shows the analysis of the effects of social security reductions targeted at the lowest wages. It can be seen that because the measure is self-financing, the required rate of taxation is very low (and negative), which renders in this case the three modes of policy financing almost equivalent.

Transitional dynamics
Figure 10.5 shows the evolution over time of the most significant variables (unemployment rates (u), wages (w), policy cost and consumption (c)) [3] in response to the reduction in employer social security contributions targeted at the lowest wages and financed by lump sum taxation. The unemployment of the low skilled falls gradually. Consequently, the cost of the measure remains

Table 10.2   *Effects of a reduction in social security contributions costing 1 % of GDP, financed by lump sum taxation.*

		Targeted sector			
		(a)	*(b)*	*(c)*	*(d)*
		B	B+M	M	T
Tax cut (in percentage points)		26.7	8.5	12.5	2.7
Ex ante change in total wage cost (in %)	B	-20.0	-6.0		
	M		-6.0	-9.0	
	T				-2.0
Ex post change in total wage cost (in %)	B	-18.8	-5.8	0.2	1.8
	M	1.32	-0.3	-1.2	0.0
	T	1.33	0.6	1.2	-0.2
Employment variation	B	89 229	28 171	30	-7984
	M	348	6061	8845	84
	T	895	345	144	2708
	TOTAL	90 472	34 577	9019	-5.193
Cost per job created (in thousands of euros per year)		-1.86	14.9	112	-
Variation of : (in %)	production	1.36	0.58	0.17	-0.06
	productivity	-1.03	-0.33	-0.06	0.08
Wealth changes (in %)	L	0.77	0.29	0.05	0.52
	M	0.70	0.46	0.30	-0.11
	H	1.37	0.63	0.08	-0.23

Table 10.3   *Effects of a reduction in social security contributions costing 1 % of GDP and targeted at the least skilled, with different methods of policy financing*

		Financing taxes		
		(a1)	(a2)	(a3)
		T	τ_h	τ_T
Tax cut (in percentage points)			-0.25	-0.43
Ex ante change in total wage cost (in %)	B	-20.0	-20.0	-20.0
	M	0.0	0.0	0.0
	T	0.0	0.0	0.0
Ex post change in total wage cost (in %)	B	-18.82	-18.83	-18.57
	M	1.32	1.35	1.32
	T	1.33	1.32	1.63
Employment variation	B	89 229	89 379	88 267
	M	348	357	339
	T	895	1878	1332
	TOTAL	90 472	91 614	89 938
Cost per job created (in thousands of Euros per year)		-1.86	-2.11	-3.62
Variation of : (in %)	production	1.36	1.39	1.36
	productivity	-1.03	-1.03	-1.01
Wealth changes (in %)	L	0.77	0.77	0.85
	M	0.70	0.72	0.7
	H	1.37	1.43	1.35

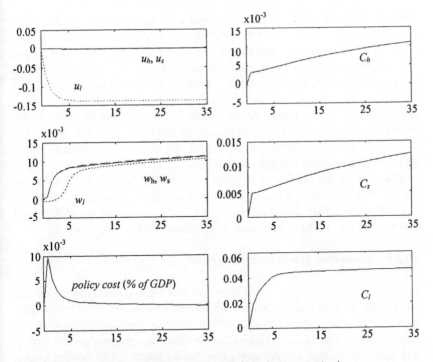

Figure 10.5   Transitional dynamics (with lump sum taxation)

positive for a few quarters. The workers who bear this cost in the meantime are, however, rational agents. Since they have access to capital markets, they can immediately increase their level of consumption and welfare (the latter not shown in the graphs). Therefore we do not observe a fall in the quality of life, neither in the long run nor during the transition.

10.3   JOB COMPETITION AND LADDER EFFECTS

Until now we have assumed a perfectly segmented labour market. This is too strong an assumption: in reality there is nothing to prevent the more qualified unemployed searching for jobs in more than one job segment simultaneously in order to maximize the probability of finding immediate employment, even for which they would be overqualified but during which they could continue searching outside their working hours for a more suitable job. A number of studies find not only that such behaviour indeed exists, but that it becomes more widespread over time. This competition for the same jobs between the workers of different skills reduces the probability of obtaining a job by the workers in lower labour market segments, giving rise to a ladder effect characterized by more workers searching for employment in the segment below their own. In this context, it is the low skilled who most suffer from job competition: being already placed at the lowest echelon of the job market, their choice remains bottom-end jobs, unemployment or domestic activities. [4] Certain studies point to the ladder effects as one of the major causes of the low-skilled unemployment. Pierrard and Sneessens (2003a, 2003b) for example show that a strong rise in unemployment across this skill group after 1975 can be almost entirely attributed to the mix of two factors: biased technological progress and job competition.

Our aim in this section is to enrich our earlier analysis by introducing ladder effects to verify whether our earlier conclusions would be modified. We will first explain the changes to the initial model; then we will present and analyse the results of numerical simulations in the enlarged setting.

10.3.1   Modelling Job Search Behaviour

In order to incorporate job competition, we will assume that a more qualified worker can replace another worker with qualifications one level below their own and, in spite of being over qualified, have the same productivity as the initial worker. Therefore, a high-skilled worker can replace a skilled worker and a skilled worker can replace a low-skilled worker. The reverse cannot take place. Nor can a high-skilled worker apply for a very simple low-skilled job, which would be too far below their qualifications: implicitly this is equivalent to assuming that such a worker would have zero productivity in such a job.

Labour market flows
Accounting for job competition modifies the labour market flows. Figure 10.6, which can be directly compared with Figure 10.4, illustrates the nature of adjustment. The dotted and dashed arrows have been added to Figure 10.4 (in which the labour market was perfectly segmented). Job destruction rates remain unchanged. The probabilities of finding a job, on the other hand, are modified as the result of the change in job search behaviour. The probability of contracting a job of a given type now depends on three parameters: labour market tightness and matching efficiency as earlier, as well as search intensity (s).

Unemployed workers with medium and high skill levels can now search on two labour market segments simultaneously. Let $s_{u,n}$ denote the search intensity of an unemployed worker of skill n in that worker's original labour market, and be a function of the time devoted to search in that segment. On the other hand, search intensity in the labour market segment corresponding to a lower skill level is a function of the time remaining and devoted to job search in that segment.[5] Hence we have:

$$s_{u,n} = F\,(e_{u,n}) \text{ and } s_{u,n}^{o} = F\,(1 - e_{u,n}) \tag{10.18}$$

where subscript n refers to the skill level, superscript o refers to search on the alternative labour market segment and $e_{u,n}$ is the fraction of time devoted to search by a worker of skill n in that worker's optimal labour market segment. Because least-skilled workers have access to only one labour market segment, the value of $s_{u,l}$ is normalized to 1. Finally, the vertical arrows show the flow from one employment to another when a worker, as the result of on-the-job search, moves from a suboptimal to an optimal job. When on the job, workers search with an intensity which depends on their on-the-job search time: $s_{n}^{o} = F(e_{n}^{o})$.

This formulation of the labour market has been inspired by Gautier (2002). It has been enlarged to include three, rather than two, types of jobs and qualification levels. The significance of ladder effects and job competition phenomena depends on the incentives available to workers in order to apply for and accept the offers of suboptimal jobs. It is hence important to model carefully the search behaviour of the qualified workers. Therefore, contrary to Gautier (2002), we endogenize search intensities and model them along the

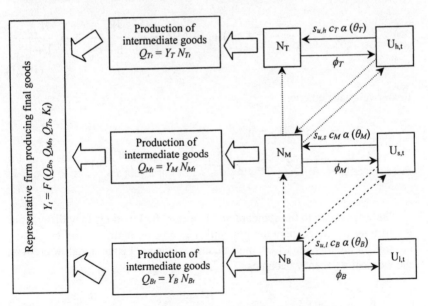

Figure 10.6   Labour market flows in the presence of job competition

lines of Pierrard and Sneessens (2003a, 2003b).[6] As well as choosing their consumption level, individuals also choose their search intensities by taking into account the probabilities of finding different job types and the expectations of wages offered in different market segments. They maximize:

$$W_{n,t}^{H} = U(C_{n,t}) - D(N_{l,t}) - D^{o}(N_{n,t}^{o}) + \beta E_{t}[W_{n,t+1}^{H}] \qquad (10.19)$$

with respect to the new budget constraint:

$$C_{n,t} = \pi_{n,t} + b_{n,t}U_{n,t} + (1 - \tau_{n})w_{l,t}N_{l,t}$$
$$+ (1 - \tau_{n}^{o})w_{l,t}^{o}N_{l,t}^{o} + (r_{t} + \delta)K_{n,t} - I_{n,t} - T_{n,t} \qquad (10.20)$$

where the added terms with a superscript pertain to the conditions in the alternative labour market segment.

On the other hand, the enterprises still choose the number of vacancies required to maximize the present value of expected profits. The optimal number of vacancies for each firm type is a function of current and expected conditions in the goods market and the relevant labour market segment (such as the probability of filling the vacancy, or the wage costs). However, some firms may now fill a vacancy with more than one type of worker. Hence they maximize profits from employing a standard worker:

$$W_{l,t}^{F} = \rho_{l,t}y_{l} - (1 + \tau_{l})w_{l} + E_{t}[(1 - \phi_{l})\frac{W_{l,t+1}^{F}}{1 + r_{t+1}} + \phi_{l}\frac{W_{l,t+1}^{V}}{1 + r_{t+1}}]$$
$$\qquad (10.21)$$

or an overqualified one:

$$W_{l,t}^{Fo} = \rho_{l,t}y_{l} - (1 + \tau_{l})w_{l}^{o}$$
$$+ E_{t}[(1 - \phi_{l} - s_{n}^{o}p_{n,t}^{o})\frac{W_{l,t+1}^{Fo}}{1 + r_{t+1}} + (\phi_{l} + s_{n}^{o}p_{n,t}^{o})\frac{W_{l,t+1}^{V}}{1 + r_{t+1}}] \qquad (10.22)$$

The wages paid to the standard and overqualified workers may differ since the firm takes into account the probability of an overqualified worker quitting the job for another for which their qualifications are better suited. Moreover, the value of a vacancy becomes:

$$W_{l,t}^{V} = -a_{l} + E_{t}[q_{l,t}\frac{W_{l,t+1}^{F}}{1 + r_{t+1}} + q_{l,t}^{o}\frac{W_{l,t+1}^{Fo}}{1 + r_{t+1}} + (1 - q_{l,t} - q_{l,t}^{o})\frac{W_{l,t+1}^{V}}{1 + r_{t+1}}] \qquad (10.23)$$

and involves the probabilities $q_{l,t}$ and $q_{l,t}^o$, of employing a standard or an overqualified job seeker.

It should be stressed that the measure of tightness in each market segment, defined initially as the ratio of vacancies to job seekers in that segment, must also be adjusted for both the enlarged pool of eligible job seekers and their search intensities:

$$\theta_{l,t} = \frac{V}{s_{u,n}U_{n,t} + s_{u,n}^o U_{n,t}^o + s_n^o N_{n,t}^o}$$ (10.24)

where the notation has been generalized to describe the unemployed looking for standard jobs, the unemployed looking for suboptimal jobs and the employed on suboptimal jobs searching for better employment.

Wage formation

Wages are bargained in sectors T and M, and fixed at the agreed minimum (which evolves exactly as before) for all employed in sector B. However, in sector M we can now observe different wages offered to the workers of different skills: although their productivity is the same, their alternative employment and replacement incomes differ. Hence the possible partition of the match surplus is:

$$[\frac{W_{N_{l,t}}^H}{U_{C_{n,t}}}]^\eta [W_{l,t}^{Fo} - W_{l,t}^V]^{1-\eta}$$ (10.25)

or

$$[\frac{W_{N_{l,t}^o}^H}{U_{C_{n,t}}}]^\eta [W_{l,t}^{Fo} - W_{l,t}^V]^{1-\eta}$$ (10.26)

10.3.2   Quantitative Analysis

The model incorporating job competition and ladder effects shall be used in the manner used earlier in order to evaluate the effects of targeted reductions in social security contributions.

Calibration

We must first specify search behaviour and the relationship between search time and search efficiency. The existing information on the subject is rather modest. To limit the number of additional parameters to be calibrated, we represent search intensity as a concave function (implying a decreasing marginal productivity of search time) for all workers and markets:

$$S_{u,n} = s_{u,n}^0 + s_{u,n}^1 \sqrt{e_{u,n}} \tag{10.27}$$

$$s_{u,n}^o = s_{u,n}^{o,0} + s_{u,n}^{o,1} \sqrt{1 - e_{u,n}} \tag{10.28}$$

$$s_n^o = s_n^{o,0} + s_n^{o,1} \sqrt{e_n^o} \tag{10.29}$$

The parameters for each of these functions are chosen to reproduce a percentage of overqualified workers close to that suggested by empirical studies – in the region of 10 per cent and the realistic fractions of time spent on search.[7]

The disutility of on-the-job search is assumed to be linear:

$$D^o(N_{I,t}^o) = d_n^o N_{I,t}^o \tag{10.30}$$

with the slope coefficient set to 0.1 for both the high-skilled and skilled workers to ensure the non-negativity of asset values entering into the wage bargaining equations.

Long run

As in Table 10.2, Table 10.5 summarizes the information effects of a reduction in social security contributions costing 1 per cent of GDP, financed

Table 10.4   Calibration of the model with job competition

		Parameters and parameter values		
Search intensities	$s_{u,h}^0$	0.75	$s_{u,s}^0$	0.6
	$s_{u,h}^1$	0.175	$s_{u,s}^1$	0.3
	$s_{u,h}^{o,0}$	0	$s_{u,s}^{o,0}$	0
	$s_{u,h}^{o,1}$	0.45	$s_{u,s}^{o,1}$	0.5
	$s_h^{o,0}$	0.15	$s_s^{o,0}$	0.1
	$s_h^{o,1}$	0.2	$s_s^{o,1}$	0.1
Disutility of on-the-job search	d^p	0.1		

by lump sum taxation, but now in the presence of job competition and ladder effects. The following is observed:

1. As, in Table 10.2, the targeting of social security reductions at the lowest wages leads to the creation of nearly 90000 jobs.
2. This similarity in terms of numbers is however misleading: search behaviour and ladder effects result in a non-negligible fraction of newly created low-skilled jobs being occupied by overqualified workers; employment changes listed in column (a) show clearly the importance of ladder effects; the reduction of social security contributions targeted at the lowest wages is therefore less effective than in the case of a perfectly segmented labour market.
3. With job competition present, the measure is no longer self-financing; cost per job created remains however rather low, at around 2000 euro per year; on the other hand, the measure does not benefit all workers: the welfare of the low skilled rises but that of the other two groups (who constitute 85 per cent of the population) falls, which is significant in terms of political decision-making.
4. As seen earlier, a broader targeting $(B+M)$ stimulates employment of both the low skilled and the skilled but the number of jobs created is again much lower (although not as low as in the previous formulation) and cost per job created still remains reasonable, in particular compared with a reduction targeted at the high-skilled workers.
5. A reduction targeted at the high skilled (column (d)) reduces job competition and the ladder effects recede, so that the result is improved compared with Table 10.2. The number of jobs created is positive but the cost per new job is exorbitant; in spite of a rise in average productivity, employment and aggregate production, all workers enjoy lower welfare.[8]

It must be remembered that the reduction of social security contributions would also have a positive effect on employment through lower job destruction, which has not been taken into account here. It might then also be that the measure is still self-financing. While this channel of transmission has not been explored here, the cost of the policy is very low in the long run: less than 0.2 per cent of GDP for a reduction in the unemployment rate of the least skilled by some 10 per cent. In addition, as before, the mode of financing does not significantly change the results.

Compared with Figure 10.5, two points should be emphasized: a gradual rise in the proportion of overqualified workers (which reaches some 12 per cent – a realistic figure close to the lower bound of available estimations) and a fall by some 2.5 per cent of high-skilled consumption (slightly more in the short run).

Table 10.5 *Effects of a reduction in social security contributions costing 1 % of GDP, financed by lump sum taxation, in the presence of job competition and ladder effects*

			Targeted Sector			
			(a)	(b)	(c)	(d)
			B	B+M	M	T
Tax cut (in percentage points)			26.67	8.5	12.5	2.7
Ex ante change in total wage cost (in %)	B		-20.0	-6.0		
	M			-6.0	-9.0	
	T					-2.0
Ex post change in total wage cost (in %)	B	l	-19.0	-5.3	1.1	1.6
		s	-19.0	-5.4	1.1	1.6
	M	s	2.8	-3.2	-4.0	1.2
		h	2.6	-3.5	-6.2	-1.5
	T	h	1.2	1.1	1.1	-0.4
Employment variation	B	l	69 855	35 810	20 392	-2018
		s	36 594	-9054	-26 328	-4725
	M	s	-22 629	13 276	27 419	5859
		h	8296	16 592	22 436	-13 920
	T	h	-4525	-11 715	-16 699	15 382
	TOTAL		87 590	44 908	27 219	578
Cost per job created (in thousands of euros per year)			2.0	9.3	25.1	1377.6

Continued

		Targeted Sector			
		(a)	(b)	(c)	(d)
		B	B+M	M	T
Proportion of overqualified workers	B	4.0	-2.1	-4.9	-0.8
	M	1.3	1.7	2.1	-1.7
	B+M	2.5	0.2	-0.6	-1.3
Variation of: (in %)	Production	0.99	0.64	0.4	0.21
	Productivity	-1.31	-0.74	-0.32	0.19
Wealth changes (in %)	l	0.84	0.59	-0.47	-0.45
	s	-0.72	-0.71	-0.93	-0.94
	h	-1.65	-1.63	-2.02	-2.17

10.4 CONCLUDING REMARKS

In addition to the comments already made, it is useful to recall the reach of these simulation exercises. The exercises have allowed us to better understand why micro- and macroeconometric estimations might be so different and to shed light on the relative importance of the two transmission channels, job creation and job destruction, the importance of policy targeting, the efficiency loss induced by job competition and ladder effects, as well as the importance of the criteria used to evaluate the merit of policy (employment and production versus welfare).

A number of dimensions have not been considered in our analysis. In particular:

1. It would be useful to enlarge the analysis to account for both skill and age groups. A large number of the least qualified workers are too old and this affects their search behaviour and wage bargaining.

2. A shift in the demand for the low skilled resulting from a reduction in wage costs is larger the more growth dynamics it causes. A rise in low-skilled employment stimulates, and is itself stimulated by, a subsequent rise in high-skilled employment and investment. Since the low-skilled unemployed tend to be clustered in declining regions where there is relatively little skilled labour and capital, these growth dynamics would be much less powerful.

3. We have considered a closed economy – considering an open economy would involve two modifications, one of secondary and the other of primary importance. The secondary change concerns capital mobility which would alter the transitional dynamics (Figure 10.7). The crucial modification concerns the problem of competitiveness which is presented as an argument in favour of non-targeted tax cuts. This argument poses a fundamental question: are reductions in social security contributions the most appropriate means of lowering wage costs and stimulating competitiveness? The analysis in a closed economy provides at least an elementary answer: a targeted measure is not problematic as long as it is beneficial (or it is perceived as such) for all categories of workers.

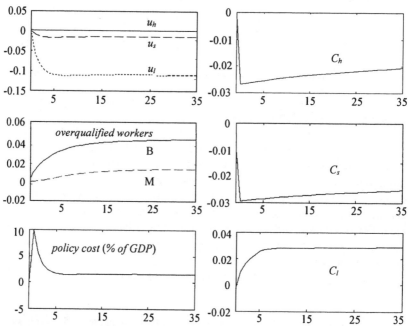

Figure 10.7 Transitional dynamics (with job competition and lump sum taxation)

NOTES

1. The introduction of public debt would not change our results since the assumption of perfect capital markets and the absence of nominal rigidities imply the ricardian equivalence: taxation today or tomorrow does not change the consumption or capital accumulation profile.
2. There is no information on the parameters of productivity y_l which link employment and production in the intermediate goods sectors and the value of which determine the contribution of each worker type to the total factor productivity. With a Cobb-Douglas final goods production function these values influence only total production.
3. The numbers on the x-axis are the number of quarters.
4. Or indeed work in the hidden economy.
5. For sake of readability, this intensity is not represented in Figure 10.6.
6. Dolado et al. (2002) or Albrecht and Vroman (2002) use a similar model but assume that all firms produce the same intermediate good, albeit with different technologies. This formulation effectively means that the workers of different skills are perfect substitutes in spite of having different productivities.
7. Around 80 per cent for search in the optimal market segment and the remaining 20 per cent in the suboptimal market segment, and around 10 per cent of spare time devoted to on-the-job search) as in previous literature, as well as the realistic values for the sensitivity of search effort to labour market tensions so that first order conditions are satisfied and the slope parameters are as large as possible.
8. This illustrates that employment and production are not necessarily good indicators of the merits of an economic policy.

REFERENCES

Abowd, J.M. and F. Kramarz (2003), 'The cost of hiring and separations', *Labour Economics,* **10**, 499–530.

Albrecht, J. and S. Vroman (2002), 'A matching model with endogenous skill requirements', *International Economic Review*, **43**, 283–305.

Autor, D.H., L.F. Katz and A.B. Krueger (1998), 'Computing inequality: have computers changed the labor market?', *Quarterly Journal of Economics*, **113**, 1169–1213.

Berman, E., J. Bound and S. Machin (1998), 'Implications of skill-biased technological change: international evidence', *Quarterly Journal of Economics*, **113**, 1245–79.

Bulletin Social (1997), 'Le précompte professionnel 1997', *Bulletin Social,* January.

Bureau fédéral du Plan (2005), 'Variantes de réduction des cotisations sociales et modalités de financement alternatif', *Planning Paper 97*, January, Federal Planning Bureau, Brussels.

Burggraeve, K. and P. du Caju (2003), 'The labour market and fiscal impact of labour tax reductions', *Working Paper 36*, National Bank of Belgium.

Cockx, B. and M. Dejemeppe (2002), 'Do the higher educated unemployed crowd out the lower educated ones in a competition for jobs?', *Discussion Paper 541*, IZA (Institute for the Study of Labor), Bonn, Germany.

Crépon, B. and R. Desplatz (2001), 'Une nouvelle évaluation des effets des allégements des charges sociales sur les bas salaires', *Economie et Statistique*, **348**, 1–24.

Delmotte J., G. van Hootegem and J. Dejonckheere (2001), 'Les entreprises et le recrutement en Belgique en 2000', *Publication nr. 7446*, Hoger instituut voor de arbeid, Katholieke universiteit Leuven, Belgium.

Dolado, J., M. Jansen and J. Jimeno (2002), 'A matching model of crowding-out and on-the-job search (with an application to Spain)', *Discussion paper No. 3466*, Center for Economic Policy Research (CEPR).

Gautier, P.A. (2002), 'Unemployment and search externalities in a model with heterogeneous jobs and heterogeneous workers', *Economica*, **69**, 21–40.

Hartog, J. (2000), 'Over-education and earnings: where are we, where should we go?', *Economics of Education Review*, **19**, 131–147.

Hendrickx, K., C. Joyeux, L. Masure and P. Stockman (2003), 'Une nouvelle modèle econométrique du marche du travail: estimation, simulation de base et simulation de politiques d'emploi', *Working Paper No. 13–03*, Federal Planning Bureau, Brussels.

INS National Institute of Statistics (1995–99) *Enquêtes sur la structure et la répartition des salaires*, Brussels: INS.

INS National Institute of Statistics (1996–97) *Enquêtes sur les budgets des ménages*, Brussels: INS.

INS National Institute of Statistics (1997) *Enquêtes sur les forces de travail*, Brussels: INS.

Laroque, G. and B. Salanié (2000), 'Une décomposition du non-emploi en France', *Economie et Statistique*, **331**, 47–66.

Linden, B. van der and E. Dor (2001), 'Labour market policies and equilibrium employment: theory and application for Belgium', *Discussion Paper 2001–05*, IRES (Institut de Recherches Economiques et Sociales), Université catholique de Louvain, Louvain-la-Neuve, Belgium.

Machin S. and J. van Reenen (1998), 'Technology and changes in skill structure: evidence from seven OECD countries', *Quarterly Journal of Economics*, **113**, 1215–44.

Manacorda, M. and B. Petrongolo (1999), 'Skill mismatch and unemployment in OECD countries', *Economica*, **66**, 181–207.

OECD (1996), *Employment Outlook*, Paris: OECD.

OECD (1997), *Benefits and Wages*, Paris: OECD.

OECD (1998), *Employment Outlook*, Paris: OECD.

OECD (2000), *Taxing Wages*, Paris: OECD.

ONEM (National Employment Office) (1997), *Stat Info*, Brussels : ONEM.

Pierrard, O. (2004a), 'Impact of selective Reductions in Labour Taxation', *Discussion Paper 2004–035*, IRES (Institut de Recherches Economiques et Sociales), Université catholique de Louvain, Louvain-la-Neuve, Belgium.

Pierrard, O. (2004b), 'Pourquoi faut-il cibler la réduction du coût du travail sur les très bas salaires?', *Regards Economiques No 24*, September, Department of Economics, Université catholique de Louvain, Louvain-la-Neuve, Belgium.

Pierrard, O. and H. Sneessens (2003a), 'Inadéquations, déqualifications et chômage', Report to the SES, Ministère de la Région wallonne, Namur.

Pierrard, O. and H. Sneessens (2003b) 'Low-Skilled unemployment, biased technological shocks and job competition', *Discussion Paper 784*, IZA (Institute for the Study of Labor), Bonn, Germany.

Pissarides, C. (2000), *Equilibrium Unemployment Theory*, Cambridge, MA: MIT Press.

Sneessens, H. and F. Shadman-Mehta (2000), 'Analyse macro-économique des effets de réductions ciblées des charges sociales', *Revue Belge de Sécurité Sociale*, **3**, 631–640.

Stockman, P. (2002), 'General and selective reductions in employer social security contributions in the 2002 vintage of HERMES', *Working Paper 06–02*, Federal Planning Bureau, Brussels.

Index

239